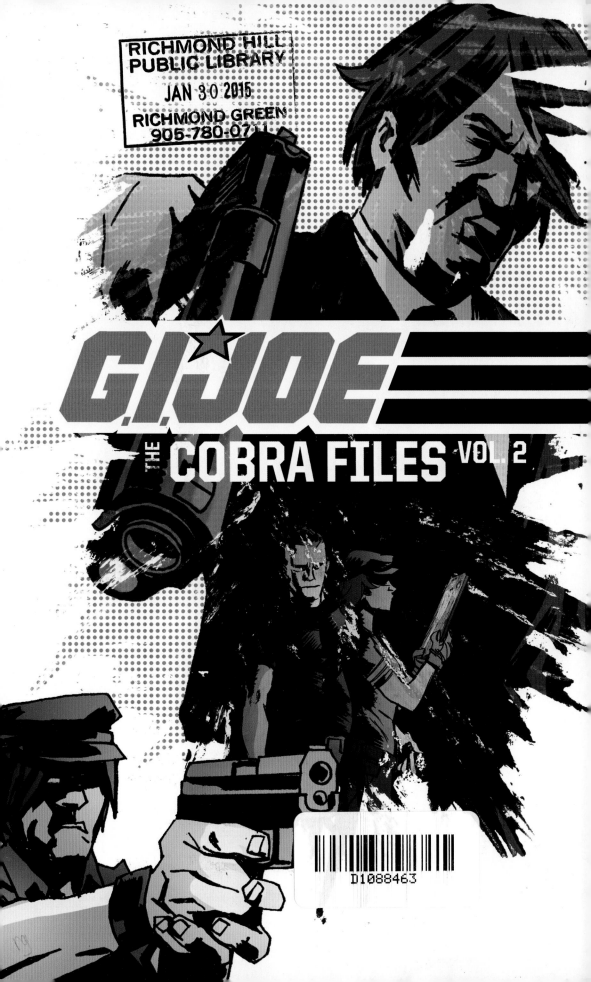

G.I.JOE

THE COBRA FILES VOL. 2

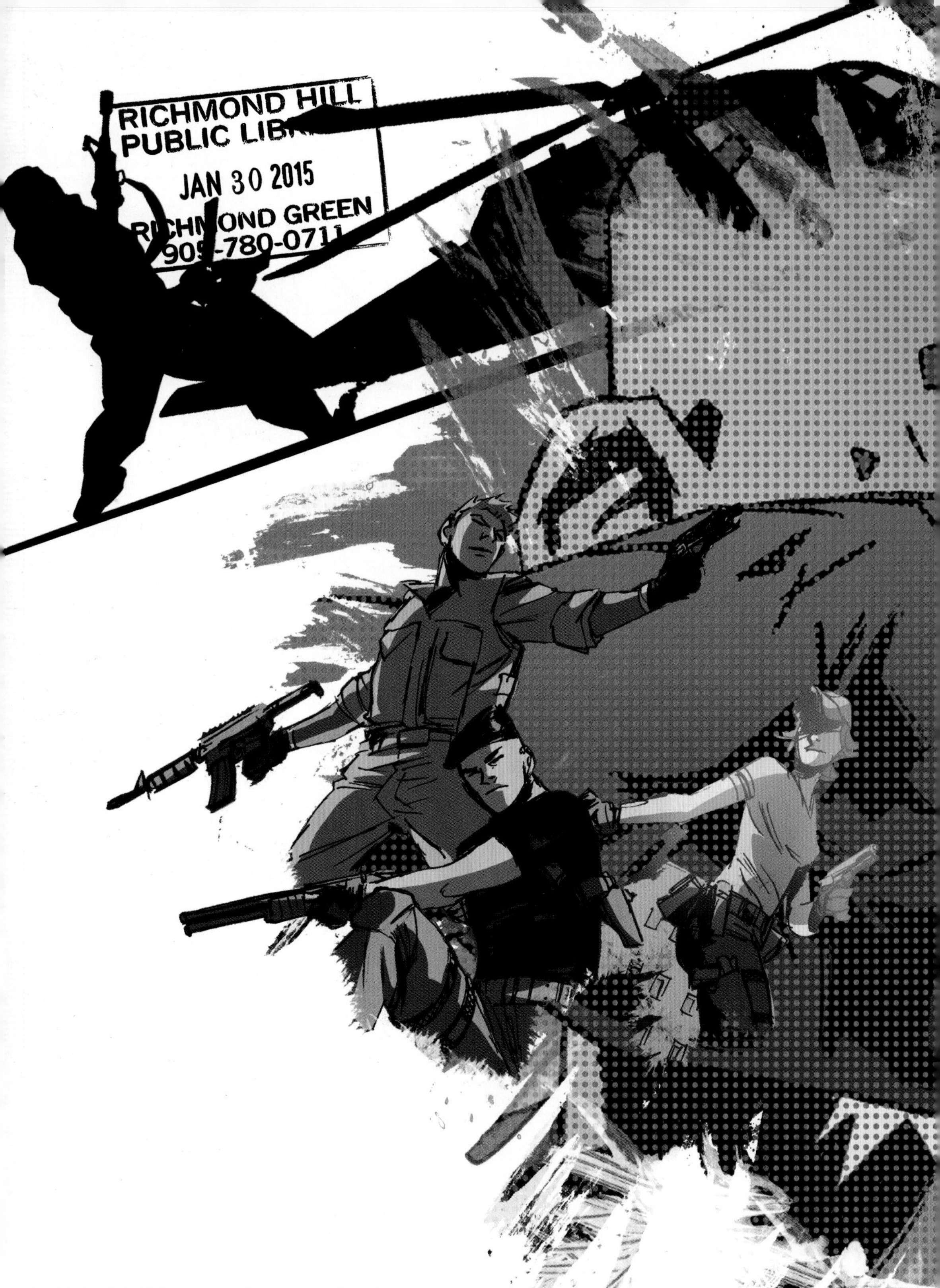

Special thanks to Hasbro's Ed Lane, Joe Furfaro, Heather Hopkins, and Michael Kelly for their invaluable assistance.

ISBN: 978-1-61377-918-7

17 16 15 14   1 2 3 4

IDW® Licensed By: Hasbro

www.IDWPUBLISHING.com
IDW founded by Ted Adams, Alex Garner, Kris Oprisko, and Robbie Robbins

Ted Adams, CEO & Publisher
Greg Goldstein, President & COO
Robbie Robbins, EVP/Sr. Graphic Artist
Chris Ryall, Chief Creative Officer/Editor-in-Chief
Matthew Ruzicka, CPA, Chief Financial Officer
Alan Payne, VP of Sales
Dirk Wood, VP of Marketing
Lorelei Bunjes, VP of Digital Services
Jeff Webber, VP of Digital Publishing & Business Development

Facebook: facebook.com/idwpublishing
Twitter: @idwpublishing
YouTube: youtube.com/idwpublishing
Instagram: instagram.com/idwpublishing
deviantART: idwpublishing.deviantart.com
Pinterest: pinterest.com/idwpublishing/idw-staff-faves

Originally published as G.I. JOE: THE COBRA FILES issues #5–9.

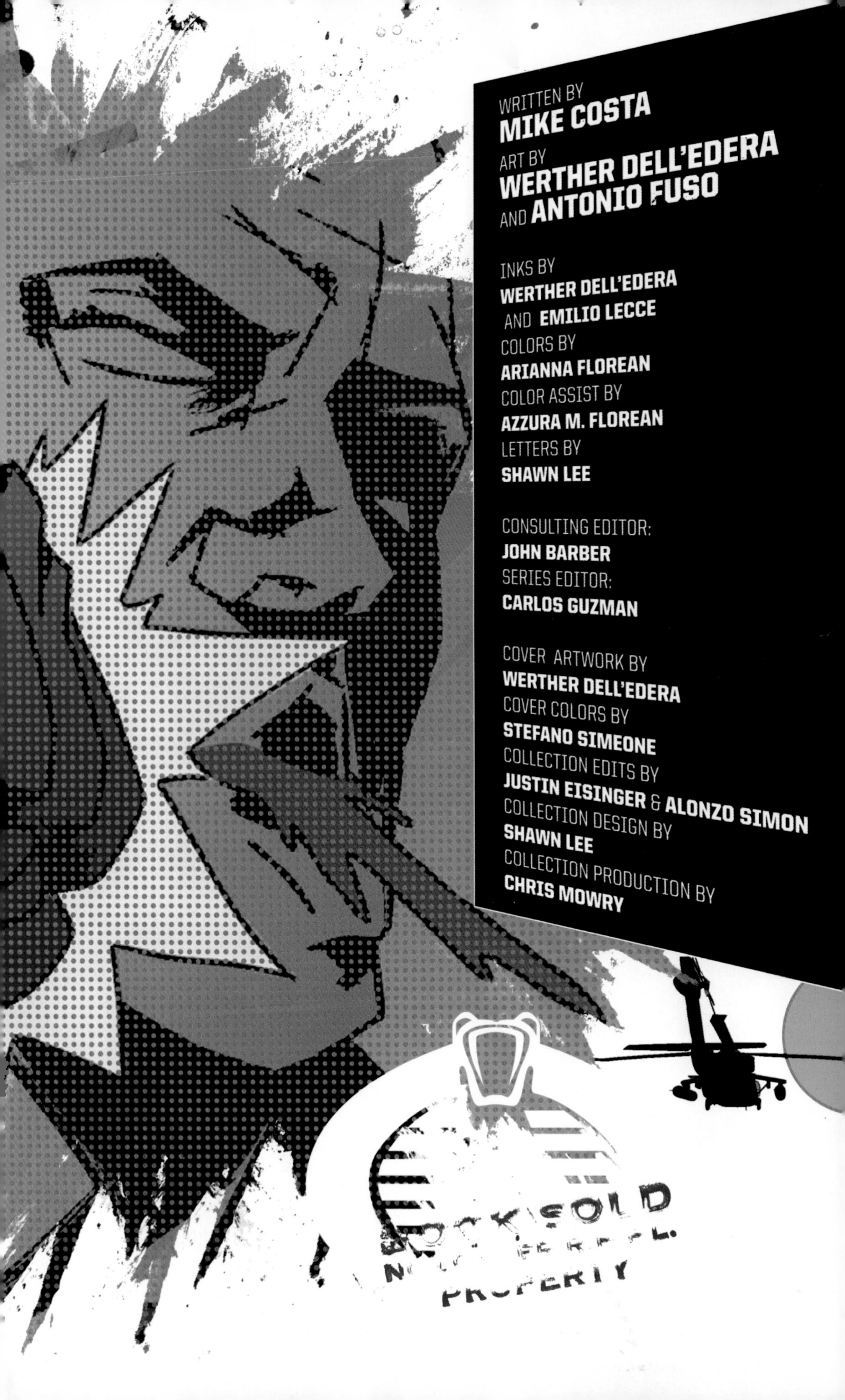

WRITTEN BY
MIKE COSTA
ART BY
WERTHER DELL'EDERA
AND **ANTONIO FUSO**

INKS BY
WERTHER DELL'EDERA
AND **EMILIO LECCE**
COLORS BY
ARIANNA FLOREAN
COLOR ASSIST BY
AZZURA M. FLOREAN
LETTERS BY
SHAWN LEE

CONSULTING EDITOR:
JOHN BARBER
SERIES EDITOR:
CARLOS GUZMAN

COVER ARTWORK BY
WERTHER DELL'EDERA
COVER COLORS BY
STEFANO SIMEONE
COLLECTION EDITS BY
JUSTIN EISINGER & **ALONZO SIMON**
COLLECTION DESIGN BY
SHAWN LEE
COLLECTION PRODUCTION BY
CHRIS MOWRY

ART BY
ANTONIO FUSO

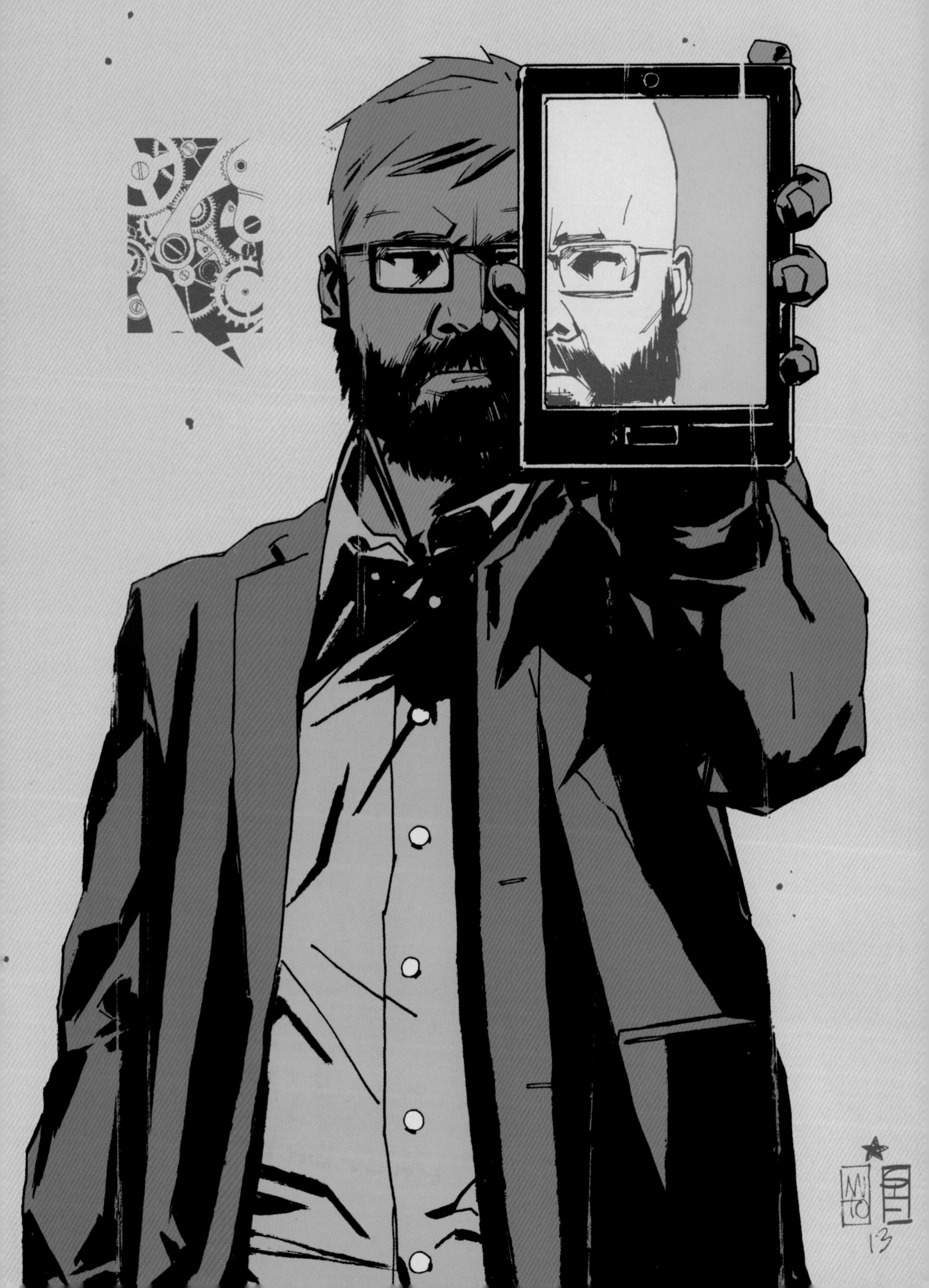

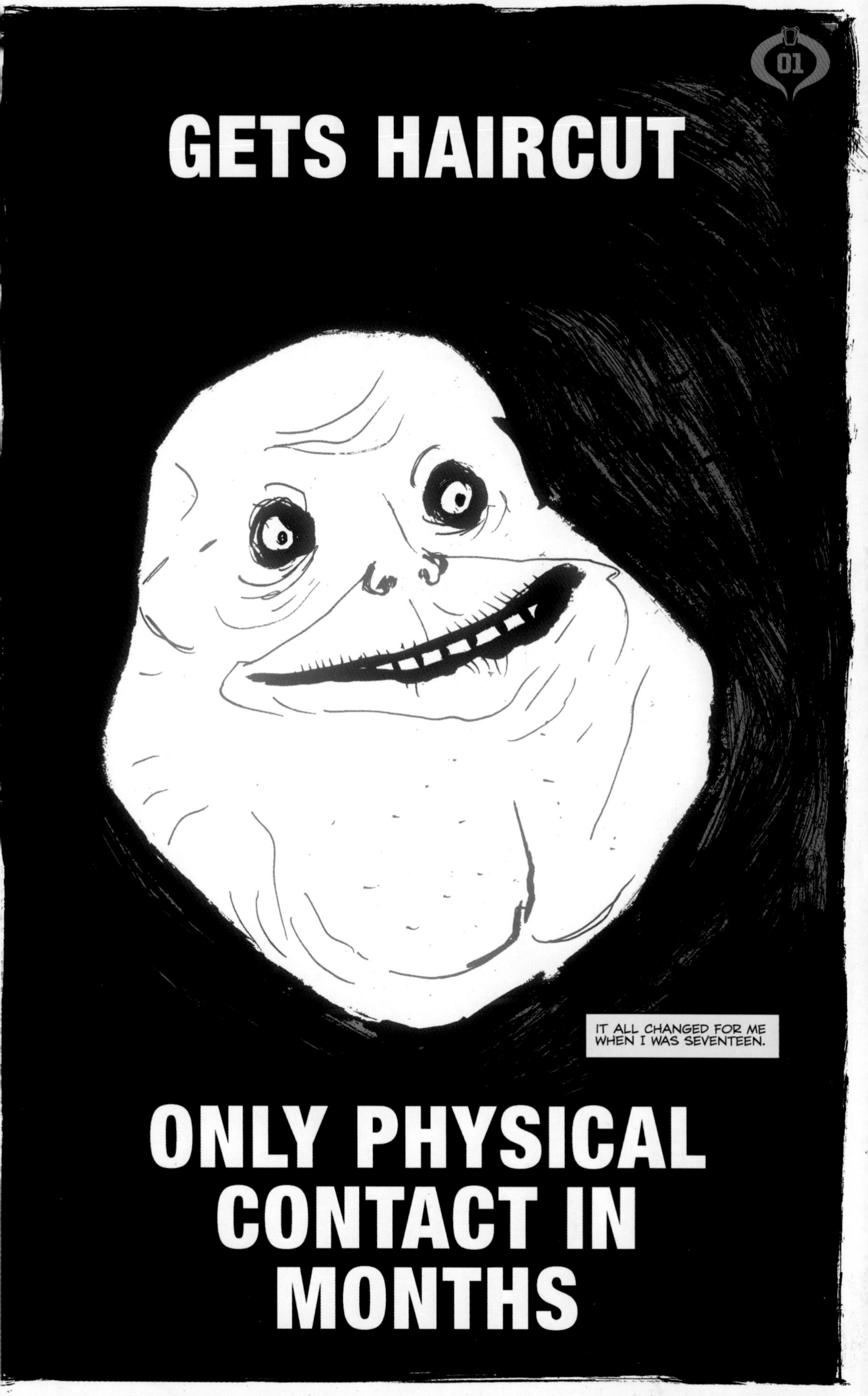

GETS HAIRCUT
IT ALL CHANGED FOR ME WHEN I WAS SEVENTEEN.
ONLY PHYSICAL CONTACT IN MONTHS

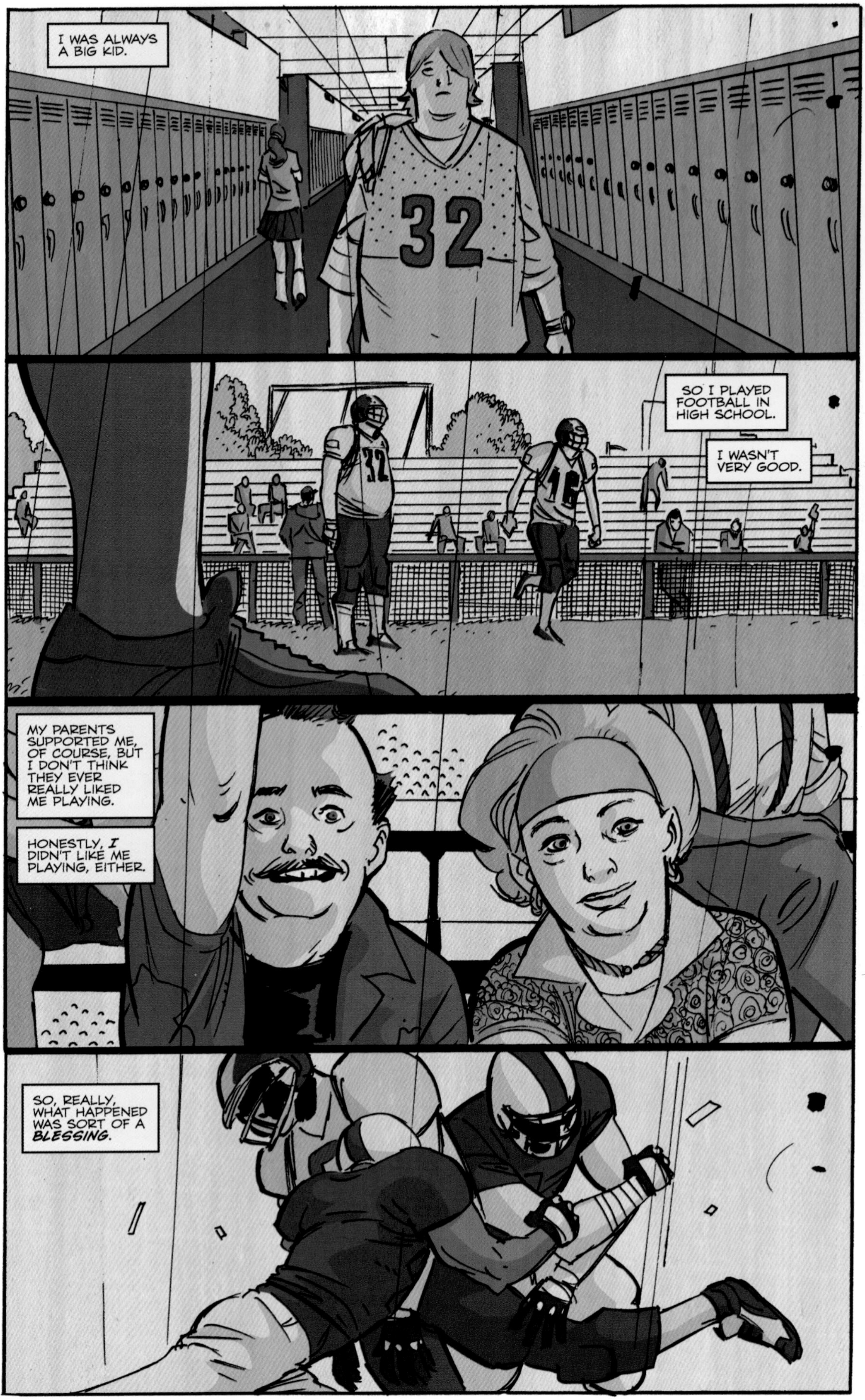
I WAS ALWAYS A BIG KID.
32
SO I PLAYED FOOTBALL IN HIGH SCHOOL.
I WASN'T VERY GOOD.
32
16
MY PARENTS SUPPORTED ME, OF COURSE, BUT I DON'T THINK THEY EVER REALLY LIKED ME PLAYING.
HONESTLY, *I* DIDN'T LIKE ME PLAYING, EITHER.
SO, REALLY, WHAT HAPPENED WAS SORT OF A ***BLESSING***.

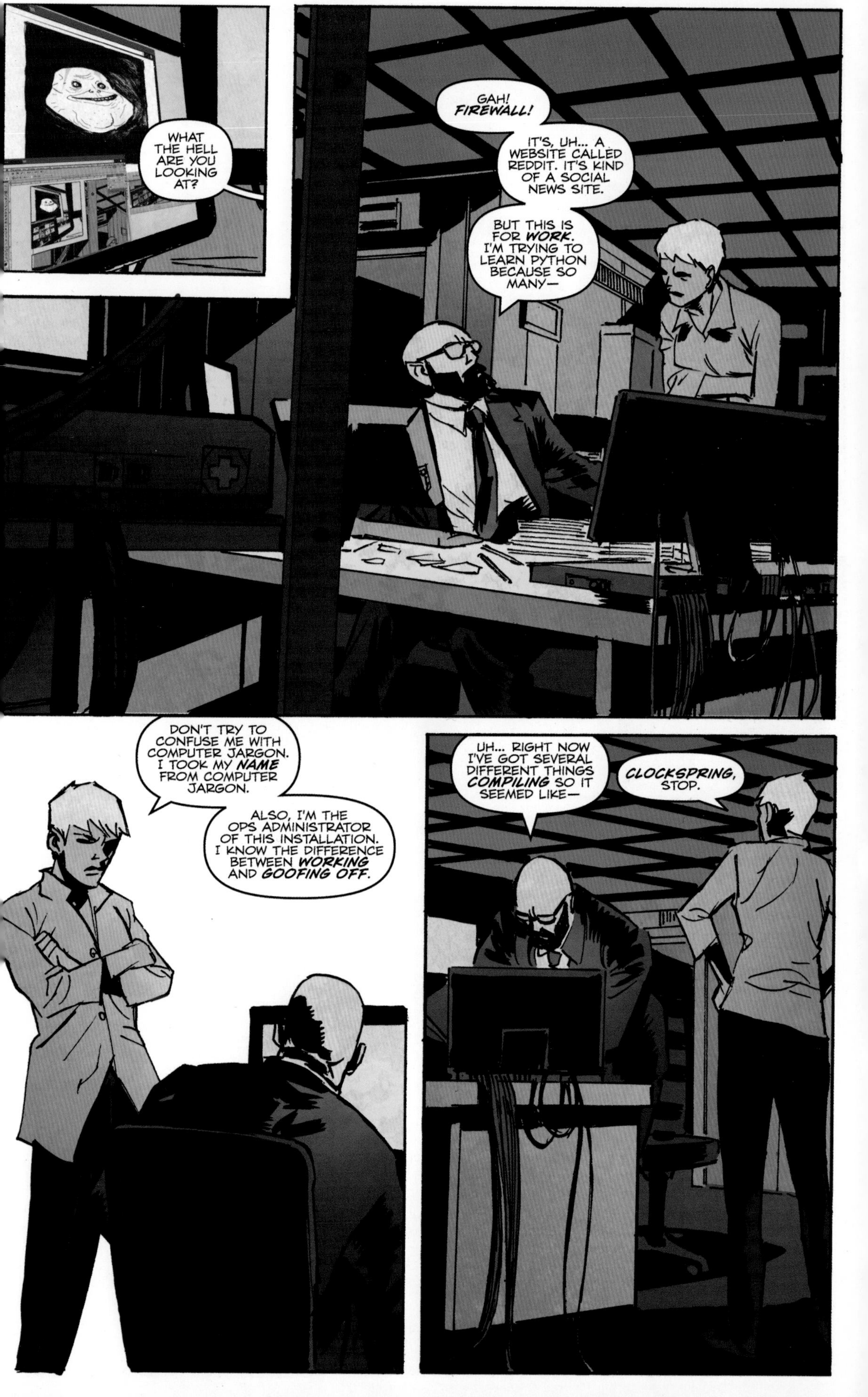
WHAT THE HELL ARE YOU LOOKING AT?
GAH! FIREWALL!
IT'S, UH... A WEBSITE CALLED REDDIT. IT'S KIND OF A SOCIAL NEWS SITE.
BUT THIS IS FOR WORK. I'M TRYING TO LEARN PYTHON BECAUSE SO MANY—
DON'T TRY TO CONFUSE ME WITH COMPUTER JARGON. I TOOK MY NAME FROM COMPUTER JARGON.
ALSO, I'M THE OPS ADMINISTRATOR OF THIS INSTALLATION. I KNOW THE DIFFERENCE BETWEEN WORKING AND GOOFING OFF.
UH... RIGHT NOW I'VE GOT SEVERAL DIFFERENT THINGS COMPILING SO IT SEEMED LIKE—
CLOCKSPRING, STOP.

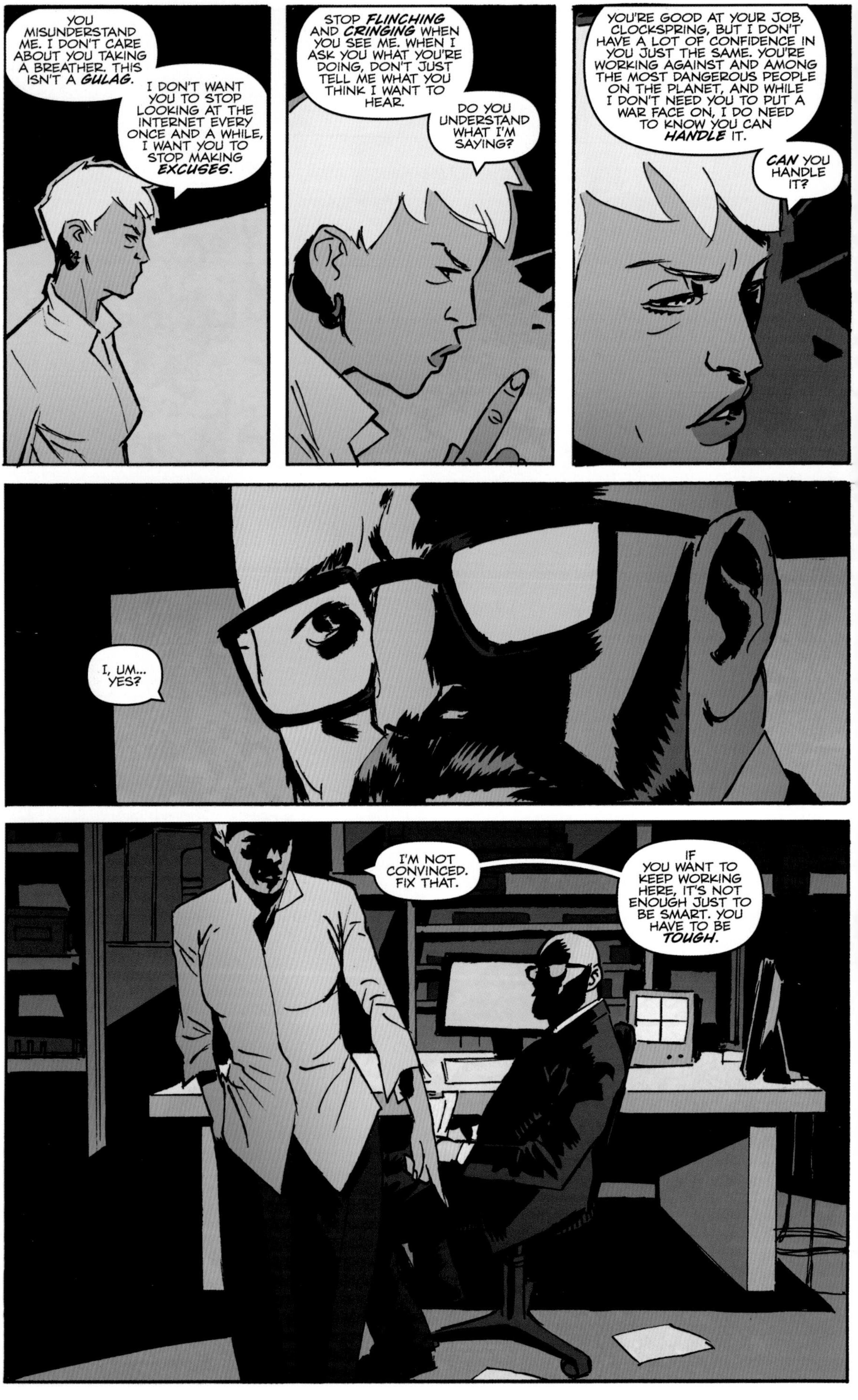

YOU MISUNDERSTAND ME. I DON'T CARE ABOUT YOU TAKING A BREATHER. THIS ISN'T A GULAG.
I DON'T WANT YOU TO STOP LOOKING AT THE INTERNET EVERY ONCE AND A WHILE, I WANT YOU TO STOP MAKING EXCUSES.
STOP FLINCHING AND CRINGING WHEN YOU SEE ME. WHEN I ASK YOU WHAT YOU'RE DOING, DON'T JUST TELL ME WHAT YOU THINK I WANT TO HEAR.
DO YOU UNDERSTAND WHAT I'M SAYING?
YOU'RE GOOD AT YOUR JOB, CLOCKSPRING, BUT I DON'T HAVE A LOT OF CONFIDENCE IN YOU JUST THE SAME. YOU'RE WORKING AGAINST AND AMONG THE MOST DANGEROUS PEOPLE ON THE PLANET, AND WHILE I DON'T NEED YOU TO PUT A WAR FACE ON, I DO NEED TO KNOW YOU CAN HANDLE IT.
CAN YOU HANDLE IT?
I, UM... YES?
I'M NOT CONVINCED. FIX THAT.
IF YOU WANT TO KEEP WORKING HERE, IT'S NOT ENOUGH JUST TO BE SMART. YOU HAVE TO BE TOUGH.

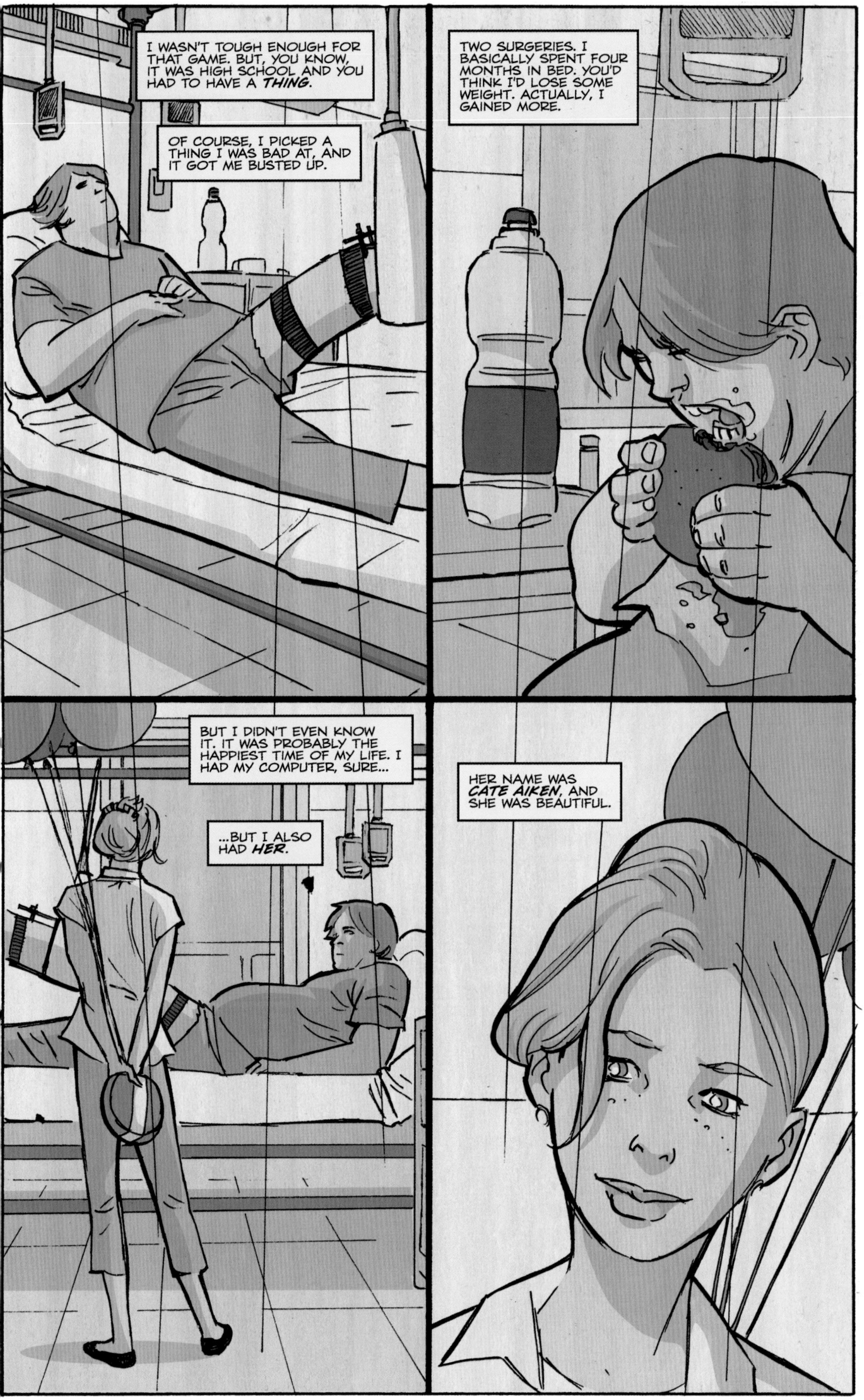
I WASN'T TOUGH ENOUGH FOR THAT GAME. BUT, YOU KNOW, IT WAS HIGH SCHOOL AND YOU HAD TO HAVE A *THING*.
OF COURSE, I PICKED A THING I WAS BAD AT, AND IT GOT ME BUSTED UP.
TWO SURGERIES. I BASICALLY SPENT FOUR MONTHS IN BED. YOU'D THINK I'D LOSE SOME WEIGHT. ACTUALLY, I GAINED MORE.
BUT I DIDN'T EVEN KNOW IT. IT WAS PROBABLY THE HAPPIEST TIME OF MY LIFE. I HAD MY COMPUTER, SURE...
...BUT I ALSO HAD *HER*.
HER NAME WAS *CATE AIKEN*, AND SHE WAS BEAUTIFUL.

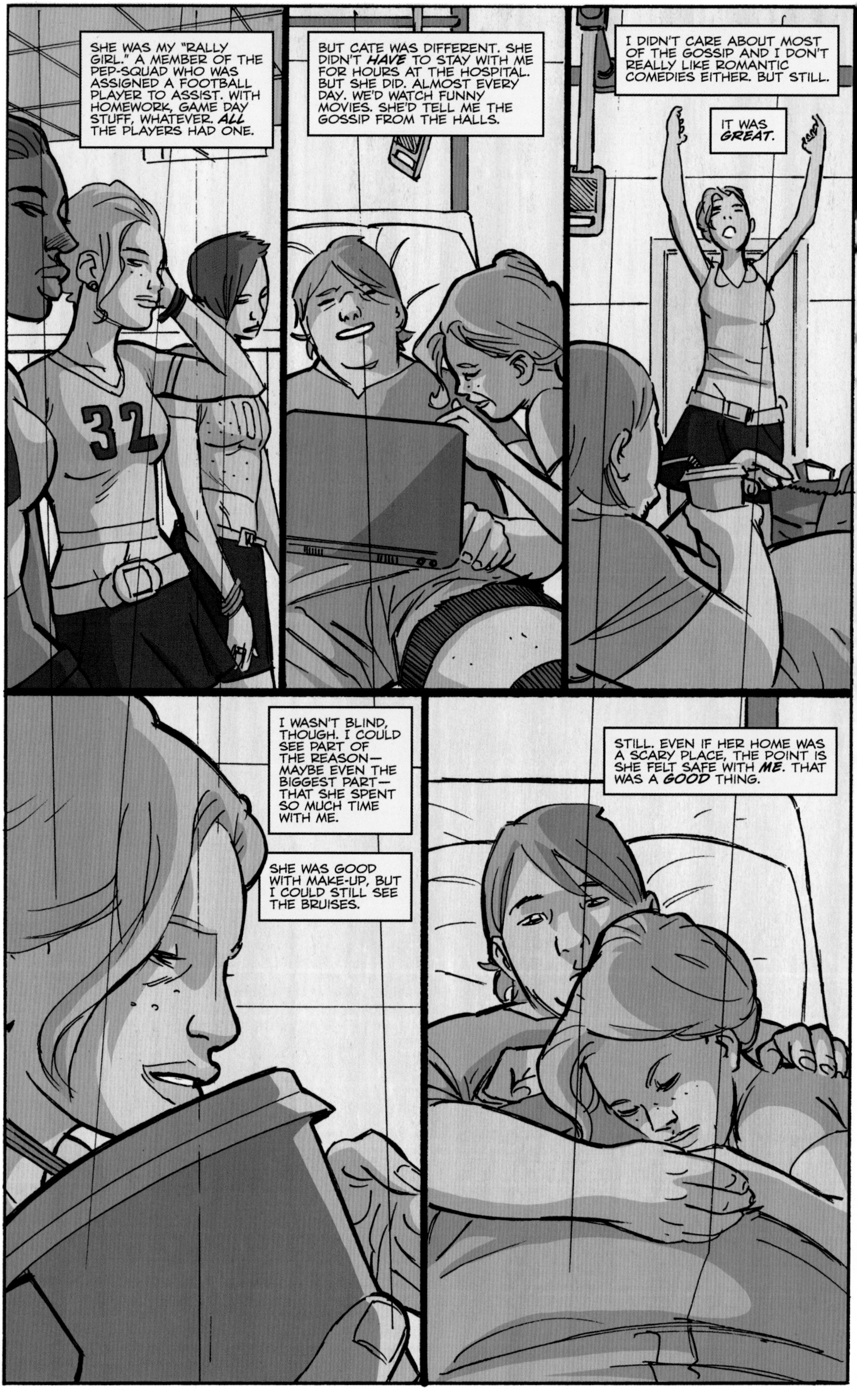
SHE WAS MY "RALLY GIRL." A MEMBER OF THE PEP-SQUAD WHO WAS ASSIGNED A FOOTBALL PLAYER TO ASSIST. WITH HOMEWORK, GAME DAY STUFF, WHATEVER. ALL THE PLAYERS HAD ONE.
32
BUT CATE WAS DIFFERENT. SHE DIDN'T HAVE TO STAY WITH ME FOR HOURS AT THE HOSPITAL. BUT SHE DID. ALMOST EVERY DAY. WE'D WATCH FUNNY MOVIES. SHE'D TELL ME THE GOSSIP FROM THE HALLS.
I DIDN'T CARE ABOUT MOST OF THE GOSSIP AND I DON'T REALLY LIKE ROMANTIC COMEDIES EITHER. BUT STILL.
IT WAS GREAT.
I WASN'T BLIND, THOUGH. I COULD SEE PART OF THE REASON— MAYBE EVEN THE BIGGEST PART— THAT SHE SPENT SO MUCH TIME WITH ME.
SHE WAS GOOD WITH MAKE-UP, BUT I COULD STILL SEE THE BRUISES.
STILL. EVEN IF HER HOME WAS A SCARY PLACE, THE POINT IS SHE FELT SAFE WITH ME. THAT WAS A GOOD THING.

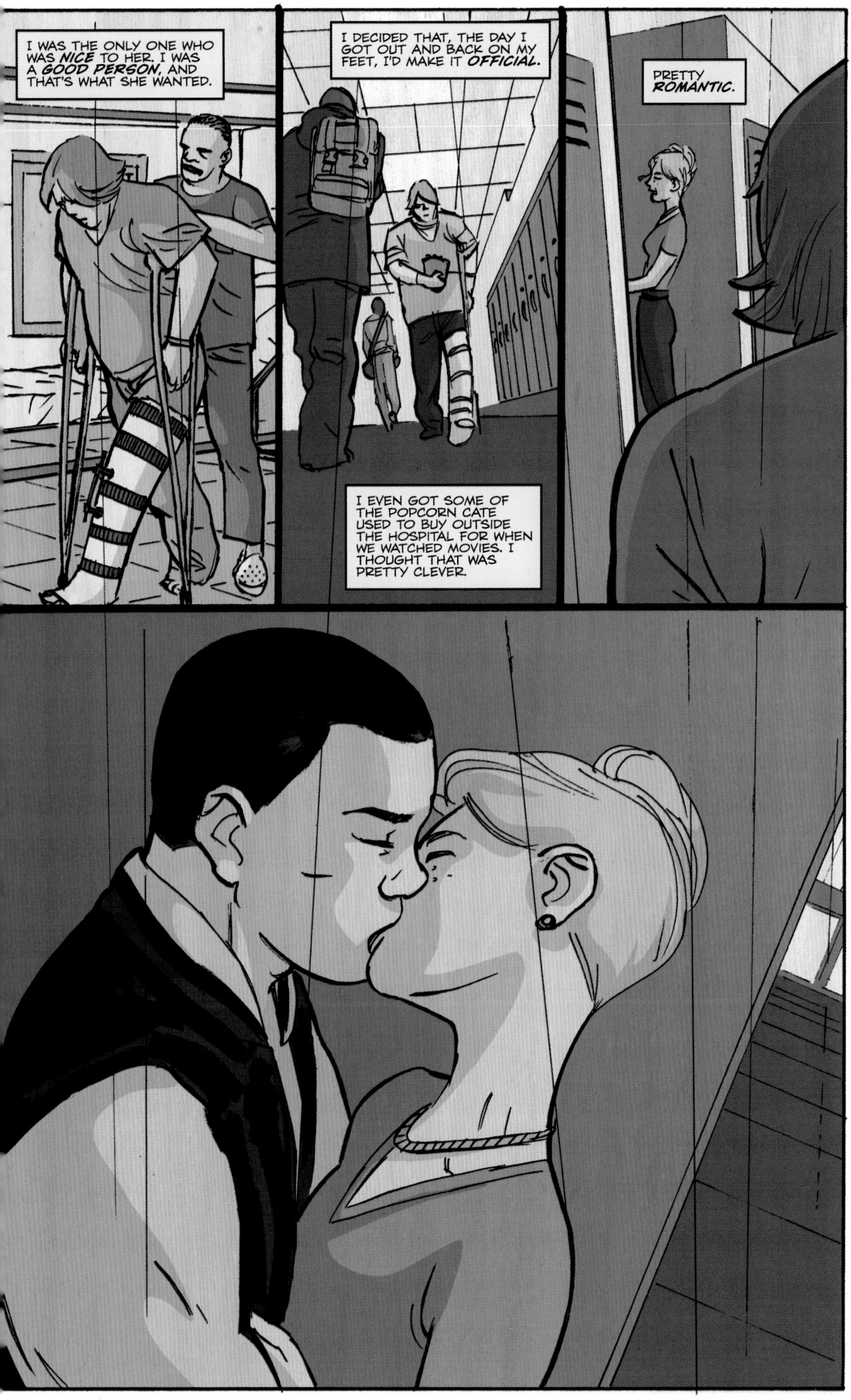

I WAS THE ONLY ONE WHO WAS NICE TO HER. I WAS A GOOD PERSON, AND THAT'S WHAT SHE WANTED.
I DECIDED THAT, THE DAY I GOT OUT AND BACK ON MY FEET, I'D MAKE IT OFFICIAL.
I EVEN GOT SOME OF THE POPCORN CATE USED TO BUY OUTSIDE THE HOSPITAL FOR WHEN WE WATCHED MOVIES. I THOUGHT THAT WAS PRETTY CLEVER.
PRETTY ROMANTIC.

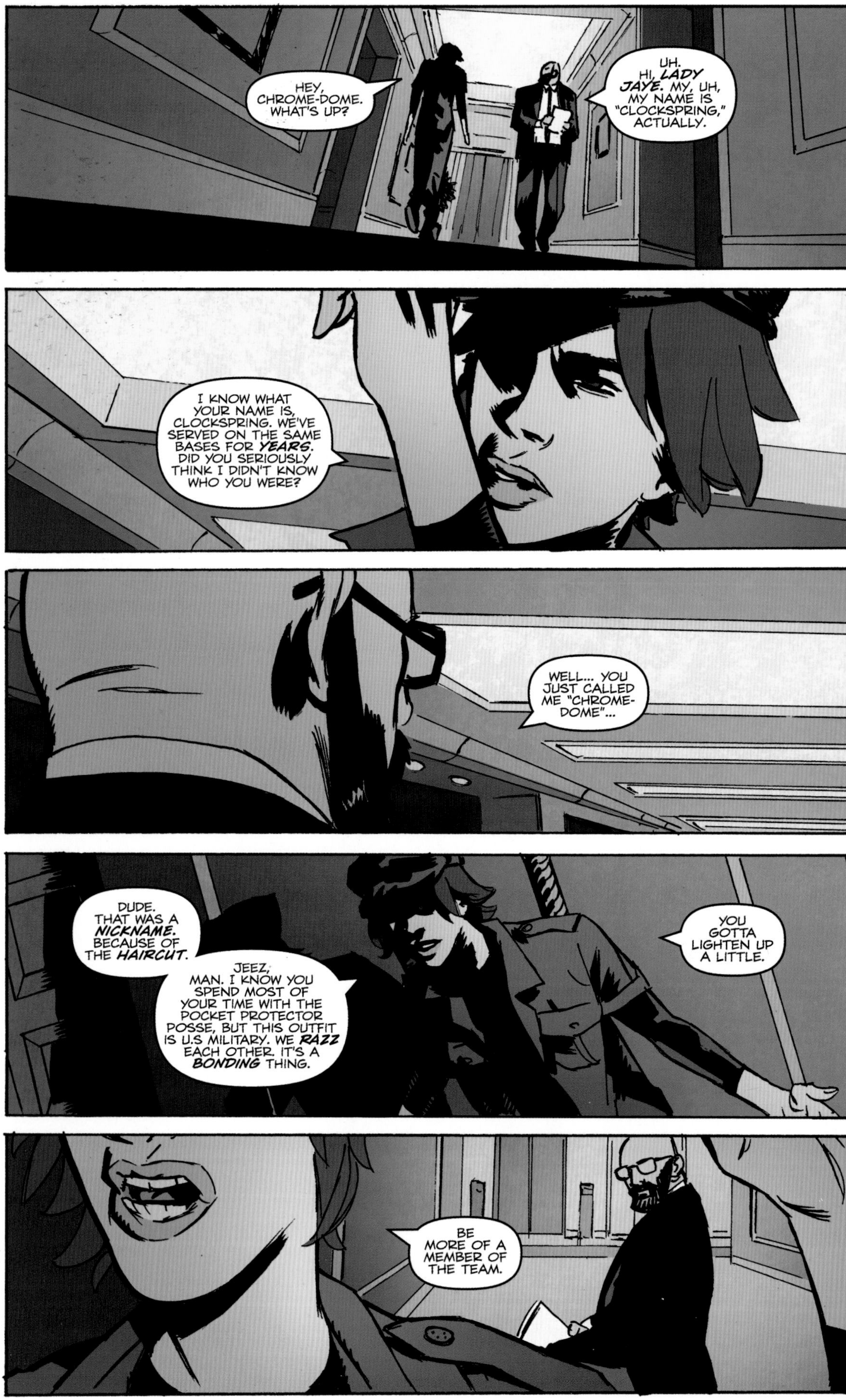
HEY, CHROME-DOME. WHAT'S UP?
UH. HI, LADY JAYE. MY, UH, MY NAME IS "CLOCKSPRING," ACTUALLY.
I KNOW WHAT YOUR NAME IS, CLOCKSPRING. WE'VE SERVED ON THE SAME BASES FOR YEARS. DID YOU SERIOUSLY THINK I DIDN'T KNOW WHO YOU WERE?
WELL... YOU JUST CALLED ME "CHROME-DOME"...
DUDE. THAT WAS A NICKNAME. BECAUSE OF THE HAIRCUT.
JEEZ, MAN. I KNOW YOU SPEND MOST OF YOUR TIME WITH THE POCKET PROTECTOR POSSE, BUT THIS OUTFIT IS U.S MILITARY. WE RAZZ EACH OTHER. IT'S A BONDING THING.
YOU GOTTA LIGHTEN UP A LITTLE.
BE MORE OF A MEMBER OF THE TEAM.

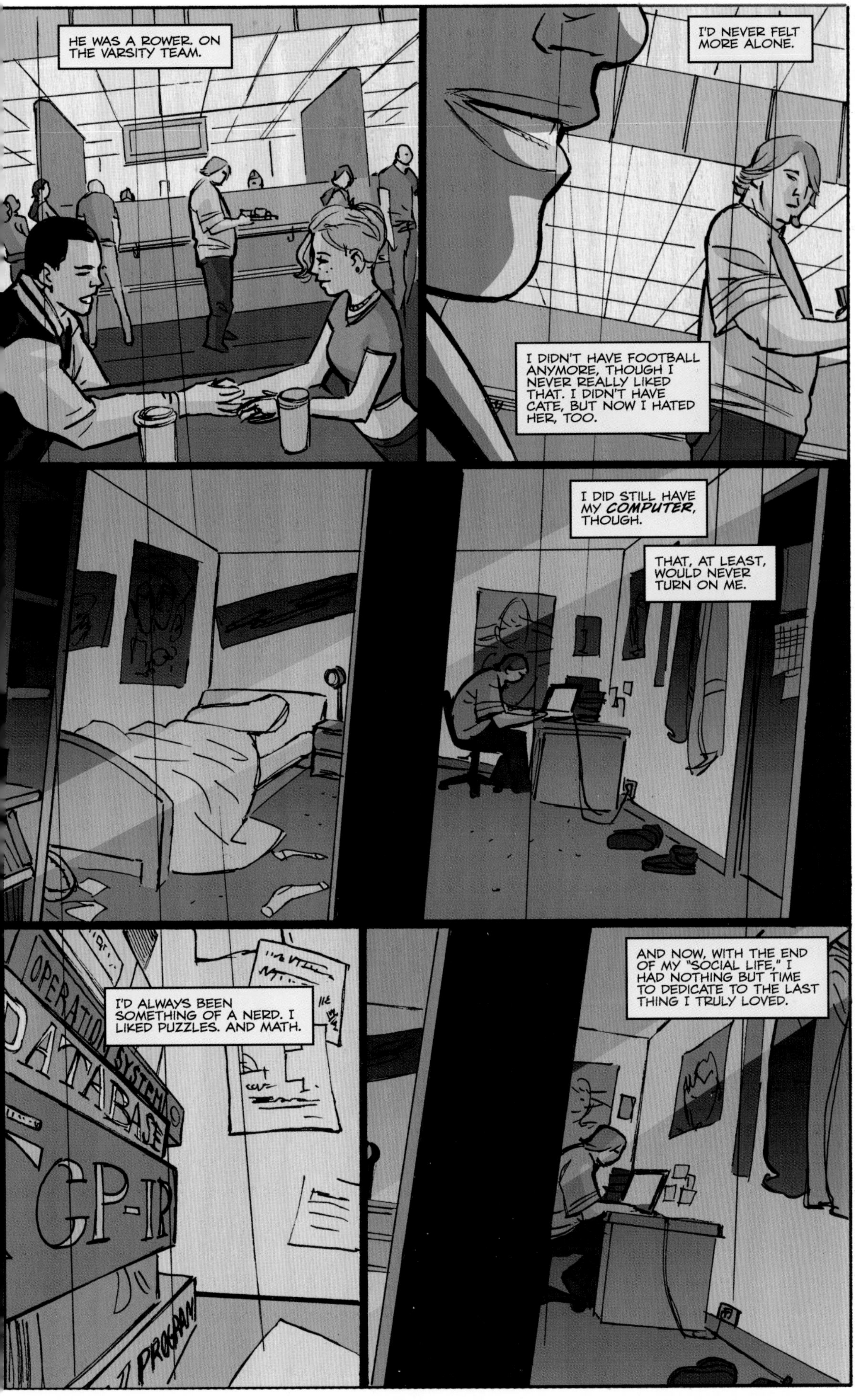
HE WAS A ROWER. ON THE VARSITY TEAM.
I'D NEVER FELT MORE ALONE.
I DIDN'T HAVE FOOTBALL ANYMORE, THOUGH I NEVER REALLY LIKED THAT. I DIDN'T HAVE CATE, BUT NOW I HATED HER, TOO.
I DID STILL HAVE MY COMPUTER, THOUGH.
THAT, AT LEAST, WOULD NEVER TURN ON ME.
I'D ALWAYS BEEN SOMETHING OF A NERD. I LIKED PUZZLES. AND MATH.
OPERATION SYSTEM
DATABASE
GP-IR
PROGRAM
AND NOW, WITH THE END OF MY "SOCIAL LIFE," I HAD NOTHING BUT TIME TO DEDICATE TO THE LAST THING I TRULY LOVED.

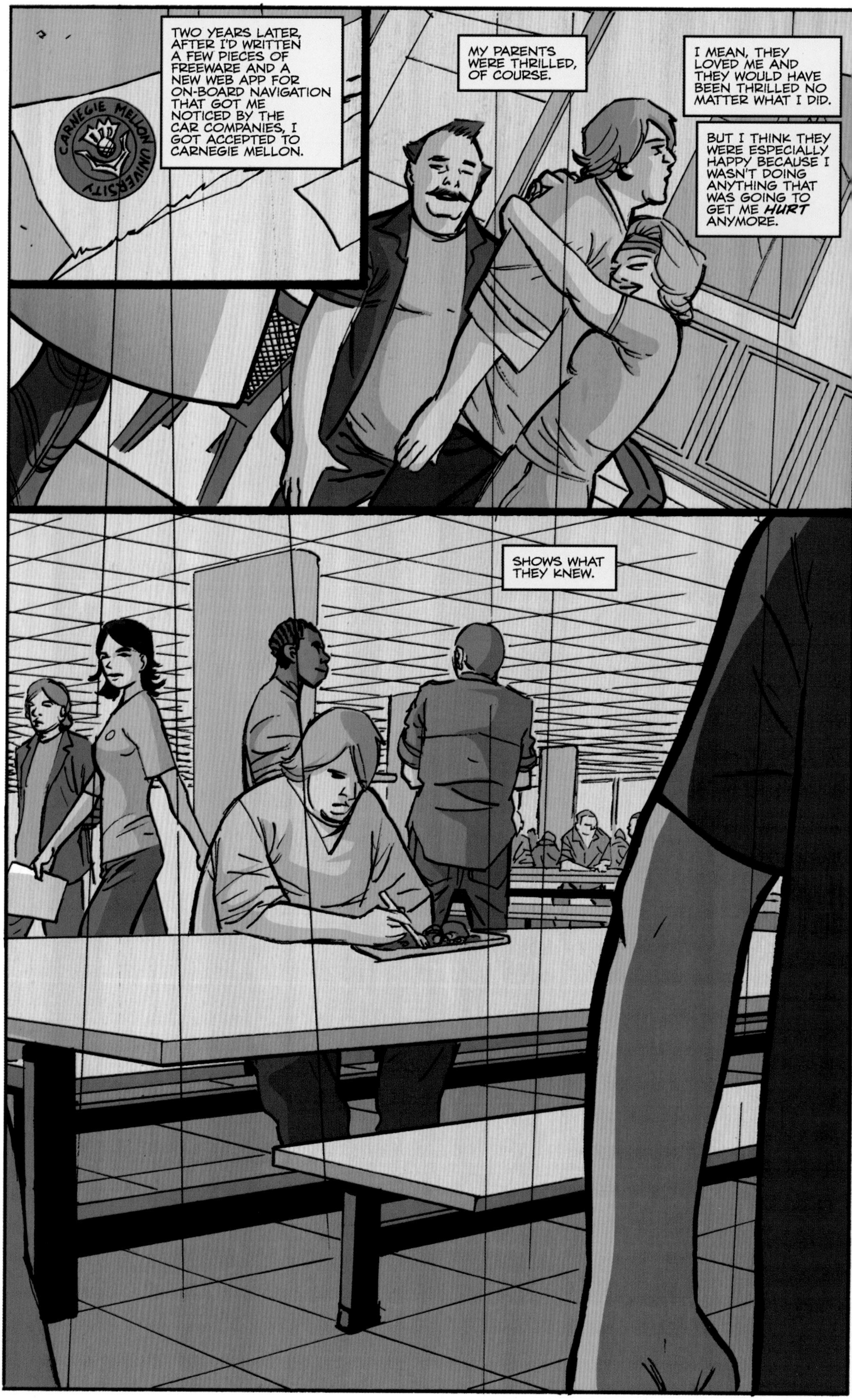
CARNEGIE MELLON UNIVERSITY
TWO YEARS LATER, AFTER I'D WRITTEN A FEW PIECES OF FREEWARE AND A NEW WEB APP FOR ON-BOARD NAVIGATION THAT GOT ME NOTICED BY THE CAR COMPANIES, I GOT ACCEPTED TO CARNEGIE MELLON.
MY PARENTS WERE THRILLED, OF COURSE.
I MEAN, THEY LOVED ME AND THEY WOULD HAVE BEEN THRILLED NO MATTER WHAT I DID.
BUT I THINK THEY WERE ESPECIALLY HAPPY BECAUSE I WASN'T DOING ANYTHING THAT WAS GOING TO GET ME ***HURT*** ANYMORE.
SHOWS WHAT THEY KNEW.

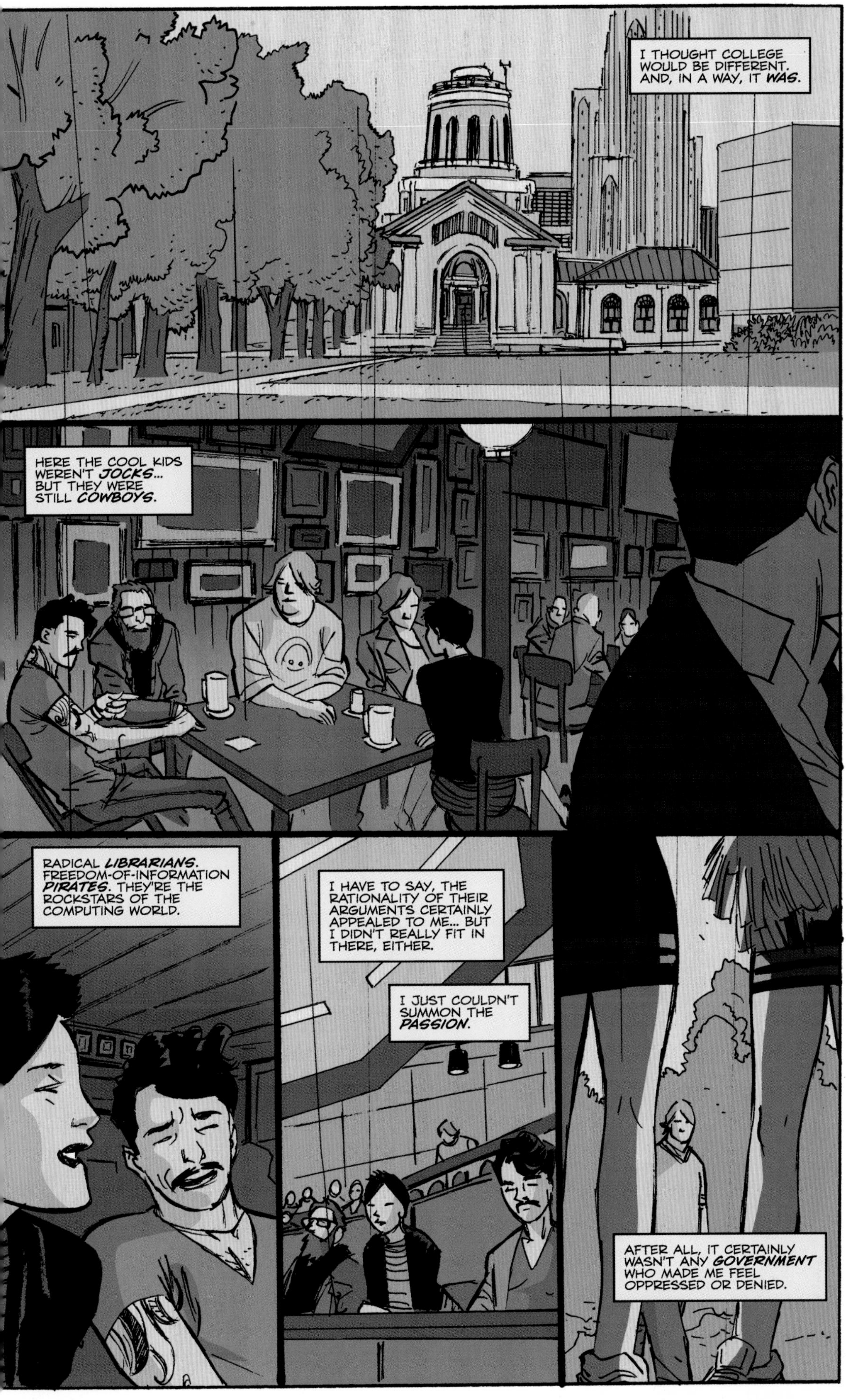
I THOUGHT COLLEGE WOULD BE DIFFERENT. AND, IN A WAY, IT WAS.
HERE THE COOL KIDS WEREN'T JOCKS... BUT THEY WERE STILL COWBOYS.
RADICAL LIBRARIANS. FREEDOM-OF-INFORMATION PIRATES. THEY'RE THE ROCKSTARS OF THE COMPUTING WORLD.
I HAVE TO SAY, THE RATIONALITY OF THEIR ARGUMENTS CERTAINLY APPEALED TO ME... BUT I DIDN'T REALLY FIT IN THERE, EITHER.
I JUST COULDN'T SUMMON THE PASSION.
AFTER ALL, IT CERTAINLY WASN'T ANY GOVERNMENT WHO MADE ME FEEL OPPRESSED OR DENIED.

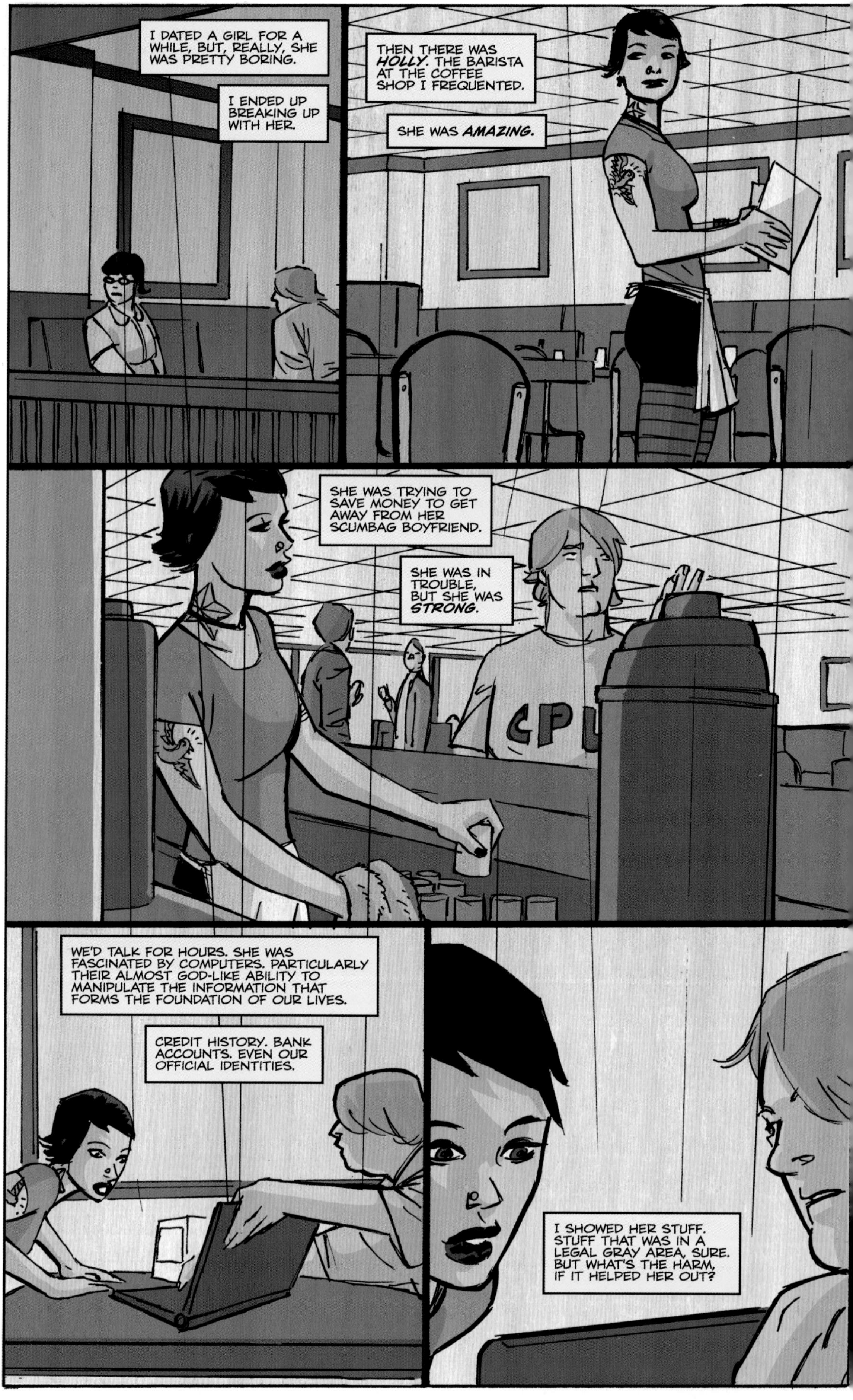

I DATED A GIRL FOR A WHILE, BUT, REALLY, SHE WAS PRETTY BORING.
I ENDED UP BREAKING UP WITH HER.
THEN THERE WAS HOLLY. THE BARISTA AT THE COFFEE SHOP I FREQUENTED.
SHE WAS AMAZING.
SHE WAS TRYING TO SAVE MONEY TO GET AWAY FROM HER SCUMBAG BOYFRIEND.
SHE WAS IN TROUBLE, BUT SHE WAS STRONG.
CPU
WE'D TALK FOR HOURS. SHE WAS FASCINATED BY COMPUTERS. PARTICULARLY THEIR ALMOST GOD-LIKE ABILITY TO MANIPULATE THE INFORMATION THAT FORMS THE FOUNDATION OF OUR LIVES.
CREDIT HISTORY. BANK ACCOUNTS. EVEN OUR OFFICIAL IDENTITIES.
I SHOWED HER STUFF. STUFF THAT WAS IN A LEGAL GRAY AREA, SURE. BUT WHAT'S THE HARM, IF IT HELPED HER OUT?

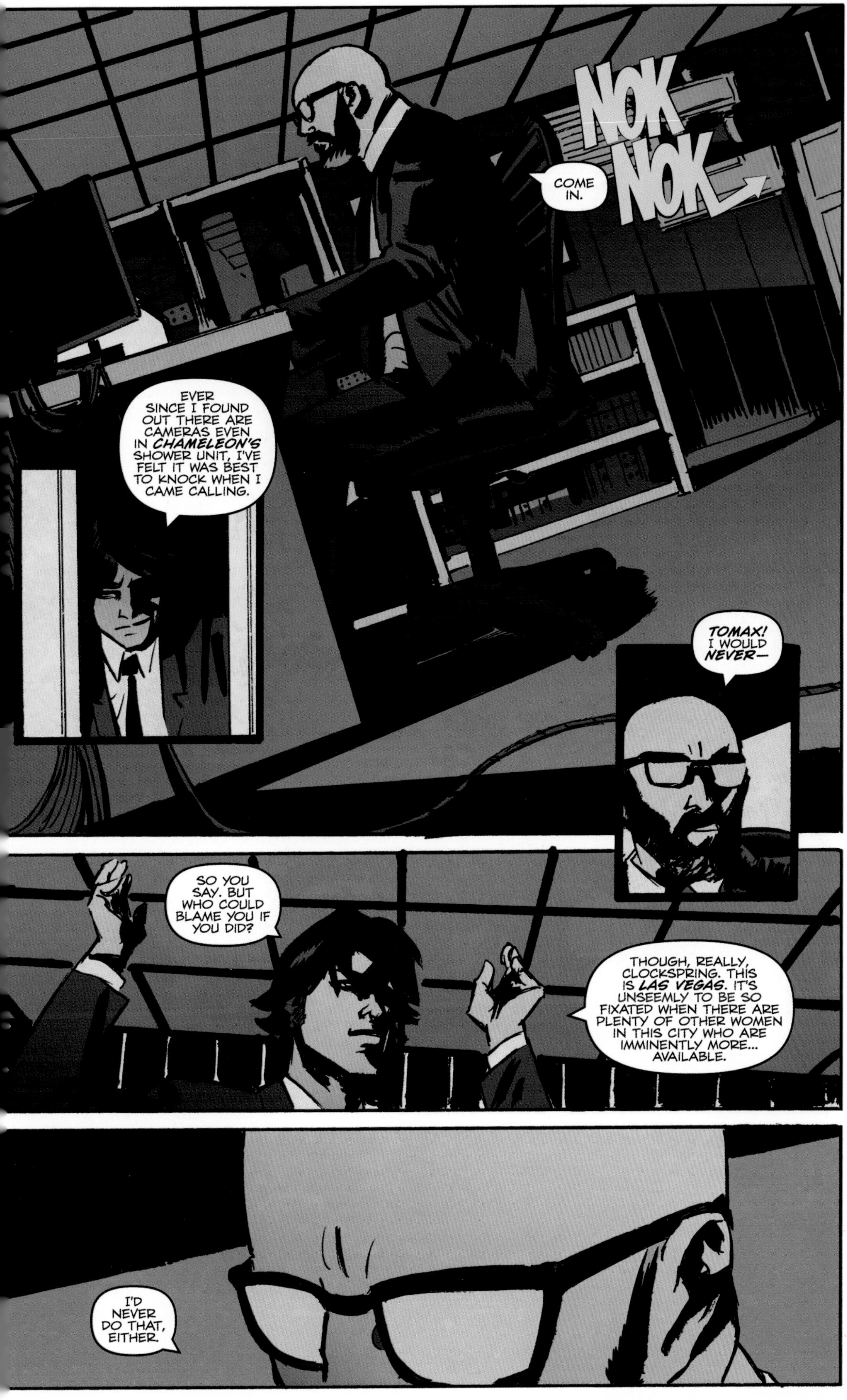

NOK NOK
COME IN.
EVER SINCE I FOUND OUT THERE ARE CAMERAS EVEN IN CHAMELEON'S SHOWER UNIT, I'VE FELT IT WAS BEST TO KNOCK WHEN I CAME CALLING.
TOMAX! I WOULD NEVER—
SO YOU SAY. BUT WHO COULD BLAME YOU IF YOU DID?
THOUGH, REALLY, CLOCKSPRING. THIS IS LAS VEGAS. IT'S UNSEEMLY TO BE SO FIXATED WHEN THERE ARE PLENTY OF OTHER WOMEN IN THIS CITY WHO ARE IMMINENTLY MORE... AVAILABLE.
I'D NEVER DO THAT, EITHER.

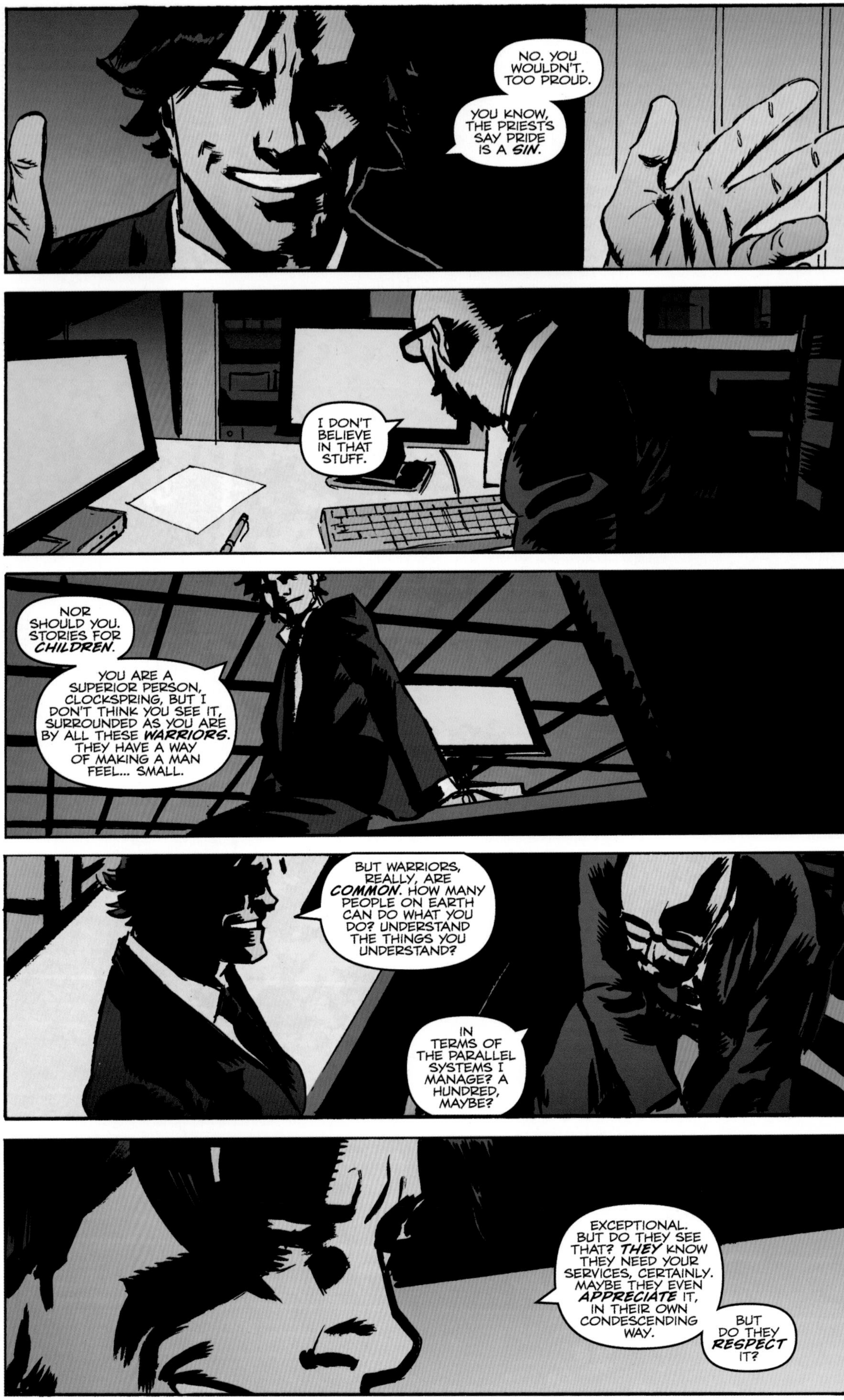
NO. YOU WOULDN'T. TOO PROUD.
YOU KNOW, THE PRIESTS SAY PRIDE IS A *SIN*.
I DON'T BELIEVE IN THAT STUFF.
NOR SHOULD YOU. STORIES FOR *CHILDREN*.
YOU ARE A SUPERIOR PERSON, CLOCKSPRING, BUT I DON'T THINK YOU SEE IT, SURROUNDED AS YOU ARE BY ALL THESE *WARRIORS*. THEY HAVE A WAY OF MAKING A MAN FEEL... SMALL.
BUT WARRIORS, REALLY, ARE *COMMON*. HOW MANY PEOPLE ON EARTH CAN DO WHAT YOU DO? UNDERSTAND THE THINGS YOU UNDERSTAND?
IN TERMS OF THE PARALLEL SYSTEMS I MANAGE? A HUNDRED, MAYBE?
EXCEPTIONAL. BUT DO THEY SEE THAT? *THEY* KNOW THEY NEED YOUR SERVICES, CERTAINLY. MAYBE THEY EVEN *APPRECIATE* IT, IN THEIR OWN CONDESCENDING WAY.
BUT DO THEY *RESPECT* IT?

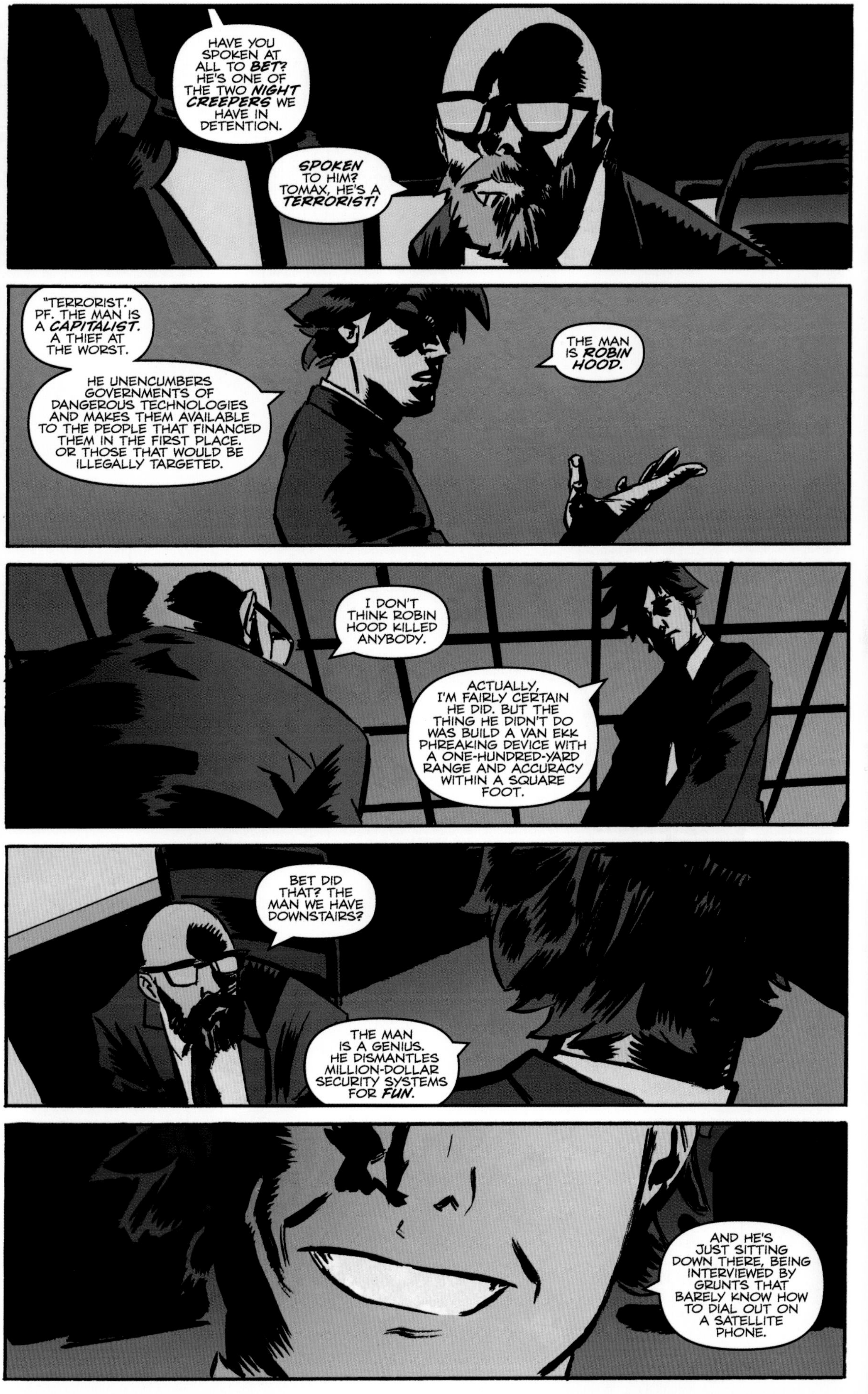
HAVE YOU SPOKEN AT ALL TO *BET?* HE'S ONE OF THE TWO *NIGHT CREEPERS* WE HAVE IN DETENTION.
SPOKEN TO HIM? TOMAX, HE'S A *TERRORIST!*
"TERRORIST." PF. THE MAN IS A *CAPITALIST*. A THIEF AT THE WORST.
HE UNENCUMBERS GOVERNMENTS OF DANGEROUS TECHNOLOGIES AND MAKES THEM AVAILABLE TO THE PEOPLE THAT FINANCED THEM IN THE FIRST PLACE. OR THOSE THAT WOULD BE ILLEGALLY TARGETED.
THE MAN IS *ROBIN HOOD*.
I DON'T THINK ROBIN HOOD KILLED ANYBODY.
ACTUALLY, I'M FAIRLY CERTAIN HE DID. BUT THE THING HE DIDN'T DO WAS BUILD A VAN EKK PHREAKING DEVICE WITH A ONE-HUNDRED-YARD RANGE AND ACCURACY WITHIN A SQUARE FOOT.
BET DID THAT? THE MAN WE HAVE DOWNSTAIRS?
THE MAN IS A GENIUS. HE DISMANTLES MILLION-DOLLAR SECURITY SYSTEMS FOR *FUN*.
AND HE'S JUST SITTING DOWN THERE, BEING INTERVIEWED BY GRUNTS THAT BARELY KNOW HOW TO DIAL OUT ON A SATELLITE PHONE.

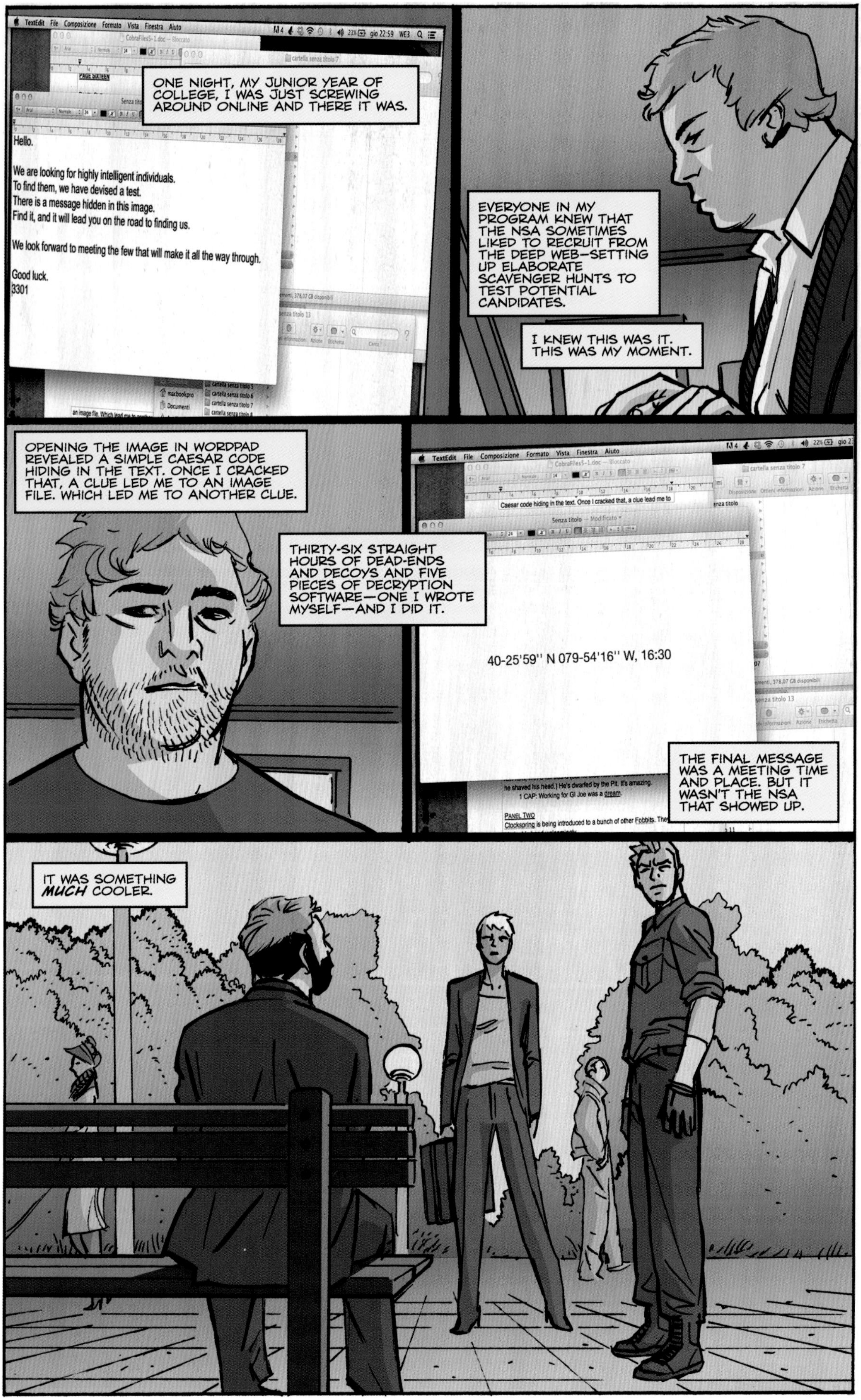
ONE NIGHT, MY JUNIOR YEAR OF COLLEGE, I WAS JUST SCREWING AROUND ONLINE AND THERE IT WAS.
Hello.
We are looking for highly intelligent individuals.
To find them, we have devised a test.
There is a message hidden in this image.
Find it, and it will lead you on the road to finding us.
We look forward to meeting the few that will make it all the way through.
Good luck.
3301
EVERYONE IN MY PROGRAM KNEW THAT THE NSA SOMETIMES LIKED TO RECRUIT FROM THE DEEP WEB—SETTING UP ELABORATE SCAVENGER HUNTS TO TEST POTENTIAL CANDIDATES.
I KNEW THIS WAS IT. THIS WAS MY MOMENT.
OPENING THE IMAGE IN WORDPAD REVEALED A SIMPLE CAESAR CODE HIDING IN THE TEXT. ONCE I CRACKED THAT, A CLUE LED ME TO AN IMAGE FILE. WHICH LED ME TO ANOTHER CLUE.
THIRTY-SIX STRAIGHT HOURS OF DEAD-ENDS AND DECOYS AND FIVE PIECES OF DECRYPTION SOFTWARE—ONE I WROTE MYSELF—AND I DID IT.
40-25'59'' N 079-54'16'' W, 16:30
THE FINAL MESSAGE WAS A MEETING TIME AND PLACE. BUT IT WASN'T THE NSA THAT SHOWED UP.
IT WAS SOMETHING *MUCH* COOLER.

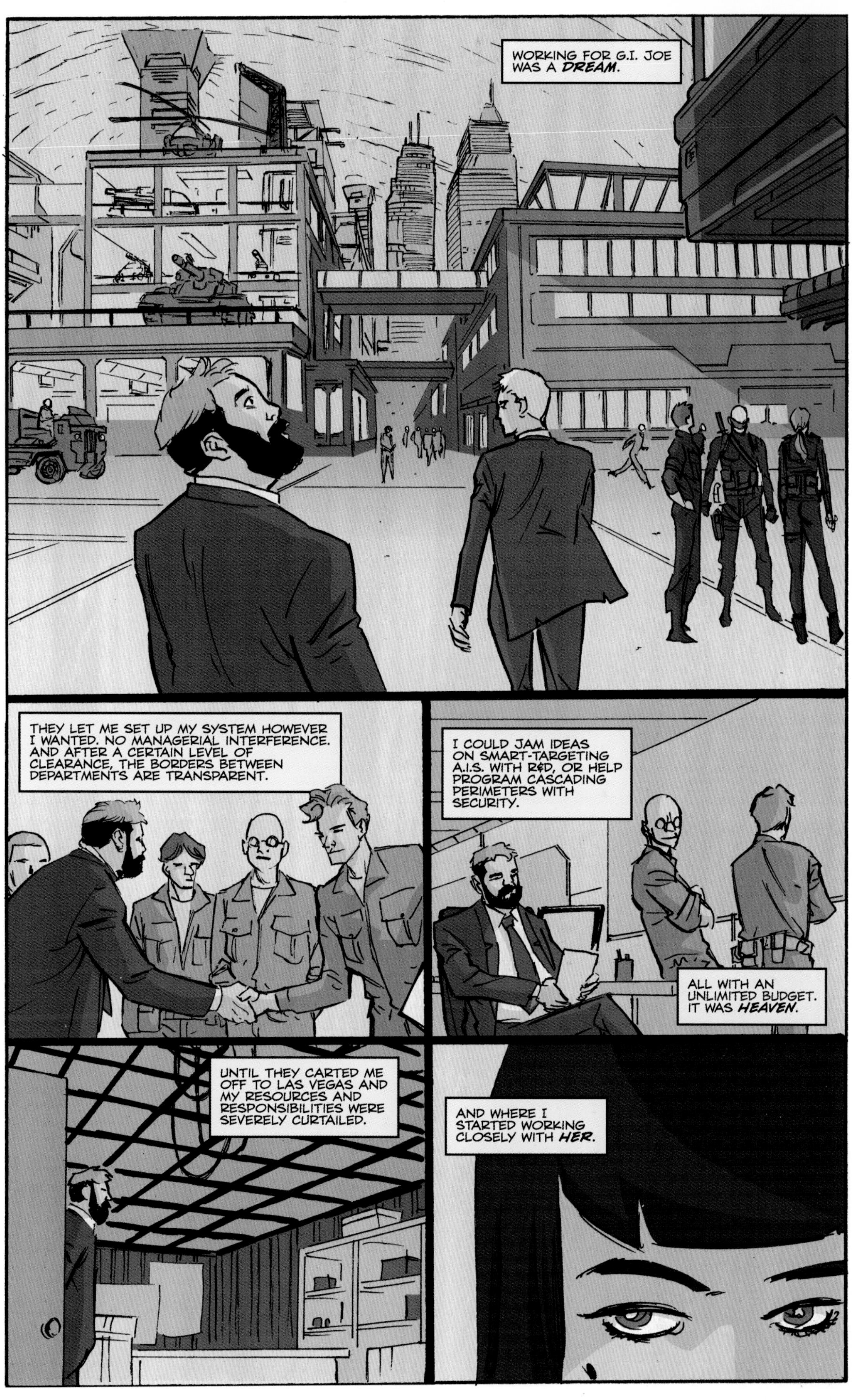
WORKING FOR G.I. JOE WAS A *DREAM*.
THEY LET ME SET UP MY SYSTEM HOWEVER I WANTED. NO MANAGERIAL INTERFERENCE. AND AFTER A CERTAIN LEVEL OF CLEARANCE, THE BORDERS BETWEEN DEPARTMENTS ARE TRANSPARENT.
I COULD JAM IDEAS ON SMART-TARGETING A.I.S. WITH R&D, OR HELP PROGRAM CASCADING PERIMETERS WITH SECURITY.
ALL WITH AN UNLIMITED BUDGET. IT WAS *HEAVEN*.
UNTIL THEY CARTED ME OFF TO LAS VEGAS AND MY RESOURCES AND RESPONSIBILITIES WERE SEVERELY CURTAILED.
AND WHERE I STARTED WORKING CLOSELY WITH *HER*.

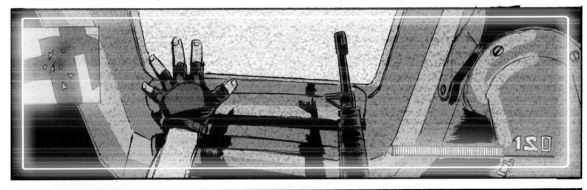

I'VE NEVER BEEN IN A WAR.

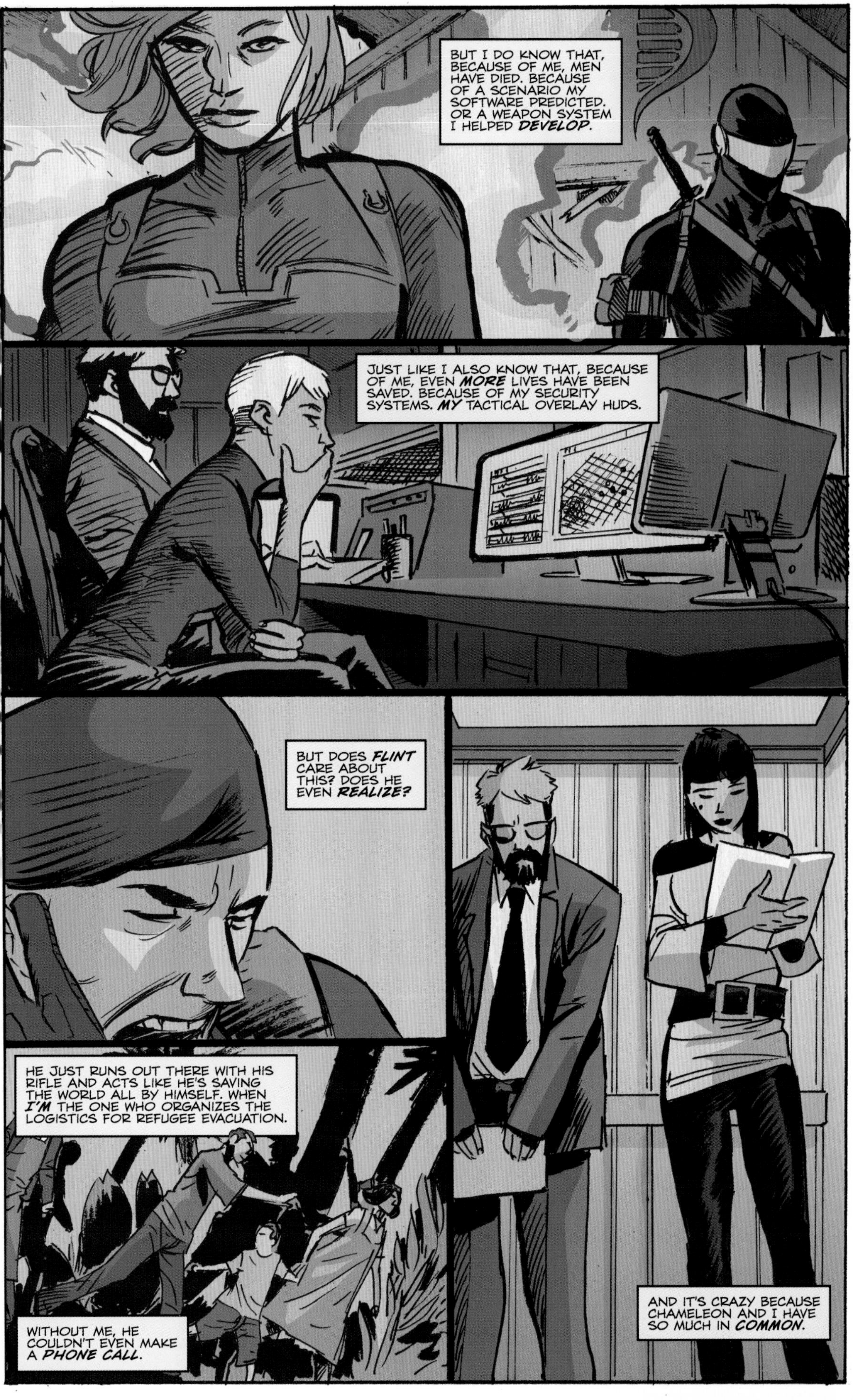
BUT I DO KNOW THAT, BECAUSE OF ME, MEN HAVE DIED. BECAUSE OF A SCENARIO MY SOFTWARE PREDICTED. OR A WEAPON SYSTEM I HELPED *DEVELOP*.
JUST LIKE I ALSO KNOW THAT, BECAUSE OF ME, EVEN *MORE* LIVES HAVE BEEN SAVED. BECAUSE OF MY SECURITY SYSTEMS. *MY* TACTICAL OVERLAY HUDS.
BUT DOES *FLINT* CARE ABOUT THIS? DOES HE EVEN *REALIZE?*
HE JUST RUNS OUT THERE WITH HIS RIFLE AND ACTS LIKE HE'S SAVING THE WORLD ALL BY HIMSELF. WHEN *I'M* THE ONE WHO ORGANIZES THE LOGISTICS FOR REFUGEE EVACUATION.
WITHOUT ME, HE COULDN'T EVEN MAKE A *PHONE CALL*.
AND IT'S CRAZY BECAUSE CHAMELEON AND I HAVE SO MUCH IN *COMMON*.

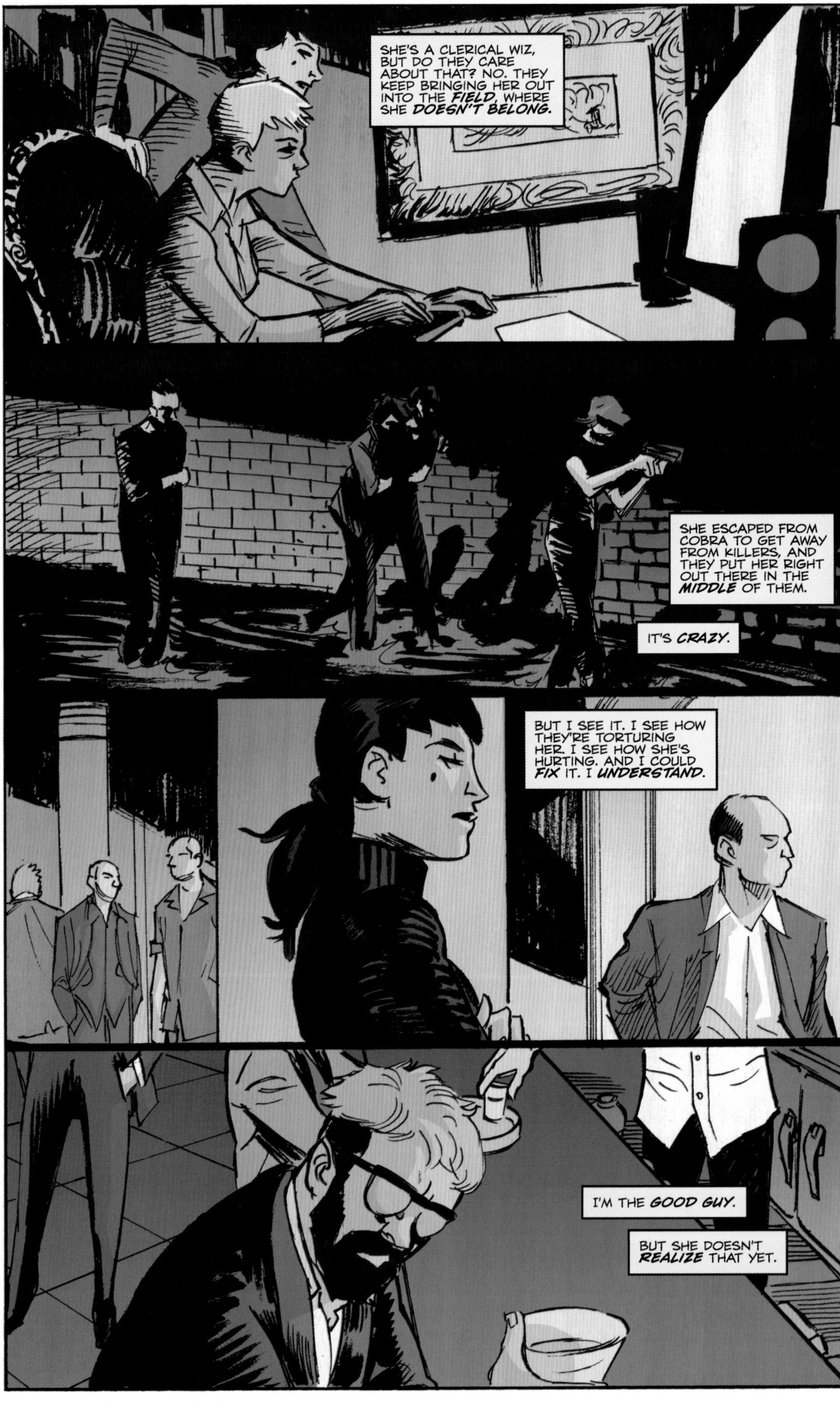
SHE'S A CLERICAL WIZ, BUT DO THEY CARE ABOUT THAT? NO. THEY KEEP BRINGING HER OUT INTO THE FIELD, WHERE SHE DOESN'T BELONG.
SHE ESCAPED FROM COBRA TO GET AWAY FROM KILLERS, AND THEY PUT HER RIGHT OUT THERE IN THE MIDDLE OF THEM.
IT'S CRAZY.
BUT I SEE IT. I SEE HOW THEY'RE TORTURING HER. I SEE HOW SHE'S HURTING. AND I COULD FIX IT. I UNDERSTAND.
I'M THE GOOD GUY.
BUT SHE DOESN'T REALIZE THAT YET.

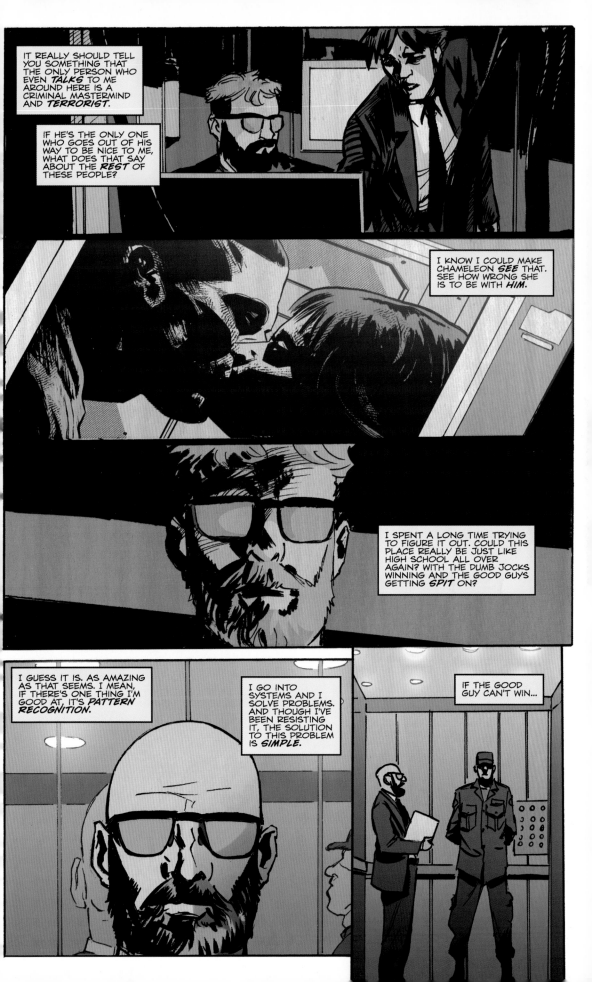

IT REALLY SHOULD TELL YOU SOMETHING THAT THE ONLY PERSON WHO EVEN *TALKS* TO ME AROUND HERE IS A CRIMINAL MASTERMIND AND *TERRORIST.*

IF HE'S THE ONLY ONE WHO GOES OUT OF HIS WAY TO BE NICE TO ME, WHAT DOES THAT SAY ABOUT THE *REST* OF THESE PEOPLE?

I KNOW I COULD MAKE CHAMELEON *SEE* THAT. SEE HOW WRONG SHE IS TO BE WITH *HIM.*

I SPENT A LONG TIME TRYING TO FIGURE IT OUT. COULD THIS PLACE REALLY BE JUST LIKE HIGH SCHOOL ALL OVER AGAIN? WITH THE DUMB JOCKS WINNING AND THE GOOD GUYS GETTING *SPIT* ON?

I GUESS IT IS. AS AMAZING AS THAT SEEMS. I MEAN, IF THERE'S ONE THING I'M GOOD AT, IT'S *PATTERN RECOGNITION.*

I GO INTO SYSTEMS AND I SOLVE PROBLEMS. AND THOUGH I'VE BEEN RESISTING IT, THE SOLUTION TO THIS PROBLEM IS *SIMPLE.*

IF THE GOOD GUY CAN'T WIN...

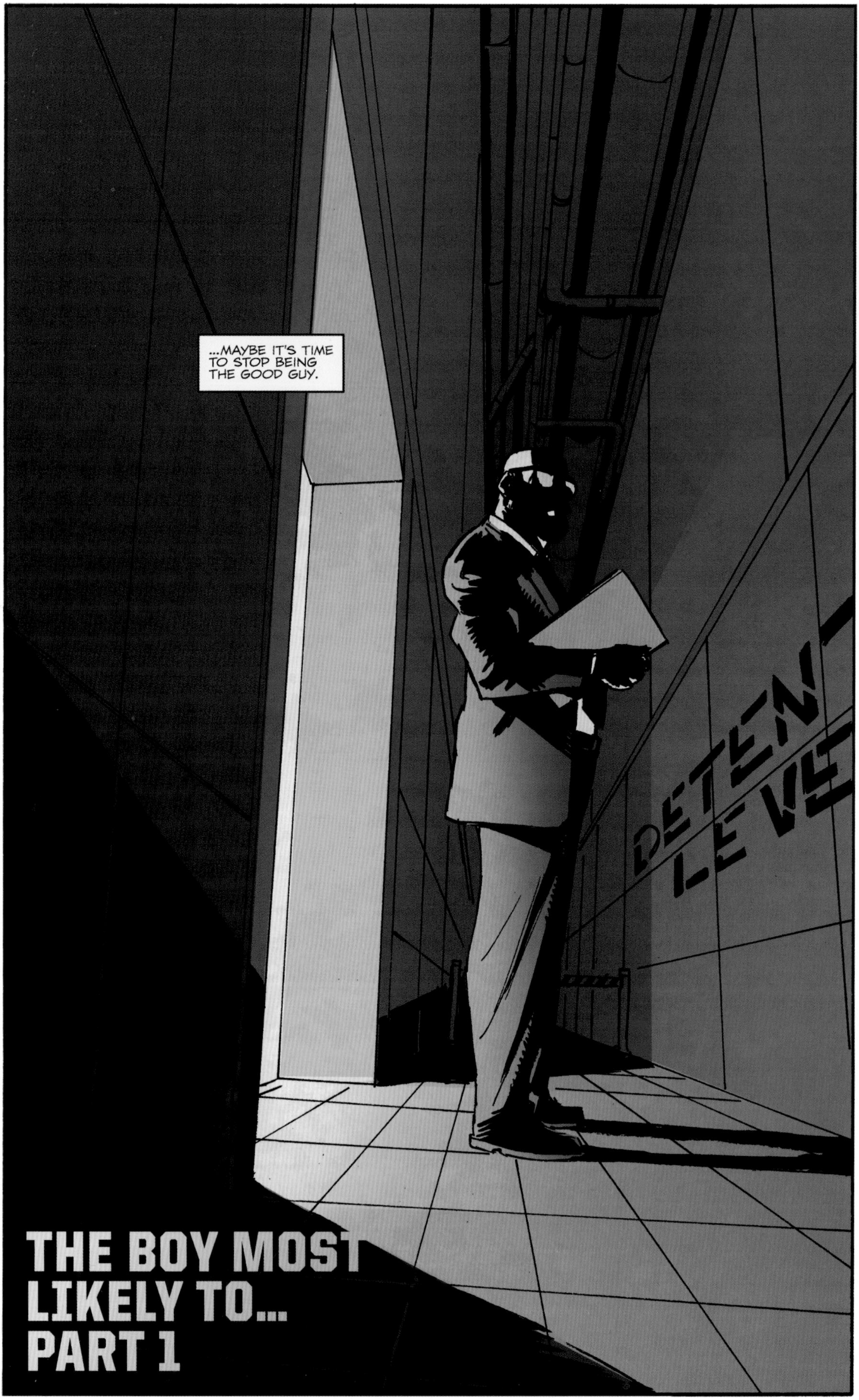
...MAYBE IT'S TIME TO STOP BEING THE GOOD GUY.
THE BOY MOST LIKELY TO... PART 1

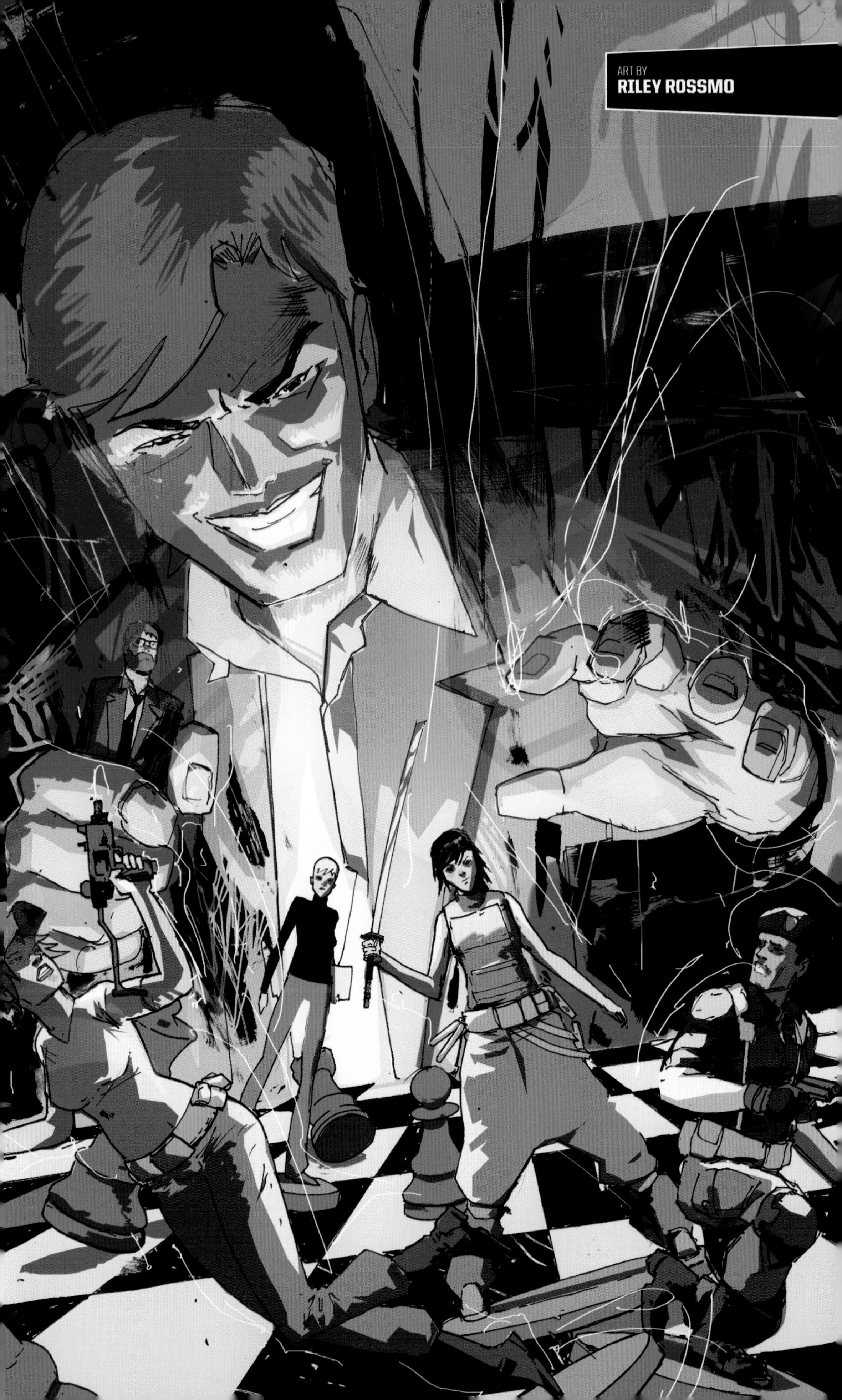

ART BY
RILEY ROSSMO

ART BY
ANTONIO FUSO
COLORS BY
STEFANO SIMEONE

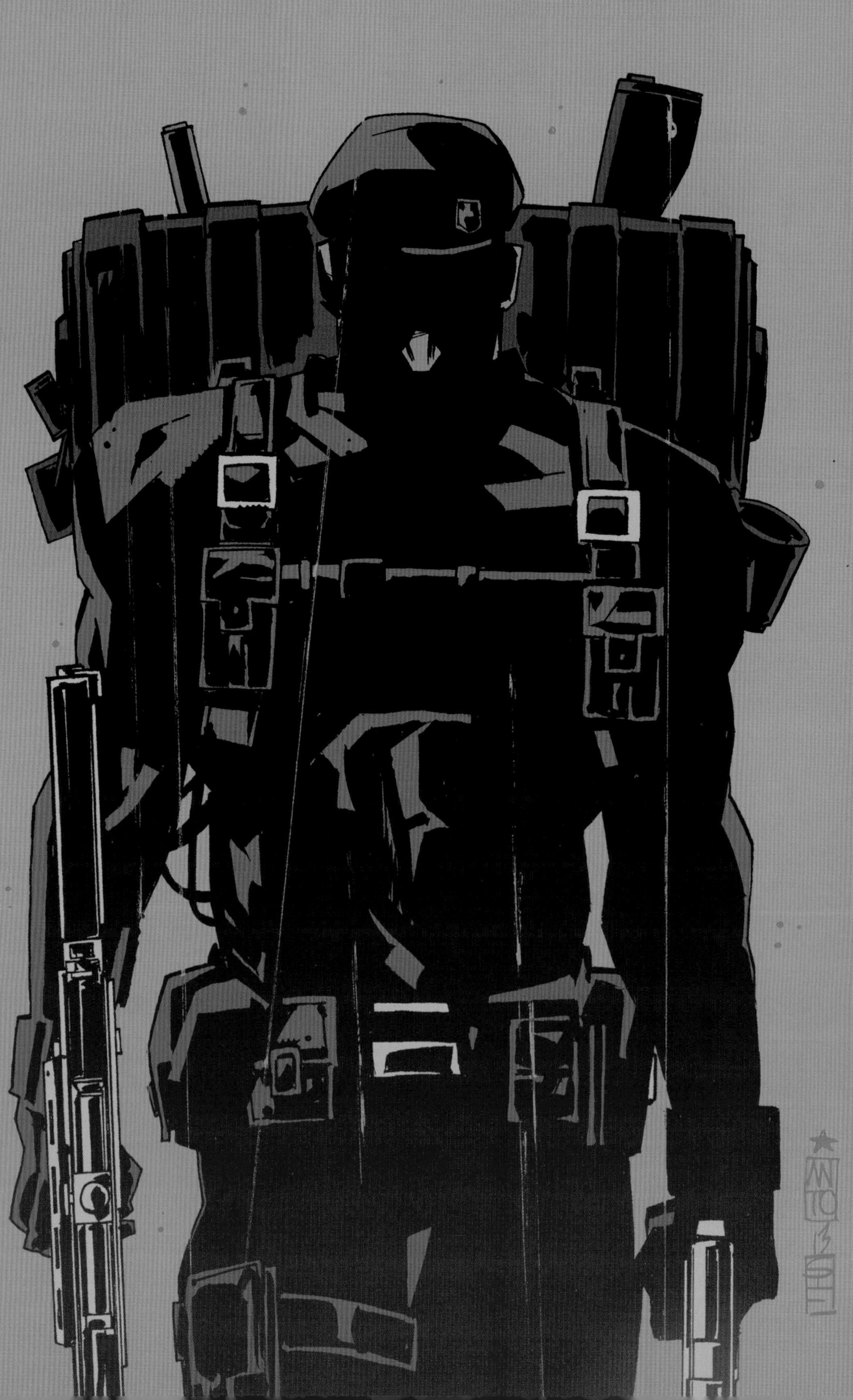

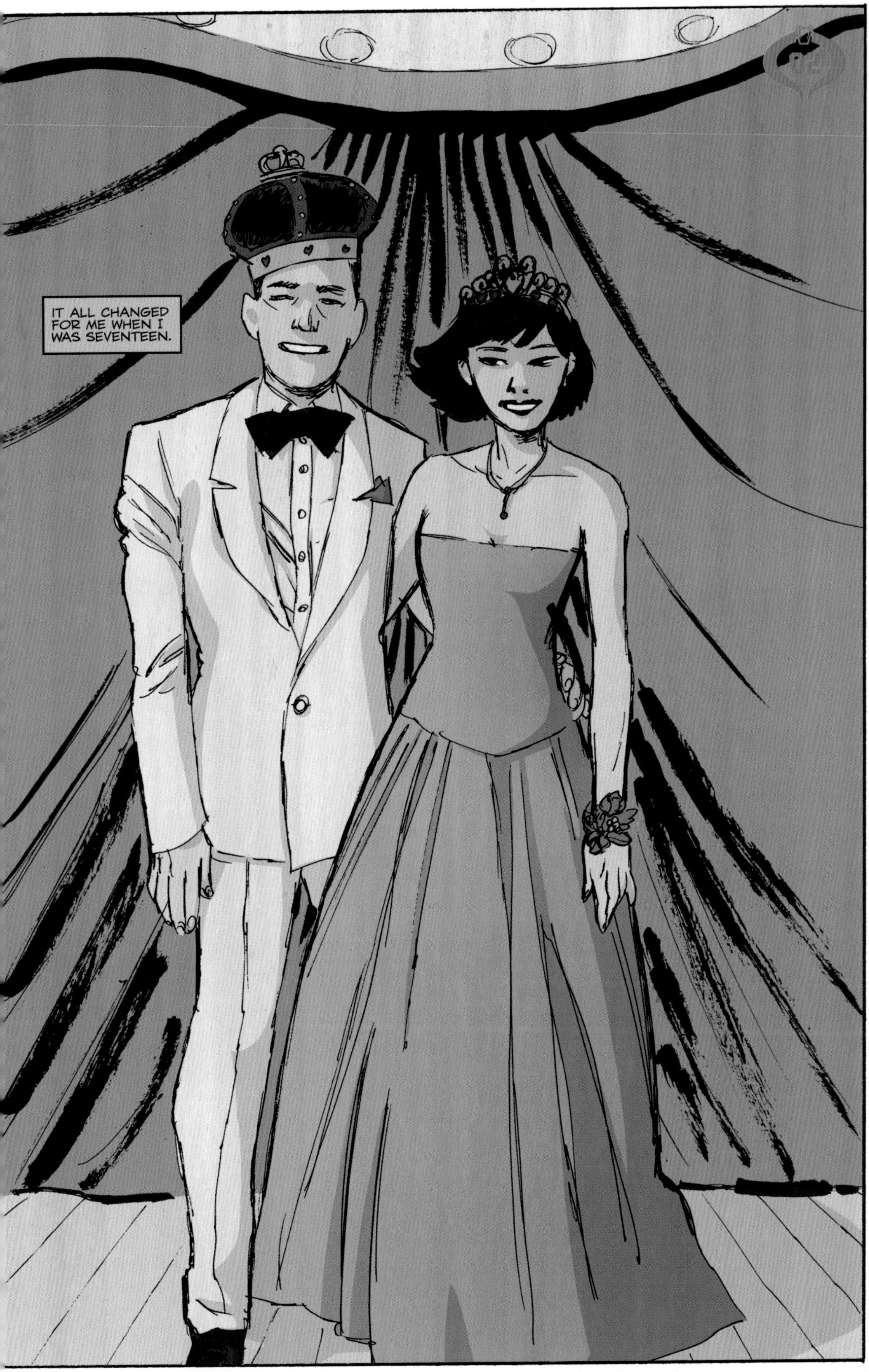
IT ALL CHANGED FOR ME WHEN I WAS SEVENTEEN.

THE BOY MOST LIKELY TO... PART 2

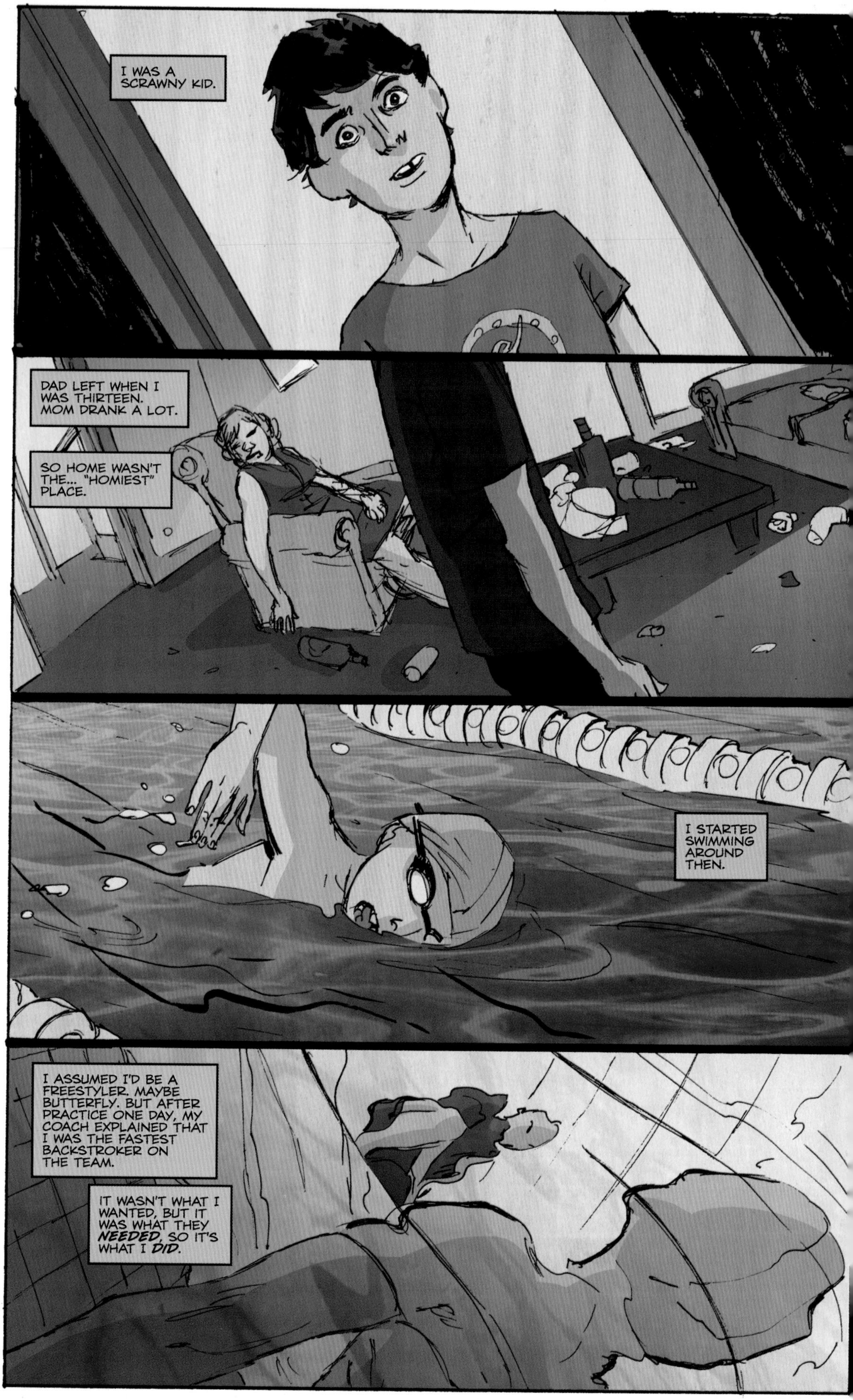

I WAS A SCRAWNY KID.
DAD LEFT WHEN I WAS THIRTEEN. MOM DRANK A LOT.
SO HOME WASN'T THE... "HOMIEST" PLACE.
I STARTED SWIMMING AROUND THEN.
I ASSUMED I'D BE A FREESTYLER. MAYBE BUTTERFLY. BUT AFTER PRACTICE ONE DAY, MY COACH EXPLAINED THAT I WAS THE FASTEST BACKSTROKER ON THE TEAM.
IT WASN'T WHAT I WANTED, BUT IT WAS WHAT THEY ***NEEDED***, SO IT'S WHAT I ***DID***.

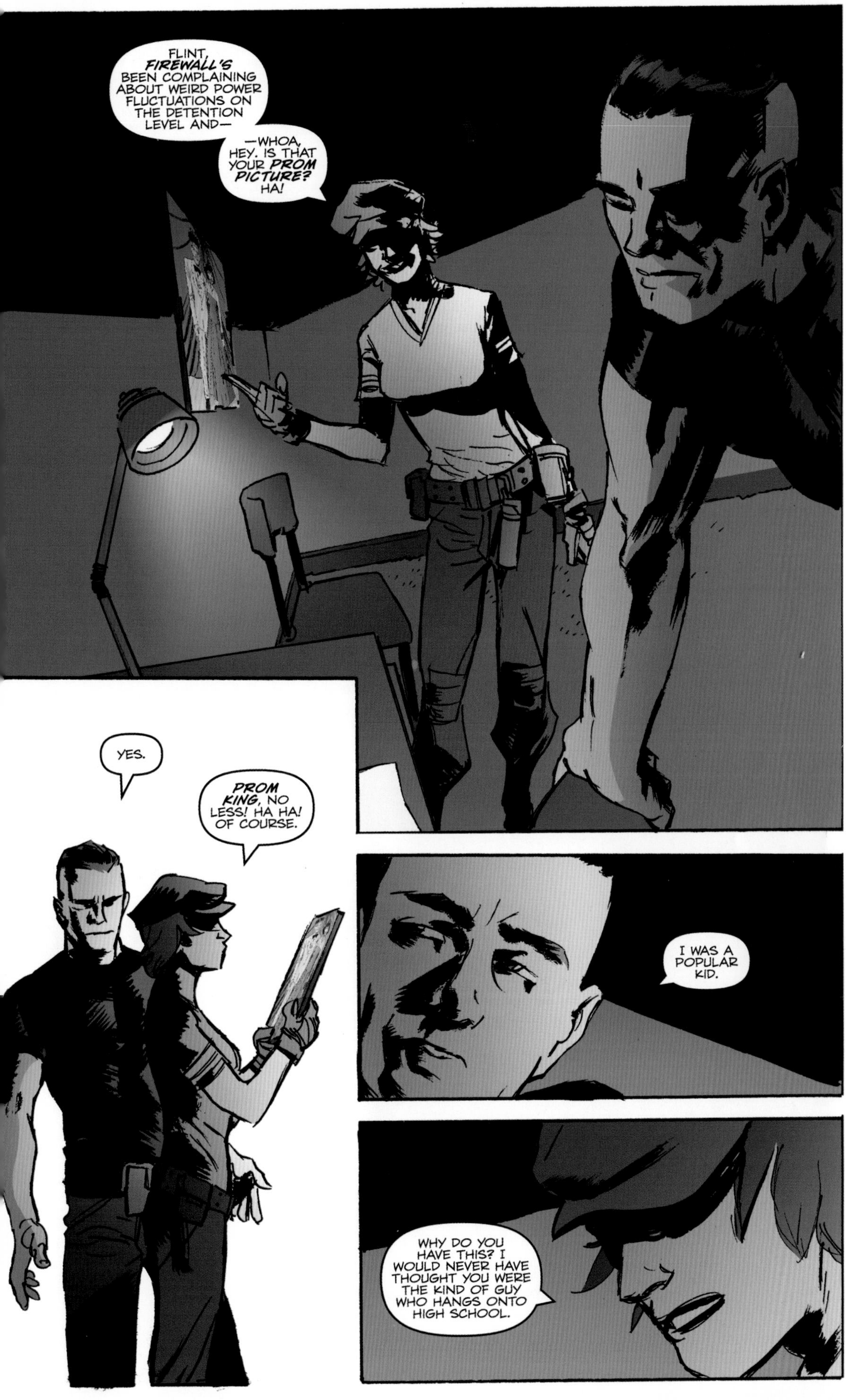
FLINT, FIREWALL'S BEEN COMPLAINING ABOUT WEIRD POWER FLUCTUATIONS ON THE DETENTION LEVEL AND—
—WHOA, HEY. IS THAT YOUR PROM PICTURE? HA!
YES.
PROM KING, NO LESS! HA HA! OF COURSE.
I WAS A POPULAR KID.
WHY DO YOU HAVE THIS? I WOULD NEVER HAVE THOUGHT YOU WERE THE KIND OF GUY WHO HANGS ONTO HIGH SCHOOL.

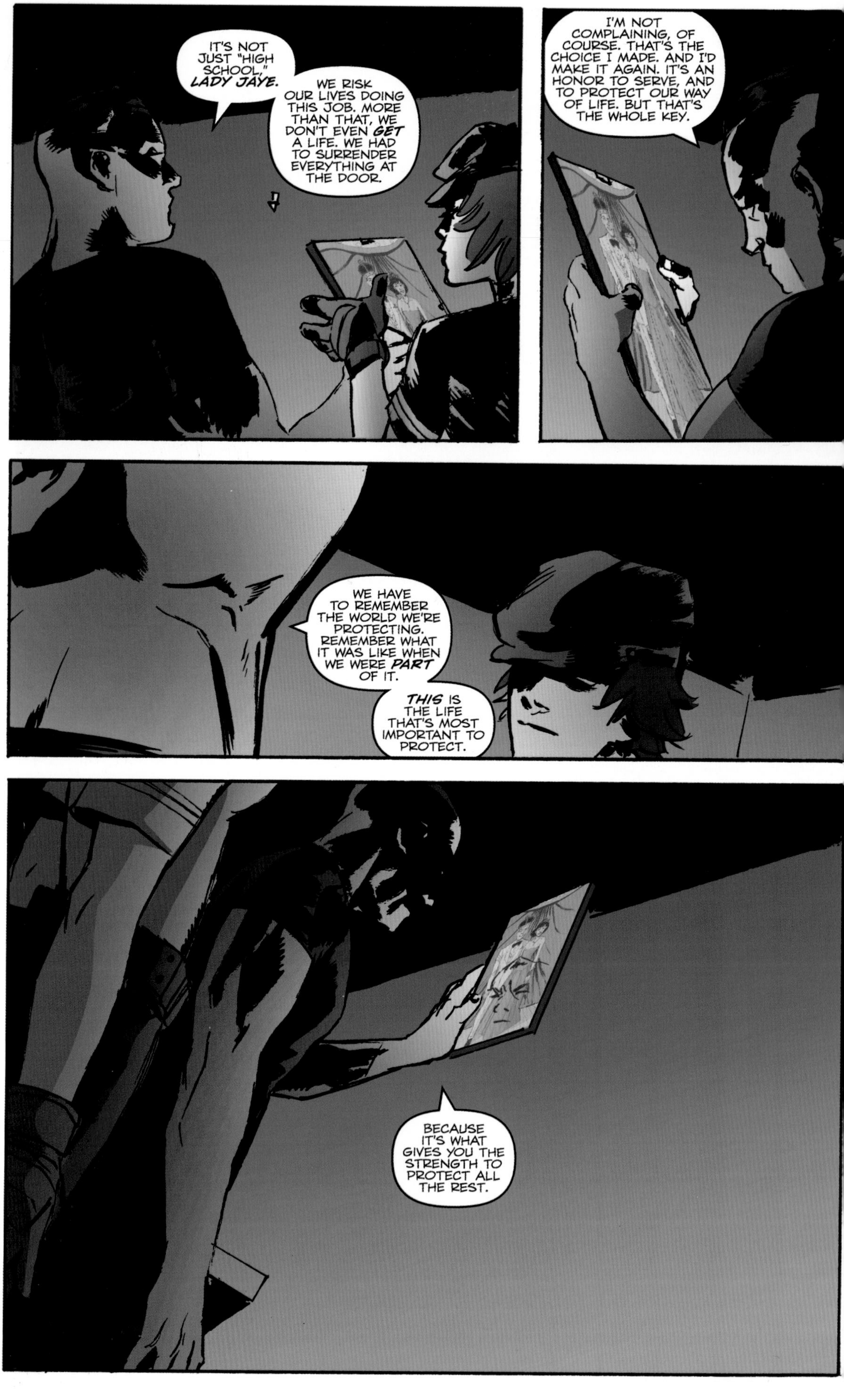
IT'S NOT JUST "HIGH SCHOOL," LADY JAYE.
WE RISK OUR LIVES DOING THIS JOB. MORE THAN THAT, WE DON'T EVEN GET A LIFE. WE HAD TO SURRENDER EVERYTHING AT THE DOOR.
I'M NOT COMPLAINING, OF COURSE. THAT'S THE CHOICE I MADE. AND I'D MAKE IT AGAIN. IT'S AN HONOR TO SERVE, AND TO PROTECT OUR WAY OF LIFE. BUT THAT'S THE WHOLE KEY.
WE HAVE TO REMEMBER THE WORLD WE'RE PROTECTING. REMEMBER WHAT IT WAS LIKE WHEN WE WERE PART OF IT.
THIS IS THE LIFE THAT'S MOST IMPORTANT TO PROTECT.
BECAUSE IT'S WHAT GIVES YOU THE STRENGTH TO PROTECT ALL THE REST.

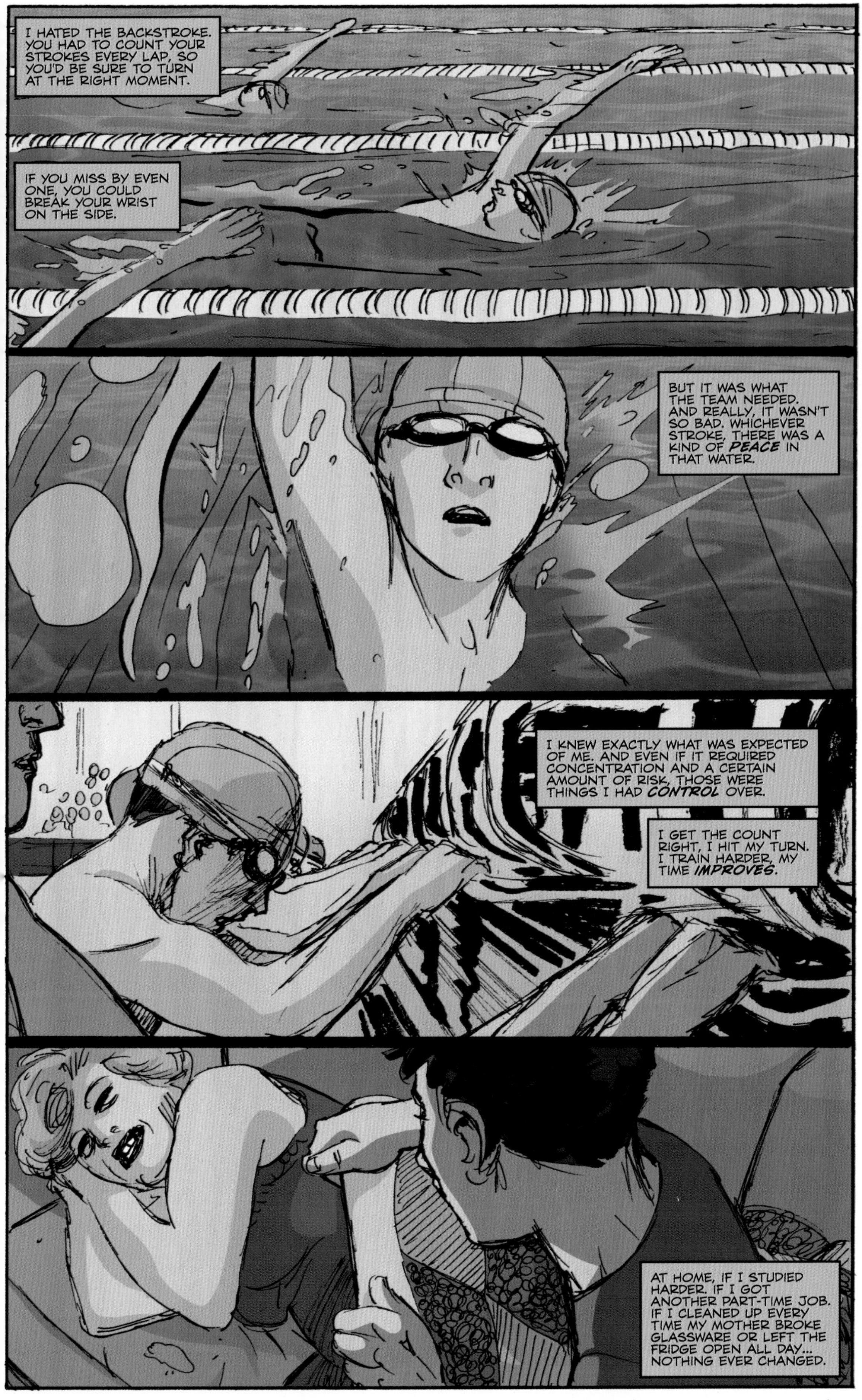
I HATED THE BACKSTROKE. YOU HAD TO COUNT YOUR STROKES EVERY LAP, SO YOU'D BE SURE TO TURN AT THE RIGHT MOMENT.
IF YOU MISS BY EVEN ONE, YOU COULD BREAK YOUR WRIST ON THE SIDE.
BUT IT WAS WHAT THE TEAM NEEDED. AND REALLY, IT WASN'T SO BAD. WHICHEVER STROKE, THERE WAS A KIND OF PEACE IN THAT WATER.
I KNEW EXACTLY WHAT WAS EXPECTED OF ME. AND EVEN IF IT REQUIRED CONCENTRATION AND A CERTAIN AMOUNT OF RISK, THOSE WERE THINGS I HAD CONTROL OVER.
I GET THE COUNT RIGHT, I HIT MY TURN. I TRAIN HARDER, MY TIME IMPROVES.
AT HOME, IF I STUDIED HARDER. IF I GOT ANOTHER PART-TIME JOB. IF I CLEANED UP EVERY TIME MY MOTHER BROKE GLASSWARE OR LEFT THE FRIDGE OPEN ALL DAY... NOTHING EVER CHANGED.

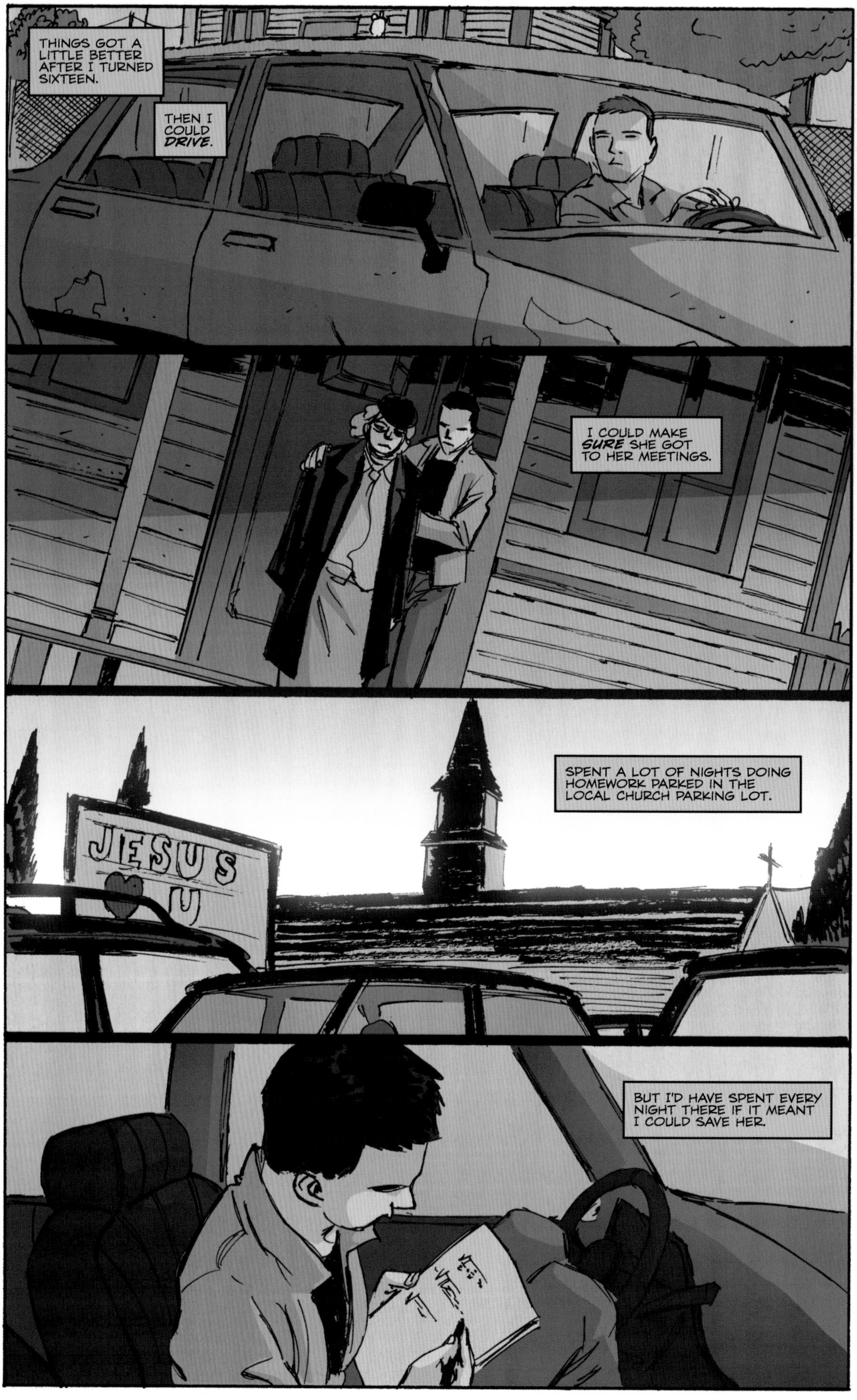
THINGS GOT A LITTLE BETTER AFTER I TURNED SIXTEEN.
THEN I COULD *DRIVE*.
I COULD MAKE *SURE* SHE GOT TO HER MEETINGS.
JESUS ♥ U
SPENT A LOT OF NIGHTS DOING HOMEWORK PARKED IN THE LOCAL CHURCH PARKING LOT.
BUT I'D HAVE SPENT EVERY NIGHT THERE IF IT MEANT I COULD SAVE HER.

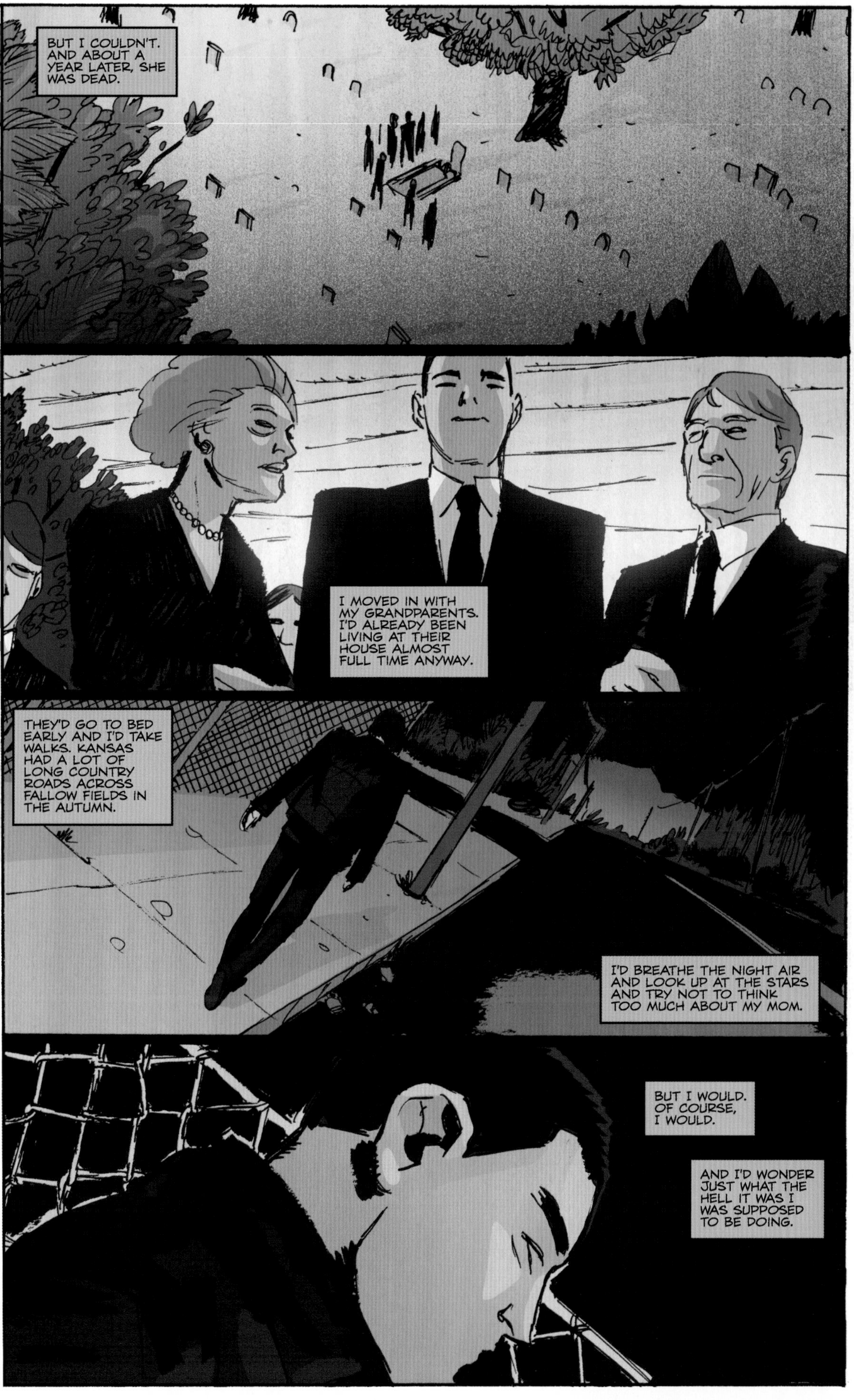
BUT I COULDN'T. AND ABOUT A YEAR LATER, SHE WAS DEAD.
I MOVED IN WITH MY GRANDPARENTS. I'D ALREADY BEEN LIVING AT THEIR HOUSE ALMOST FULL TIME ANYWAY.
THEY'D GO TO BED EARLY AND I'D TAKE WALKS. KANSAS HAD A LOT OF LONG COUNTRY ROADS ACROSS FALLOW FIELDS IN THE AUTUMN.
I'D BREATHE THE NIGHT AIR AND LOOK UP AT THE STARS AND TRY NOT TO THINK TOO MUCH ABOUT MY MOM.
BUT I WOULD. OF COURSE, I WOULD.
AND I'D WONDER JUST WHAT THE HELL IT WAS I WAS SUPPOSED TO BE DOING.

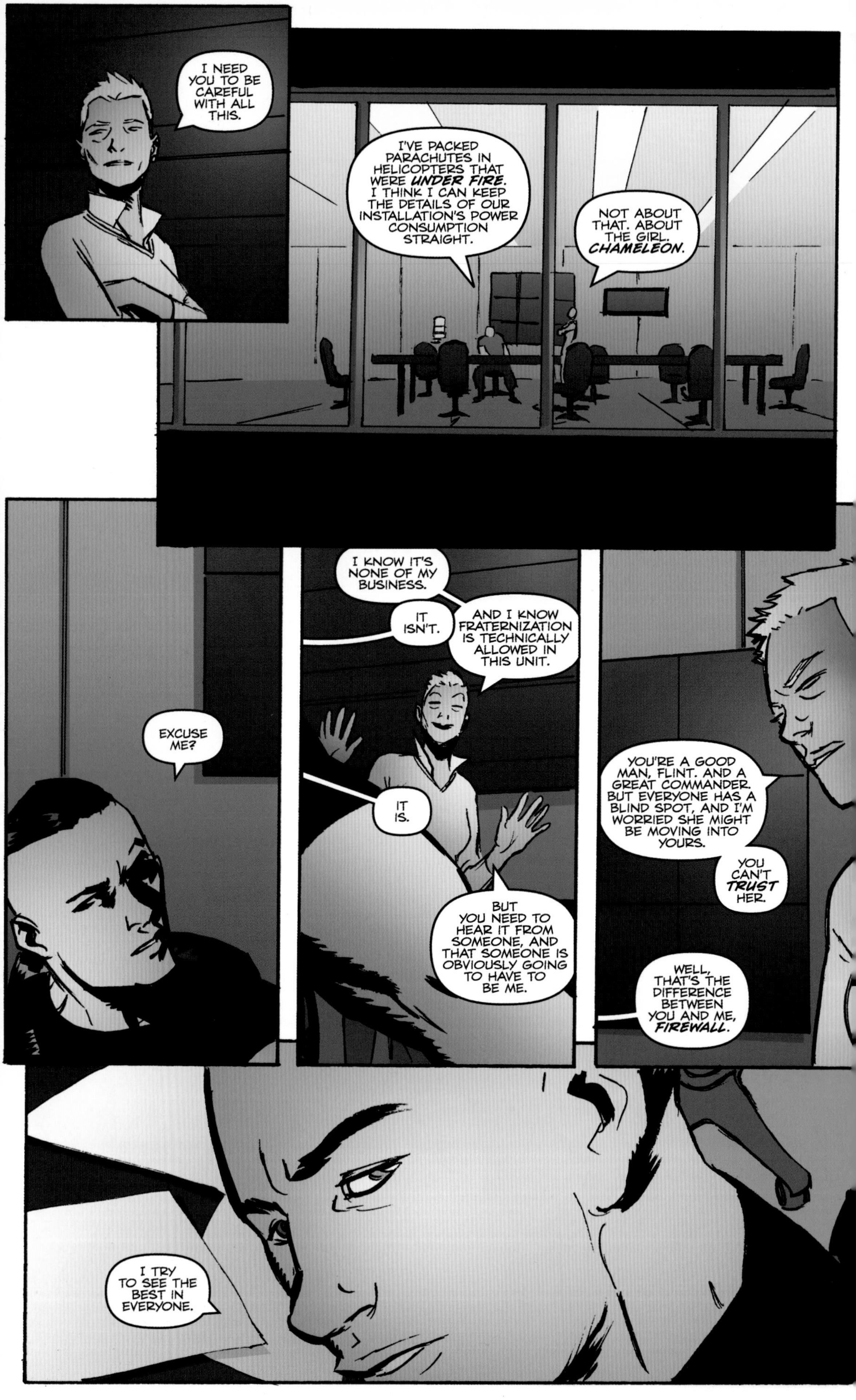
I NEED YOU TO BE CAREFUL WITH ALL THIS.
I'VE PACKED PARACHUTES IN HELICOPTERS THAT WERE UNDER FIRE. I THINK I CAN KEEP THE DETAILS OF OUR INSTALLATION'S POWER CONSUMPTION STRAIGHT.
NOT ABOUT THAT. ABOUT THE GIRL. CHAMELEON.
EXCUSE ME?
I KNOW IT'S NONE OF MY BUSINESS.
IT ISN'T.
AND I KNOW FRATERNIZATION IS TECHNICALLY ALLOWED IN THIS UNIT.
IT IS.
BUT YOU NEED TO HEAR IT FROM SOMEONE, AND THAT SOMEONE IS OBVIOUSLY GOING TO HAVE TO BE ME.
YOU'RE A GOOD MAN, FLINT. AND A GREAT COMMANDER. BUT EVERYONE HAS A BLIND SPOT, AND I'M WORRIED SHE MIGHT BE MOVING INTO YOURS.
YOU CAN'T TRUST HER.
WELL, THAT'S THE DIFFERENCE BETWEEN YOU AND ME, FIREWALL.
I TRY TO SEE THE BEST IN EVERYONE.

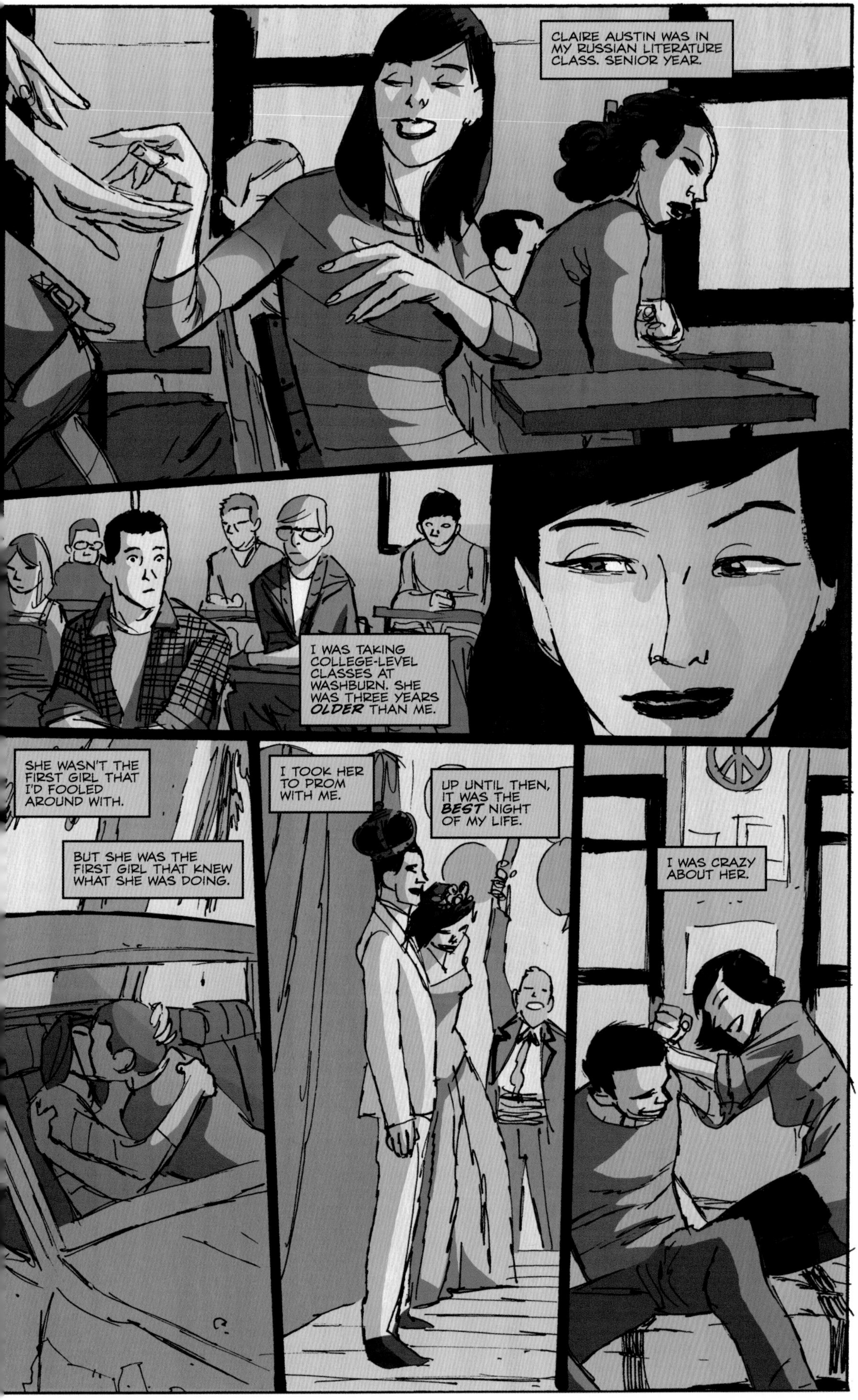
CLAIRE AUSTIN WAS IN MY RUSSIAN LITERATURE CLASS. SENIOR YEAR.
I WAS TAKING COLLEGE-LEVEL CLASSES AT WASHBURN. SHE WAS THREE YEARS *OLDER* THAN ME.
SHE WASN'T THE FIRST GIRL THAT I'D FOOLED AROUND WITH.
BUT SHE WAS THE FIRST GIRL THAT KNEW WHAT SHE WAS DOING.
I TOOK HER TO PROM WITH ME.
UP UNTIL THEN, IT WAS THE *BEST* NIGHT OF MY LIFE.
I WAS CRAZY ABOUT HER.

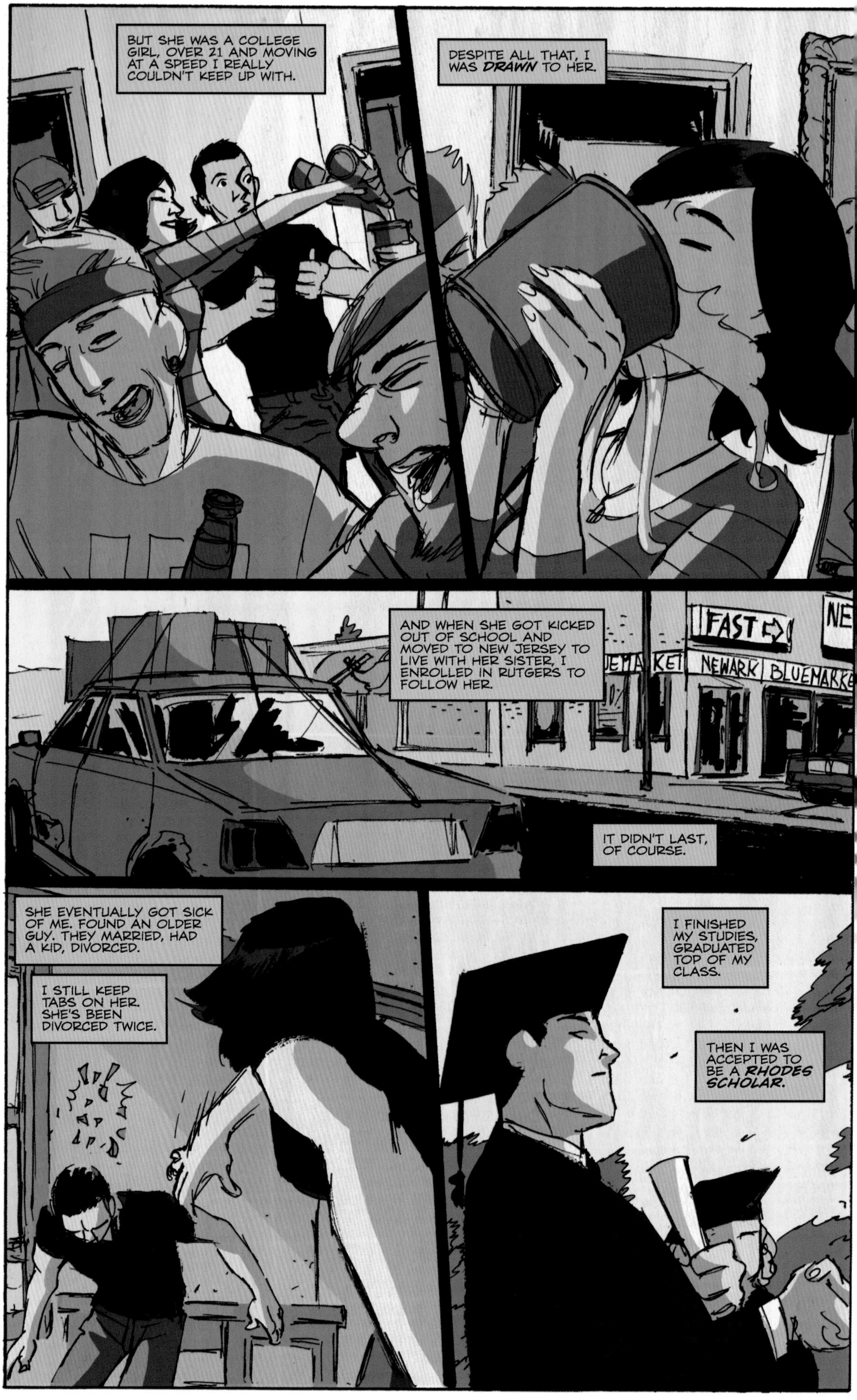

BUT SHE WAS A COLLEGE GIRL, OVER 21 AND MOVING AT A SPEED I REALLY COULDN'T KEEP UP WITH.
DESPITE ALL THAT, I WAS *DRAWN* TO HER.
AND WHEN SHE GOT KICKED OUT OF SCHOOL AND MOVED TO NEW JERSEY TO LIVE WITH HER SISTER, I ENROLLED IN RUTGERS TO FOLLOW HER.
FAST
NEWARK BLUEMARKE
IT DIDN'T LAST, OF COURSE.
SHE EVENTUALLY GOT SICK OF ME. FOUND AN OLDER GUY. THEY MARRIED, HAD A KID, DIVORCED.
I STILL KEEP TABS ON HER. SHE'S BEEN DIVORCED TWICE.
I FINISHED MY STUDIES, GRADUATED TOP OF MY CLASS.
THEN I WAS ACCEPTED TO BE A ***RHODES SCHOLAR***.

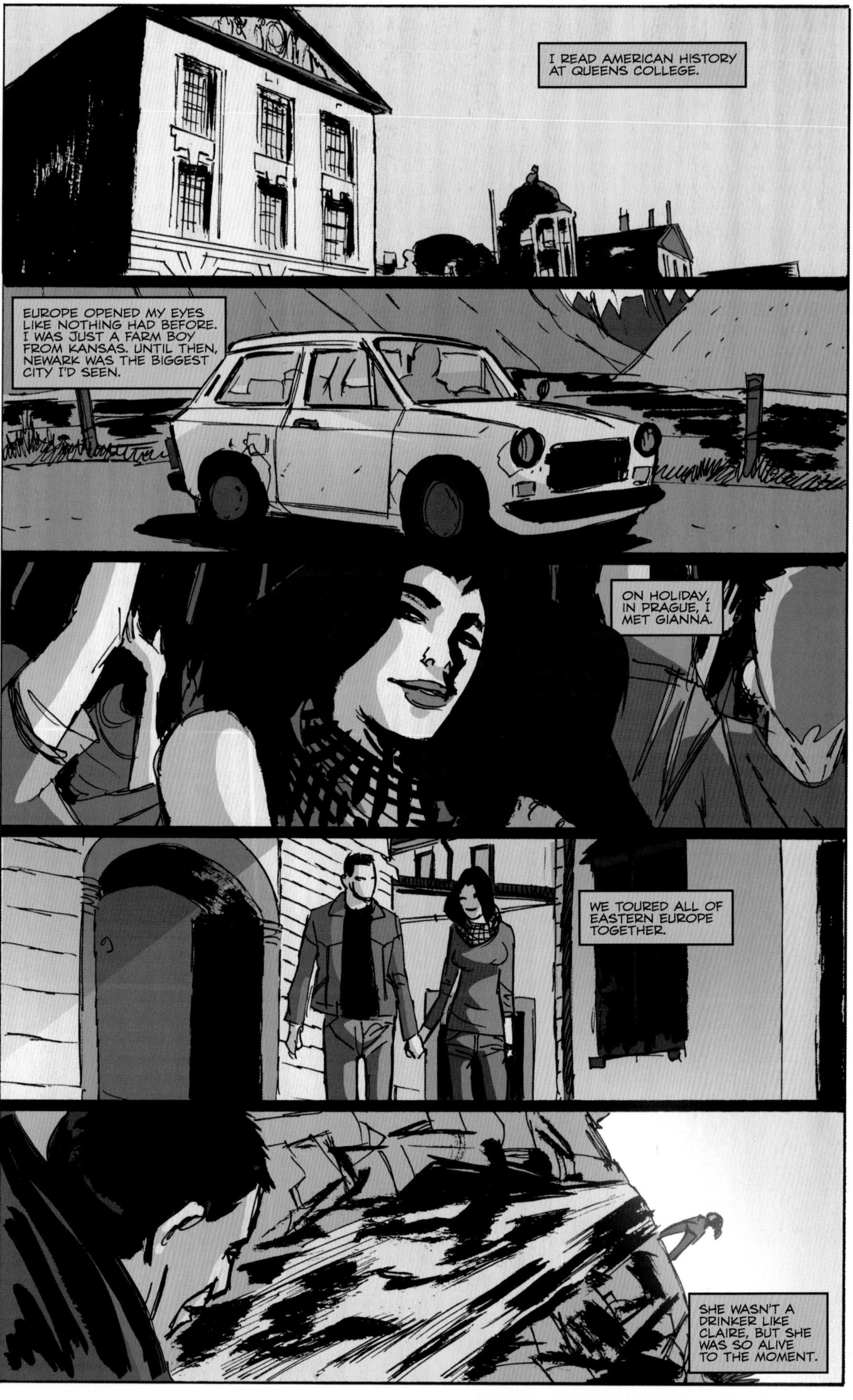
I READ AMERICAN HISTORY AT QUEENS COLLEGE.
EUROPE OPENED MY EYES LIKE NOTHING HAD BEFORE. I WAS JUST A FARM BOY FROM KANSAS. UNTIL THEN, NEWARK WAS THE BIGGEST CITY I'D SEEN.
ON HOLIDAY, IN PRAGUE, I MET GIANNA.
WE TOURED ALL OF EASTERN EUROPE TOGETHER.
SHE WASN'T A DRINKER LIKE CLAIRE, BUT SHE WAS SO ALIVE TO THE MOMENT.

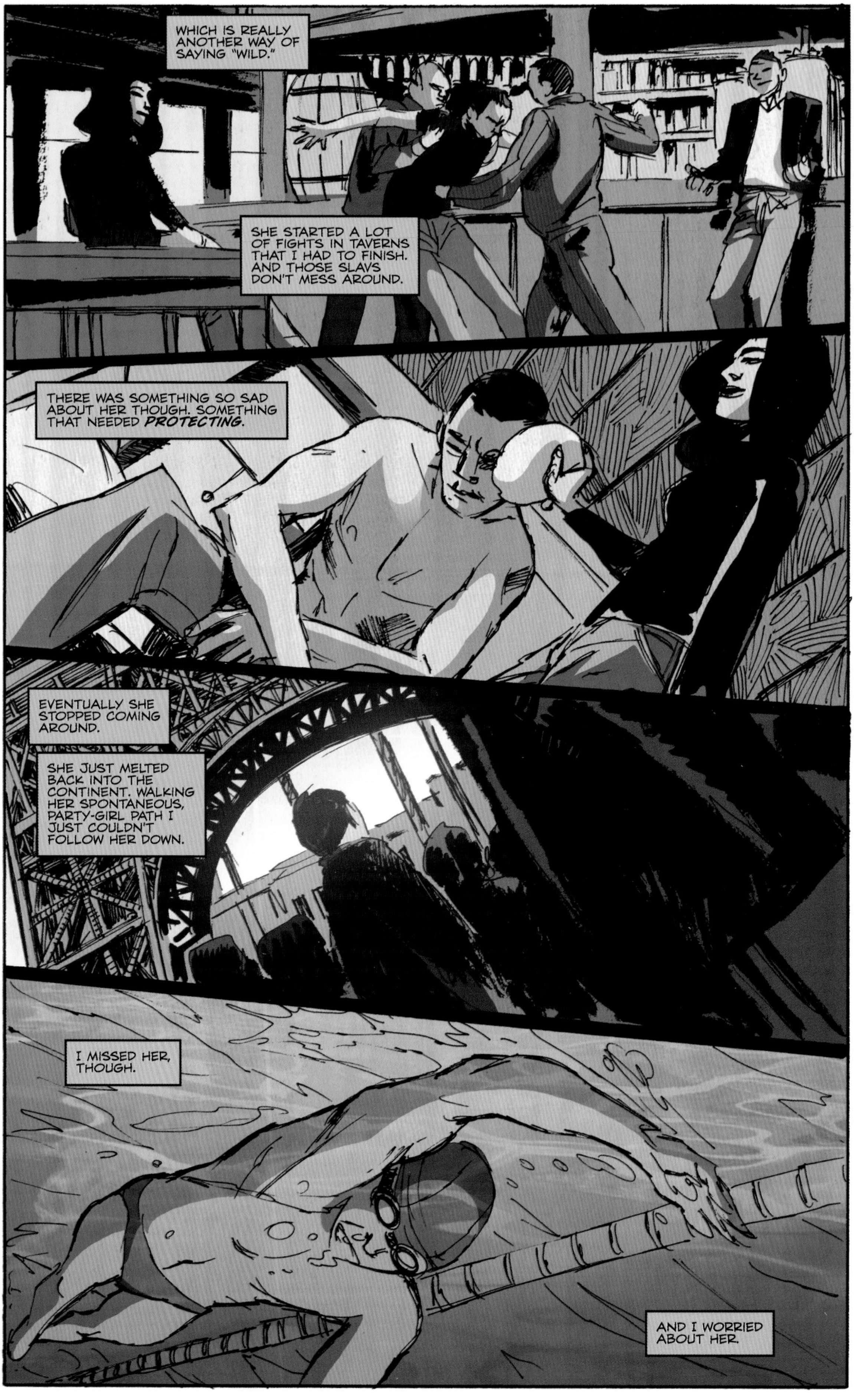
WHICH IS REALLY ANOTHER WAY OF SAYING "WILD."
SHE STARTED A LOT OF FIGHTS IN TAVERNS THAT I HAD TO FINISH. AND THOSE SLAVS DON'T MESS AROUND.
THERE WAS SOMETHING SO SAD ABOUT HER THOUGH. SOMETHING THAT NEEDED PROTECTING.
EVENTUALLY SHE STOPPED COMING AROUND.
SHE JUST MELTED BACK INTO THE CONTINENT. WALKING HER SPONTANEOUS, PARTY-GIRL PATH I JUST COULDN'T FOLLOW HER DOWN.
I MISSED HER, THOUGH.
AND I WORRIED ABOUT HER.

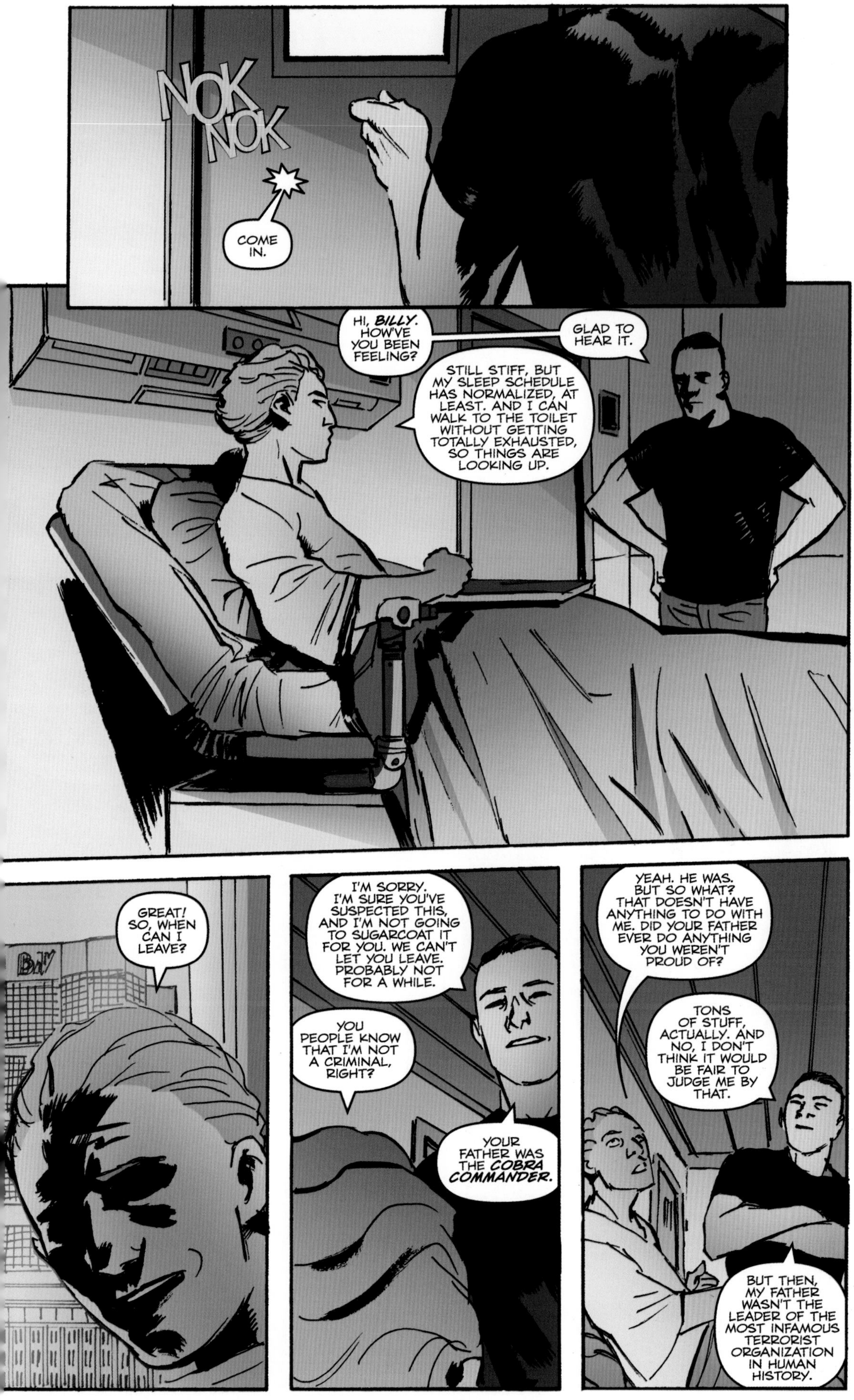
NOK NOK
COME IN.
HI, BILLY. HOW'VE YOU BEEN FEELING?
STILL STIFF, BUT MY SLEEP SCHEDULE HAS NORMALIZED, AT LEAST. AND I CAN WALK TO THE TOILET WITHOUT GETTING TOTALLY EXHAUSTED, SO THINGS ARE LOOKING UP.
GLAD TO HEAR IT.
GREAT! SO, WHEN CAN I LEAVE?
I'M SORRY. I'M SURE YOU'VE SUSPECTED THIS, AND I'M NOT GOING TO SUGARCOAT IT FOR YOU. WE CAN'T LET YOU LEAVE. PROBABLY NOT FOR A WHILE.
YOU PEOPLE KNOW THAT I'M NOT A CRIMINAL, RIGHT?
YOUR FATHER WAS THE COBRA COMMANDER.
YEAH. HE WAS. BUT SO WHAT? THAT DOESN'T HAVE ANYTHING TO DO WITH ME. DID YOUR FATHER EVER DO ANYTHING YOU WEREN'T PROUD OF?
TONS OF STUFF, ACTUALLY. AND NO, I DON'T THINK IT WOULD BE FAIR TO JUDGE ME BY THAT.
BUT THEN, MY FATHER WASN'T THE LEADER OF THE MOST INFAMOUS TERRORIST ORGANIZATION IN HUMAN HISTORY.

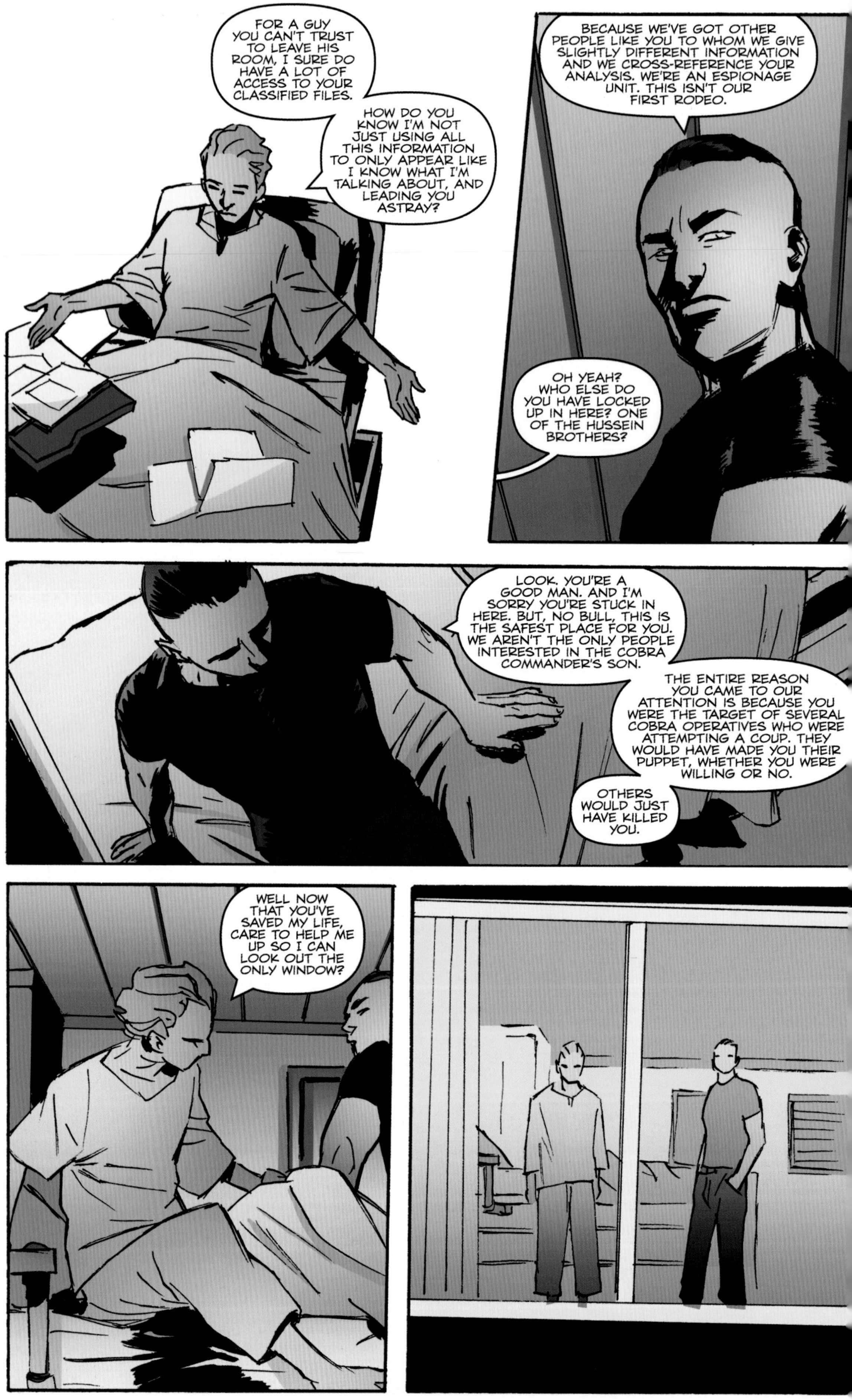
FOR A GUY YOU CAN'T TRUST TO LEAVE HIS ROOM, I SURE DO HAVE A LOT OF ACCESS TO YOUR CLASSIFIED FILES.
HOW DO YOU KNOW I'M NOT JUST USING ALL THIS INFORMATION TO ONLY APPEAR LIKE I KNOW WHAT I'M TALKING ABOUT, AND LEADING YOU ASTRAY?
BECAUSE WE'VE GOT OTHER PEOPLE LIKE YOU TO WHOM WE GIVE SLIGHTLY DIFFERENT INFORMATION AND WE CROSS-REFERENCE YOUR ANALYSIS. WE'RE AN ESPIONAGE UNIT. THIS ISN'T OUR FIRST RODEO.
OH YEAH? WHO ELSE DO YOU HAVE LOCKED UP IN HERE? ONE OF THE HUSSEIN BROTHERS?
LOOK. YOU'RE A GOOD MAN. AND I'M SORRY YOU'RE STUCK IN HERE. BUT, NO BULL, THIS IS THE SAFEST PLACE FOR YOU. WE AREN'T THE ONLY PEOPLE INTERESTED IN THE COBRA COMMANDER'S SON.
THE ENTIRE REASON YOU CAME TO OUR ATTENTION IS BECAUSE YOU WERE THE TARGET OF SEVERAL COBRA OPERATIVES WHO WERE ATTEMPTING A COUP. THEY WOULD HAVE MADE YOU THEIR PUPPET, WHETHER YOU WERE WILLING OR NO.
OTHERS WOULD JUST HAVE KILLED YOU.
WELL NOW THAT YOU'VE SAVED MY LIFE, CARE TO HELP ME UP SO I CAN LOOK OUT THE ONLY WINDOW?

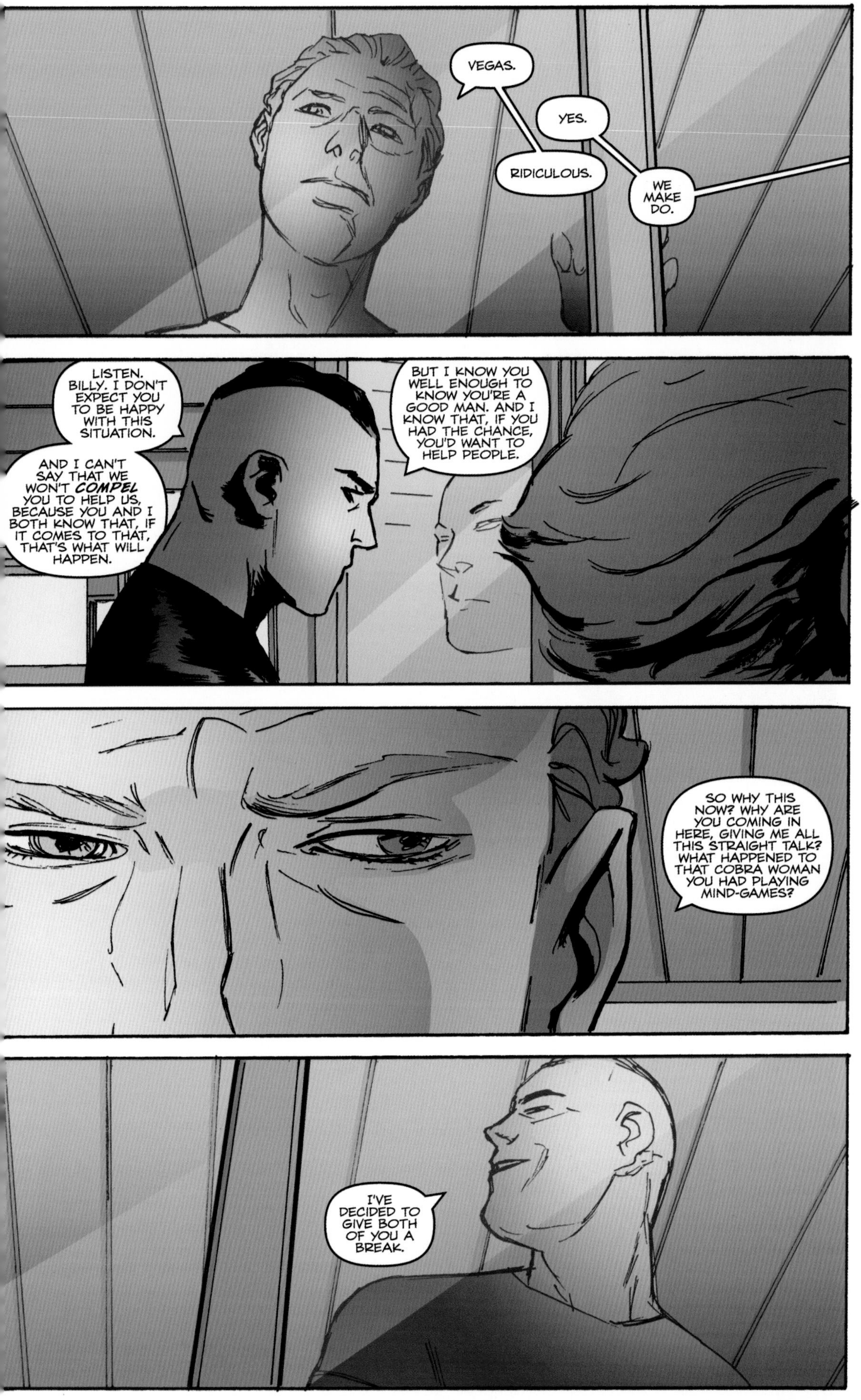
VEGAS.
RIDICULOUS.
YES.
WE MAKE DO.
LISTEN. BILLY. I DON'T EXPECT YOU TO BE HAPPY WITH THIS SITUATION.
AND I CAN'T SAY THAT WE WON'T COMPEL YOU TO HELP US, BECAUSE YOU AND I BOTH KNOW THAT, IF IT COMES TO THAT, THAT'S WHAT WILL HAPPEN.
BUT I KNOW YOU WELL ENOUGH TO KNOW YOU'RE A GOOD MAN. AND I KNOW THAT, IF YOU HAD THE CHANCE, YOU'D WANT TO HELP PEOPLE.
SO WHY THIS NOW? WHY ARE YOU COMING IN HERE, GIVING ME ALL THIS STRAIGHT TALK? WHAT HAPPENED TO THAT COBRA WOMAN YOU HAD PLAYING MIND-GAMES?
I'VE DECIDED TO GIVE BOTH OF YOU A BREAK.

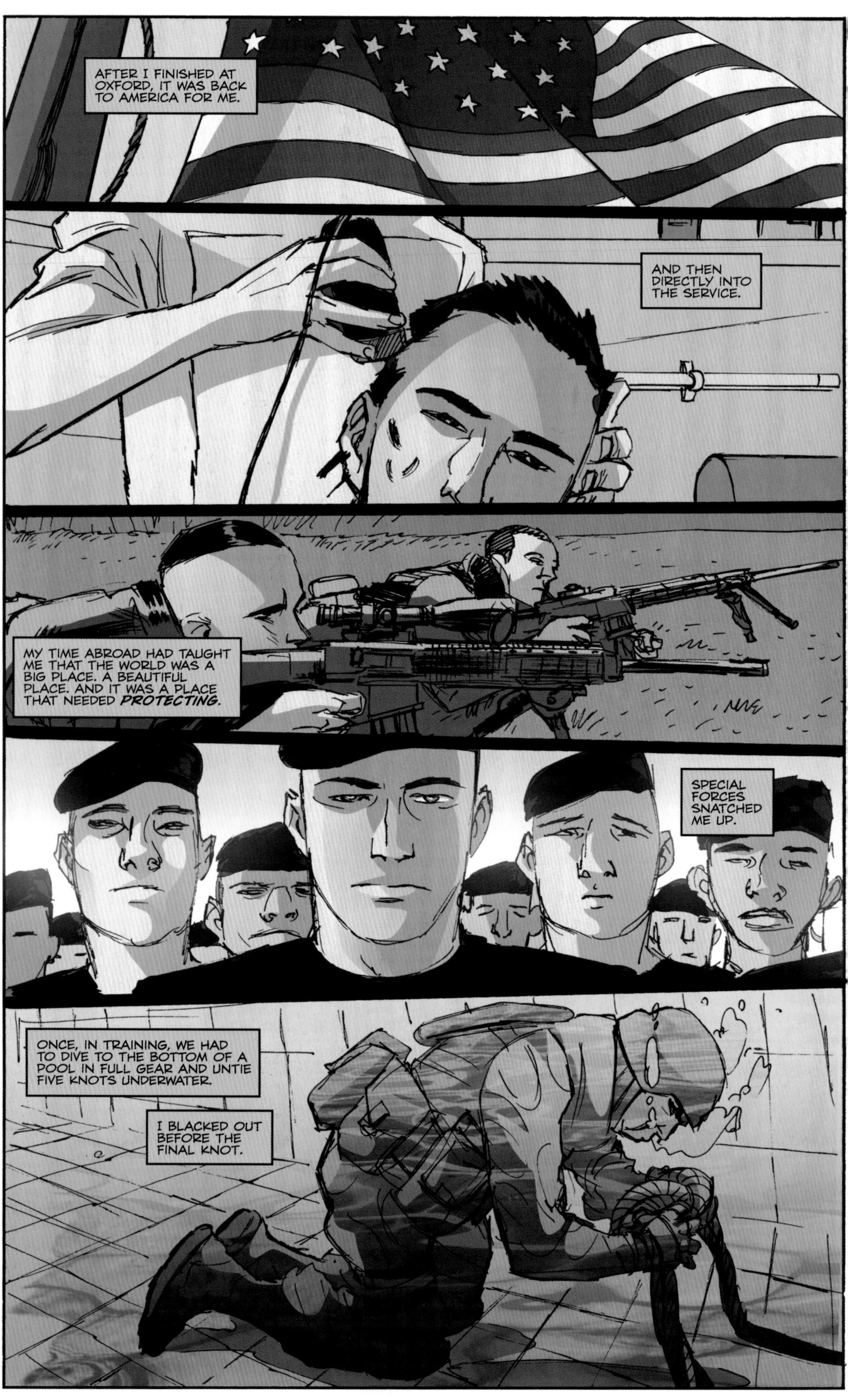
AFTER I FINISHED AT OXFORD, IT WAS BACK TO AMERICA FOR ME.
AND THEN DIRECTLY INTO THE SERVICE.
MY TIME ABROAD HAD TAUGHT ME THAT THE WORLD WAS A BIG PLACE. A BEAUTIFUL PLACE. AND IT WAS A PLACE THAT NEEDED *PROTECTING*.
SPECIAL FORCES SNATCHED ME UP.
ONCE, IN TRAINING, WE HAD TO DIVE TO THE BOTTOM OF A POOL IN FULL GEAR AND UNTIE FIVE KNOTS UNDERWATER.
I BLACKED OUT BEFORE THE FINAL KNOT.

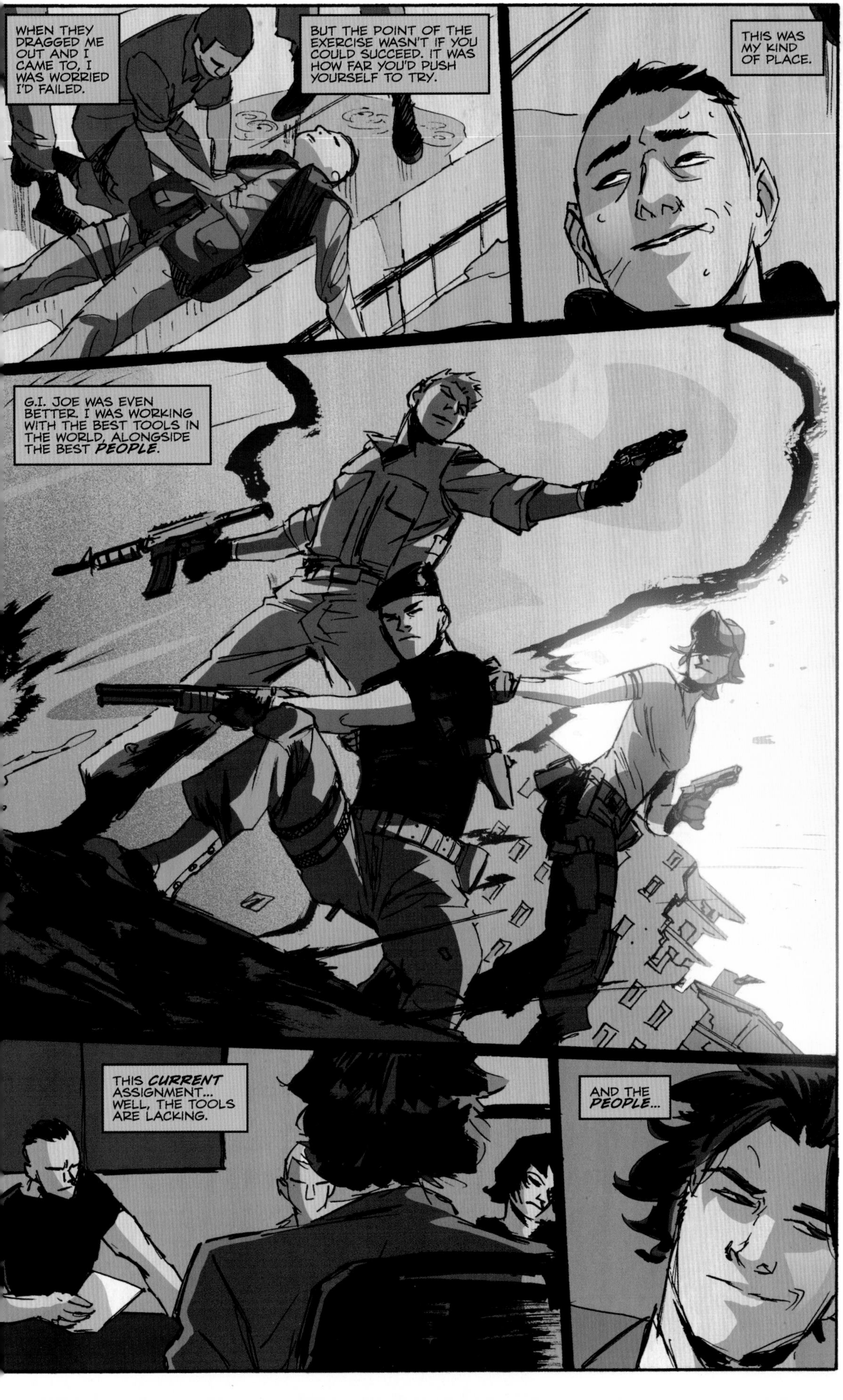
WHEN THEY DRAGGED ME OUT AND I CAME TO, I WAS WORRIED I'D FAILED.
BUT THE POINT OF THE EXERCISE WASN'T IF YOU COULD SUCCEED. IT WAS HOW FAR YOU'D PUSH YOURSELF TO TRY.
THIS WAS MY KIND OF PLACE.
G.I. JOE WAS EVEN BETTER. I WAS WORKING WITH THE BEST TOOLS IN THE WORLD, ALONGSIDE THE BEST PEOPLE.
THIS CURRENT ASSIGNMENT... WELL, THE TOOLS ARE LACKING.
AND THE PEOPLE...

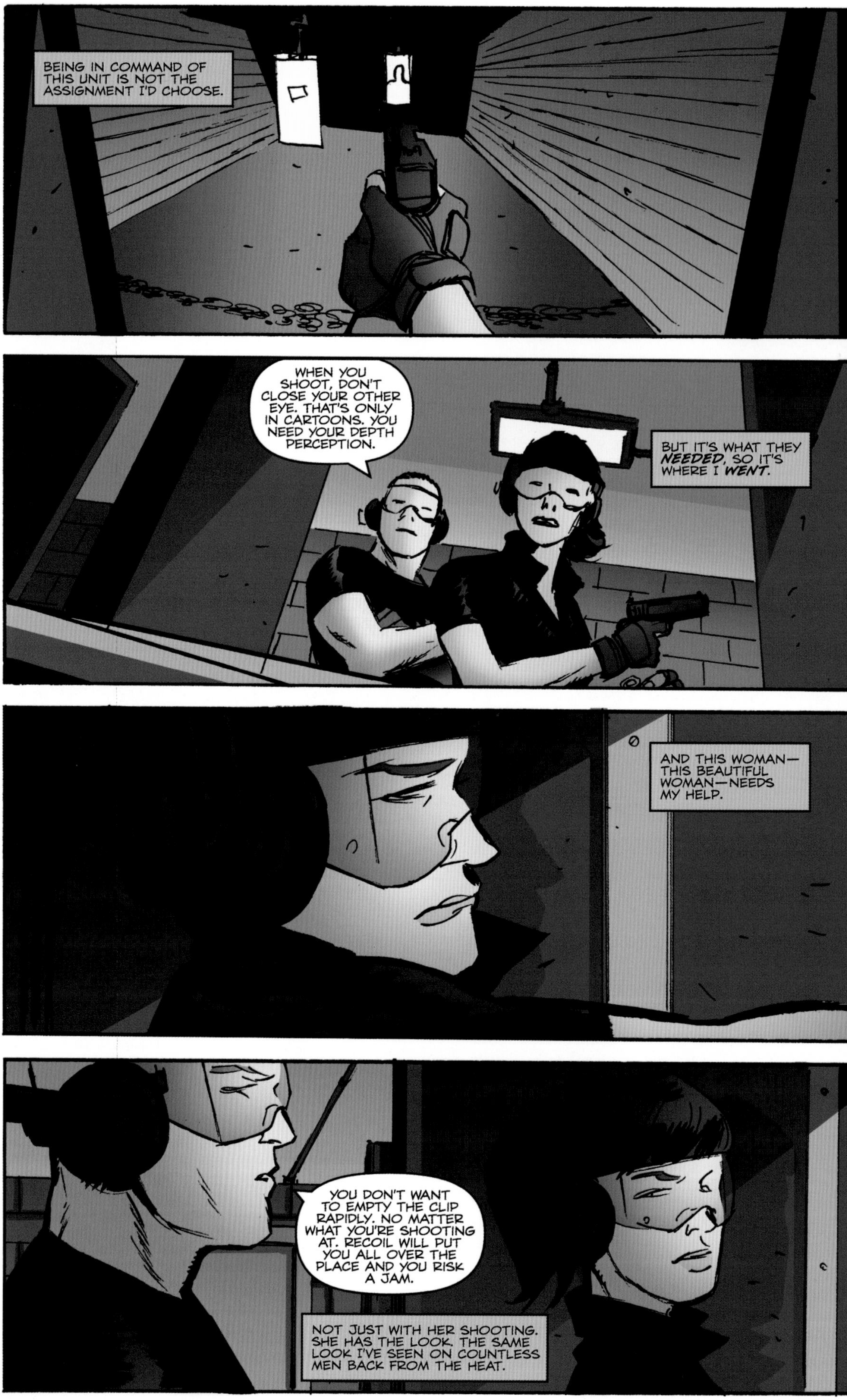
BEING IN COMMAND OF THIS UNIT IS NOT THE ASSIGNMENT I'D CHOOSE.
WHEN YOU SHOOT, DON'T CLOSE YOUR OTHER EYE. THAT'S ONLY IN CARTOONS. YOU NEED YOUR DEPTH PERCEPTION.
BUT IT'S WHAT THEY NEEDED, SO IT'S WHERE I WENT.
AND THIS WOMAN— THIS BEAUTIFUL WOMAN—NEEDS MY HELP.
YOU DON'T WANT TO EMPTY THE CLIP RAPIDLY. NO MATTER WHAT YOU'RE SHOOTING AT. RECOIL WILL PUT YOU ALL OVER THE PLACE AND YOU RISK A JAM.
NOT JUST WITH HER SHOOTING. SHE HAS THE LOOK. THE SAME LOOK I'VE SEEN ON COUNTLESS MEN BACK FROM THE HEAT.

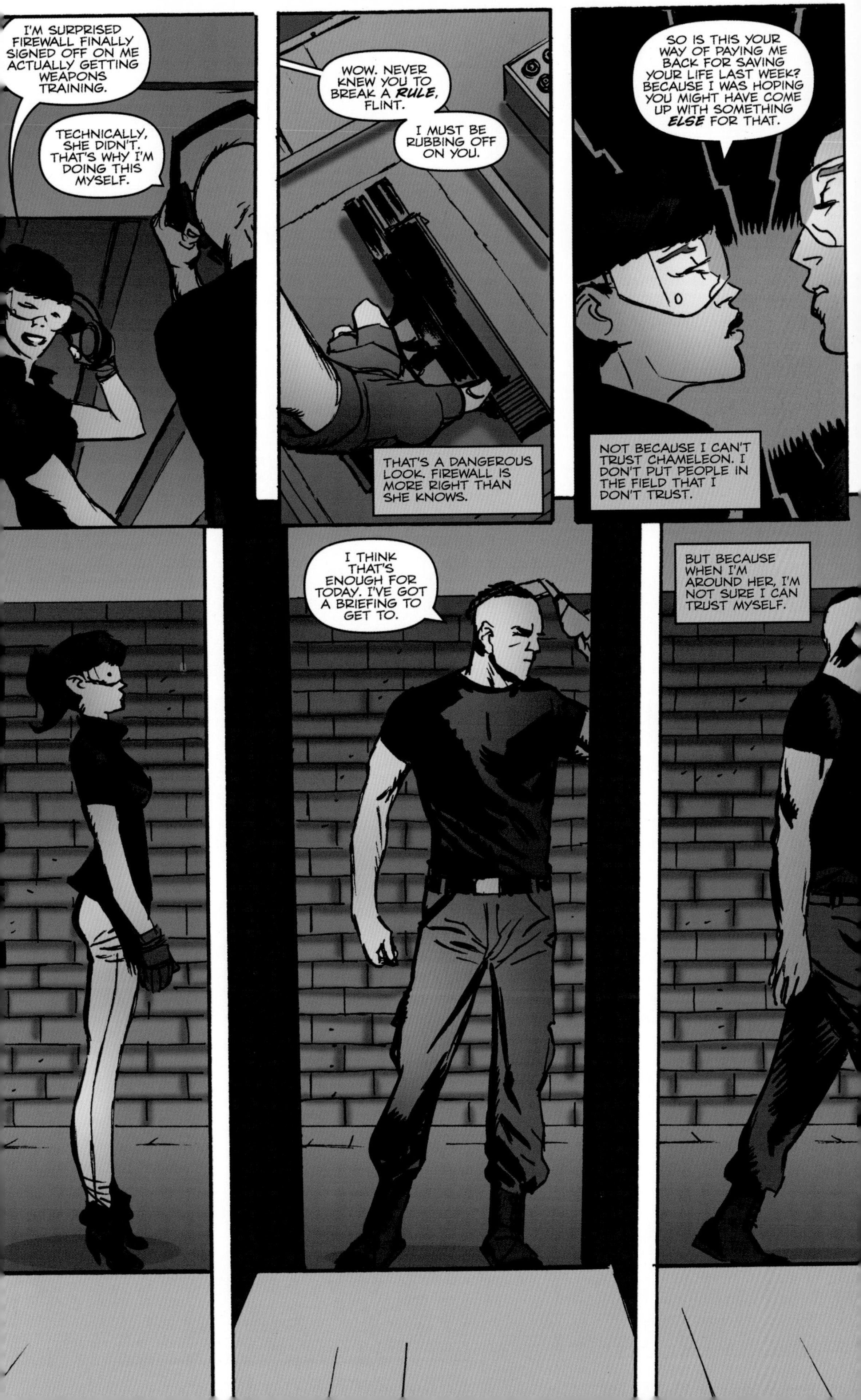
I'M SURPRISED FIREWALL FINALLY SIGNED OFF ON ME ACTUALLY GETTING WEAPONS TRAINING.
TECHNICALLY, SHE DIDN'T. THAT'S WHY I'M DOING THIS MYSELF.
WOW. NEVER KNEW YOU TO BREAK A RULE, FLINT.
I MUST BE RUBBING OFF ON YOU.
THAT'S A DANGEROUS LOOK. FIREWALL IS MORE RIGHT THAN SHE KNOWS.
SO IS THIS YOUR WAY OF PAYING ME BACK FOR SAVING YOUR LIFE LAST WEEK? BECAUSE I WAS HOPING YOU MIGHT HAVE COME UP WITH SOMETHING ELSE FOR THAT.
NOT BECAUSE I CAN'T TRUST CHAMELEON. I DON'T PUT PEOPLE IN THE FIELD THAT I DON'T TRUST.
I THINK THAT'S ENOUGH FOR TODAY. I'VE GOT A BRIEFING TO GET TO.
BUT BECAUSE WHEN I'M AROUND HER, I'M NOT SURE I CAN TRUST MYSELF.

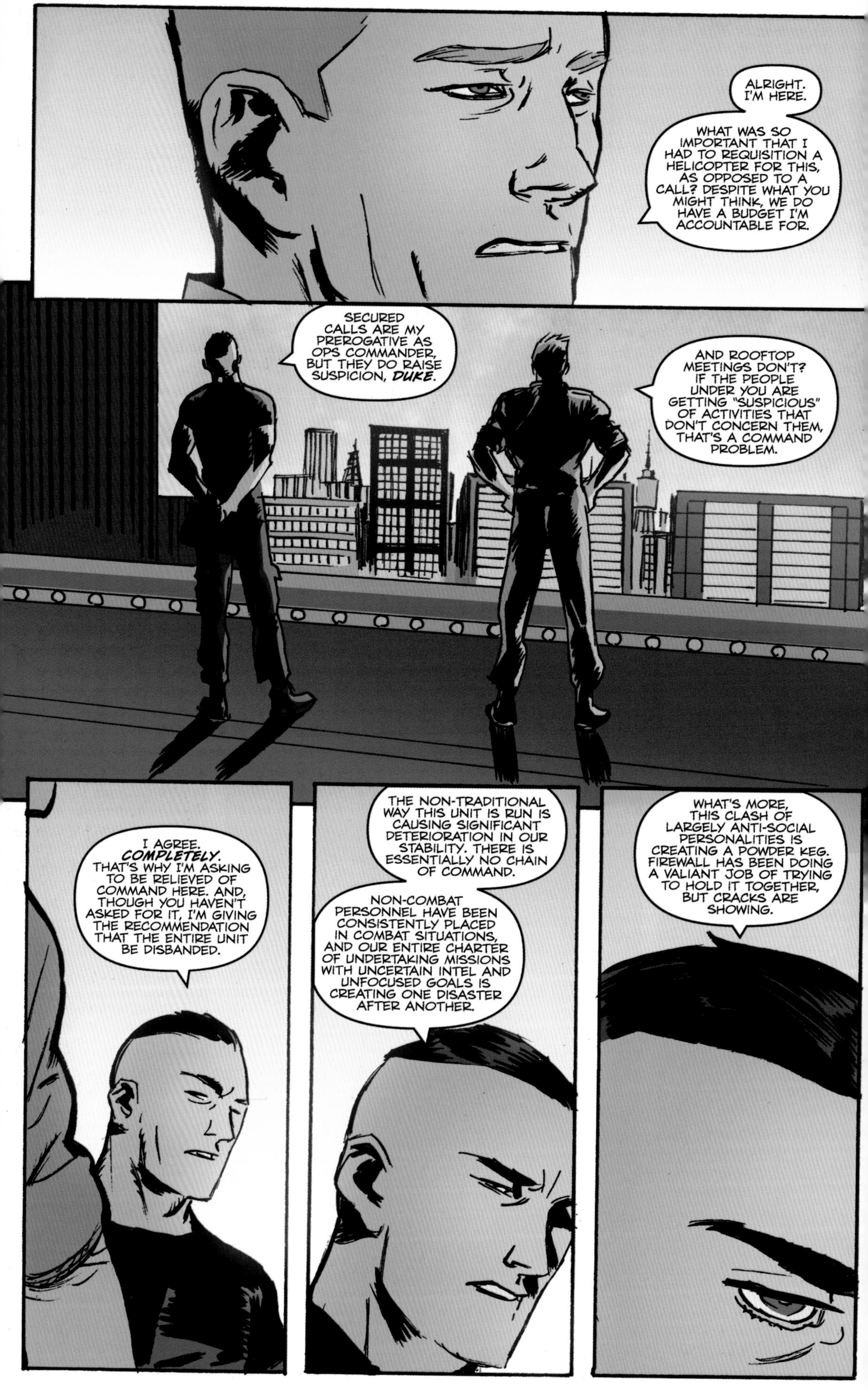
ALRIGHT. I'M HERE.
WHAT WAS SO IMPORTANT THAT I HAD TO REQUISITION A HELICOPTER FOR THIS, AS OPPOSED TO A CALL? DESPITE WHAT YOU MIGHT THINK, WE DO HAVE A BUDGET I'M ACCOUNTABLE FOR.
SECURED CALLS ARE MY PREROGATIVE AS OPS COMMANDER, BUT THEY DO RAISE SUSPICION, DUKE.
AND ROOFTOP MEETINGS DON'T? IF THE PEOPLE UNDER YOU ARE GETTING "SUSPICIOUS" OF ACTIVITIES THAT DON'T CONCERN THEM, THAT'S A COMMAND PROBLEM.
I AGREE. COMPLETELY. THAT'S WHY I'M ASKING TO BE RELIEVED OF COMMAND HERE. AND, THOUGH YOU HAVEN'T ASKED FOR IT, I'M GIVING THE RECOMMENDATION THAT THE ENTIRE UNIT BE DISBANDED.
THE NON-TRADITIONAL WAY THIS UNIT IS RUN IS CAUSING SIGNIFICANT DETERIORATION IN OUR STABILITY. THERE IS ESSENTIALLY NO CHAIN OF COMMAND.
NON-COMBAT PERSONNEL HAVE BEEN CONSISTENTLY PLACED IN COMBAT SITUATIONS, AND OUR ENTIRE CHARTER OF UNDERTAKING MISSIONS WITH UNCERTAIN INTEL AND UNFOCUSED GOALS IS CREATING ONE DISASTER AFTER ANOTHER.
WHAT'S MORE, THIS CLASH OF LARGELY ANTI-SOCIAL PERSONALITIES IS CREATING A POWDER KEG. FIREWALL HAS BEEN DOING A VALIANT JOB OF TRYING TO HOLD IT TOGETHER, BUT CRACKS ARE SHOWING.

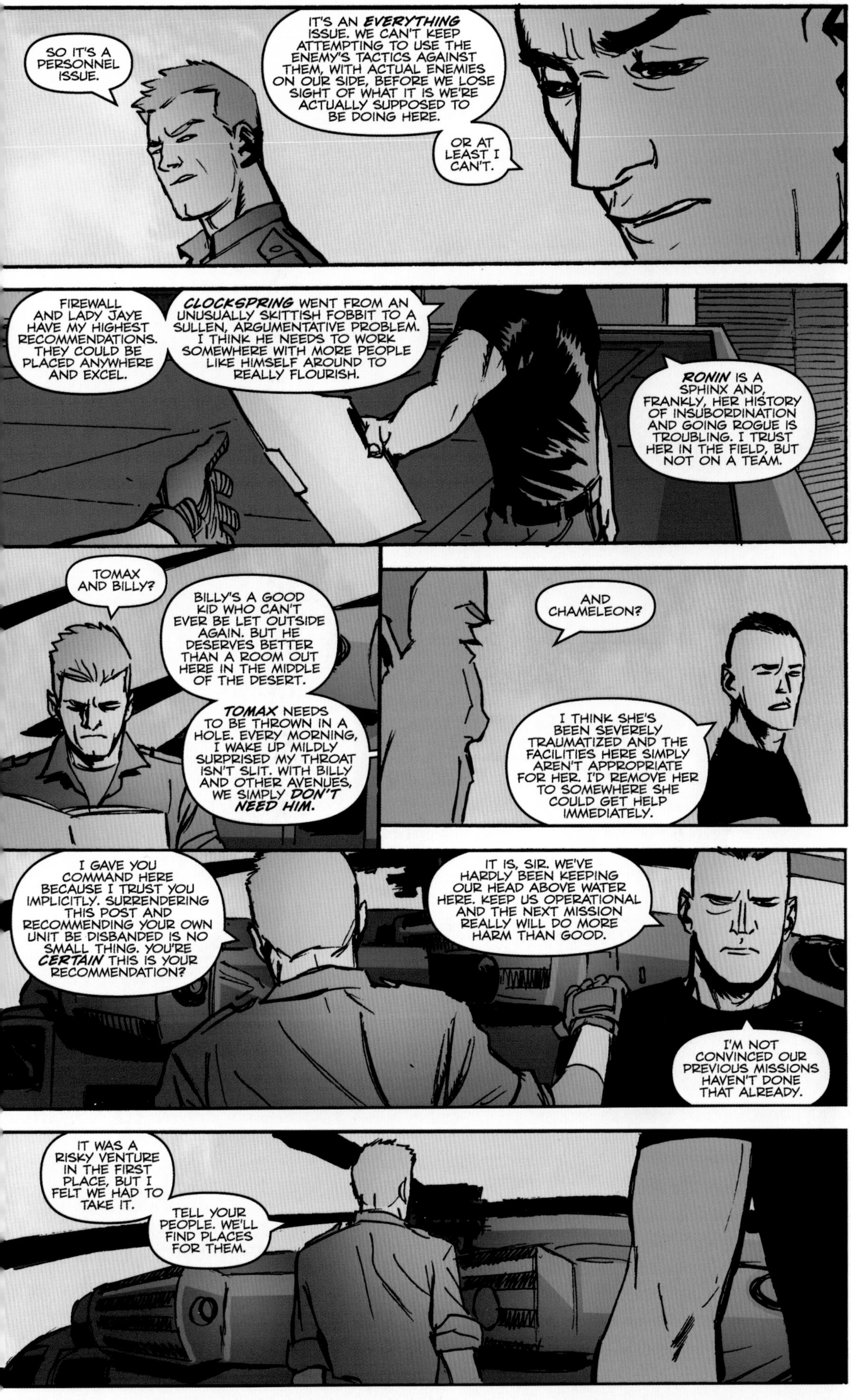
SO IT'S A PERSONNEL ISSUE.
IT'S AN EVERYTHING ISSUE. WE CAN'T KEEP ATTEMPTING TO USE THE ENEMY'S TACTICS AGAINST THEM, WITH ACTUAL ENEMIES ON OUR SIDE, BEFORE WE LOSE SIGHT OF WHAT IT IS WE'RE ACTUALLY SUPPOSED TO BE DOING HERE.
OR AT LEAST I CAN'T.
FIREWALL AND LADY JAYE HAVE MY HIGHEST RECOMMENDATIONS. THEY COULD BE PLACED ANYWHERE AND EXCEL.
CLOCKSPRING WENT FROM AN UNUSUALLY SKITTISH FOBBIT TO A SULLEN, ARGUMENTATIVE PROBLEM. I THINK HE NEEDS TO WORK SOMEWHERE WITH MORE PEOPLE LIKE HIMSELF AROUND TO REALLY FLOURISH.
RONIN IS A SPHINX AND, FRANKLY, HER HISTORY OF INSUBORDINATION AND GOING ROGUE IS TROUBLING. I TRUST HER IN THE FIELD, BUT NOT ON A TEAM.
TOMAX AND BILLY?
BILLY'S A GOOD KID WHO CAN'T EVER BE LET OUTSIDE AGAIN. BUT HE DESERVES BETTER THAN A ROOM OUT HERE IN THE MIDDLE OF THE DESERT.
TOMAX NEEDS TO BE THROWN IN A HOLE. EVERY MORNING, I WAKE UP MILDLY SURPRISED MY THROAT ISN'T SLIT. WITH BILLY AND OTHER AVENUES, WE SIMPLY DON'T NEED HIM.
AND CHAMELEON?
I THINK SHE'S BEEN SEVERELY TRAUMATIZED AND THE FACILITIES HERE SIMPLY AREN'T APPROPRIATE FOR HER. I'D REMOVE HER TO SOMEWHERE SHE COULD GET HELP IMMEDIATELY.
I GAVE YOU COMMAND HERE BECAUSE I TRUST YOU IMPLICITLY. SURRENDERING THIS POST AND RECOMMENDING YOUR OWN UNIT BE DISBANDED IS NO SMALL THING. YOU'RE CERTAIN THIS IS YOUR RECOMMENDATION?
IT IS, SIR. WE'VE HARDLY BEEN KEEPING OUR HEAD ABOVE WATER HERE. KEEP US OPERATIONAL AND THE NEXT MISSION REALLY WILL DO MORE HARM THAN GOOD.
I'M NOT CONVINCED OUR PREVIOUS MISSIONS HAVEN'T DONE THAT ALREADY.
IT WAS A RISKY VENTURE IN THE FIRST PLACE, BUT I FELT WE HAD TO TAKE IT.
TELL YOUR PEOPLE. WE'LL FIND PLACES FOR THEM.

MY IMPULSE IS ALWAYS TO SAVE PEOPLE. TO TRY AND FIX WHAT'S BROKEN. BUT I HAVE TO BE A *LEADER*.
IT'S NOT WHAT I WANT... BUT IT'S WHAT'S NEEDED.
SO IT'S WHAT I *DO*.

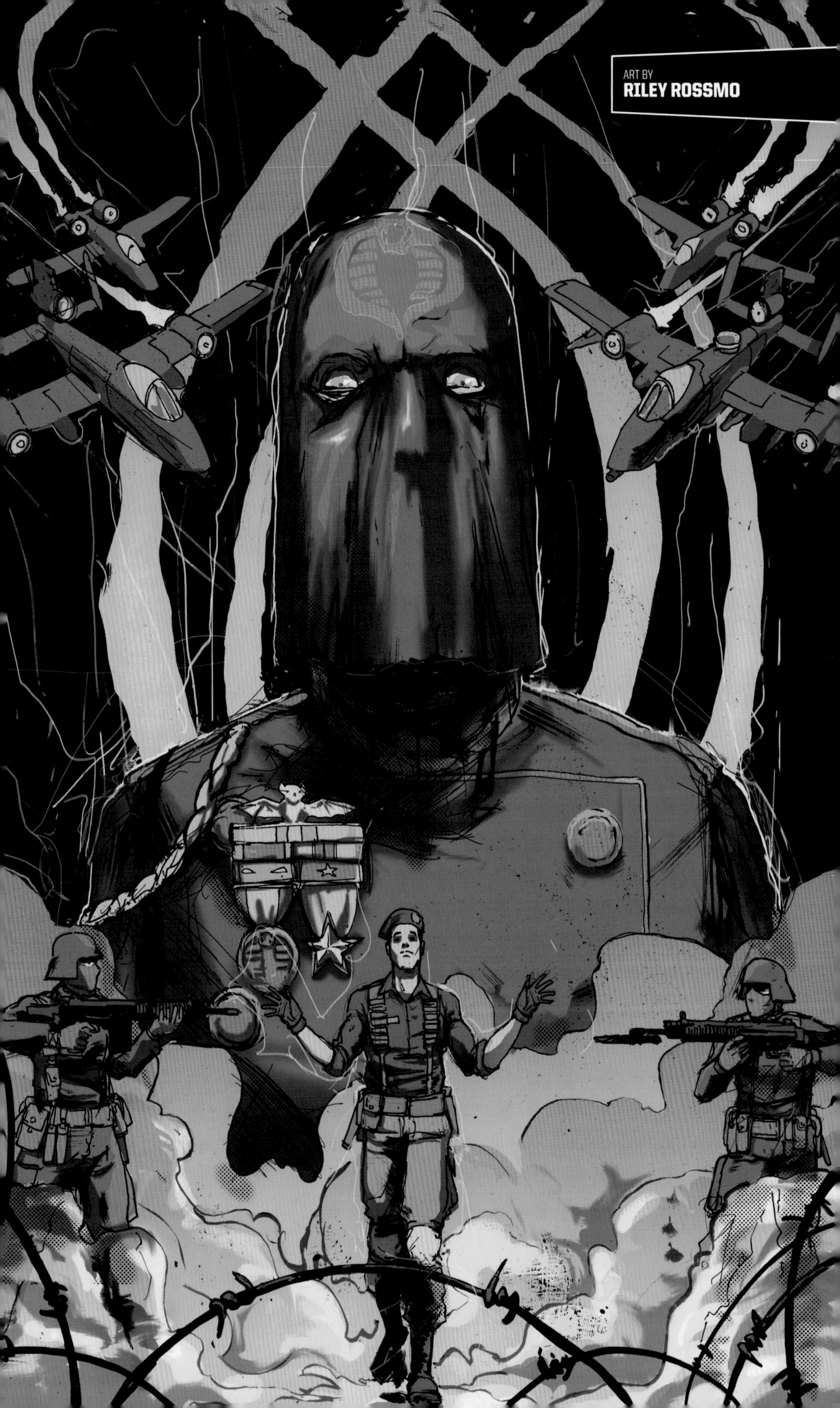
ART BY
RILEY ROSSMO

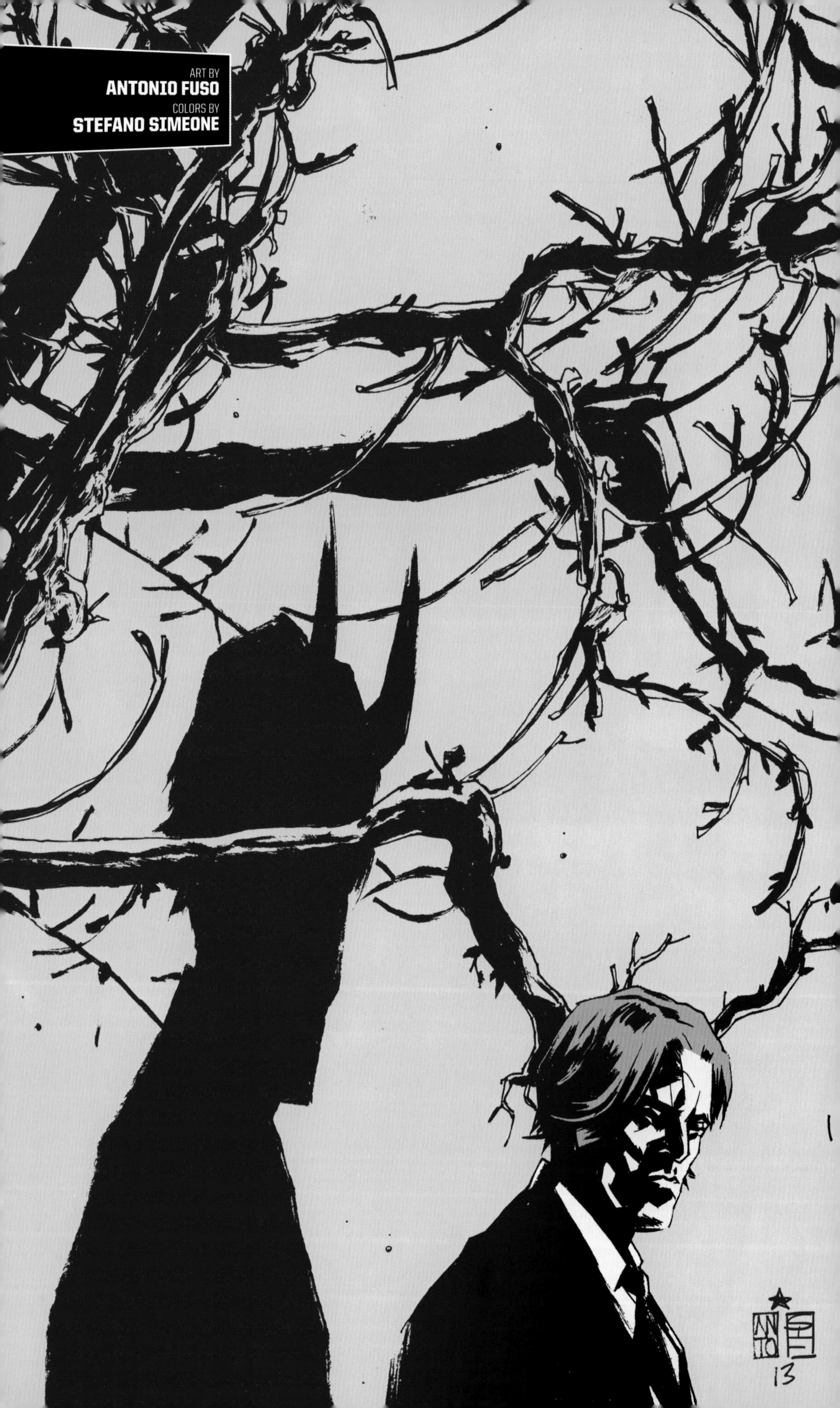

ART BY
ANTONIO FUSO
COLORS BY
STEFANO SIMEONE

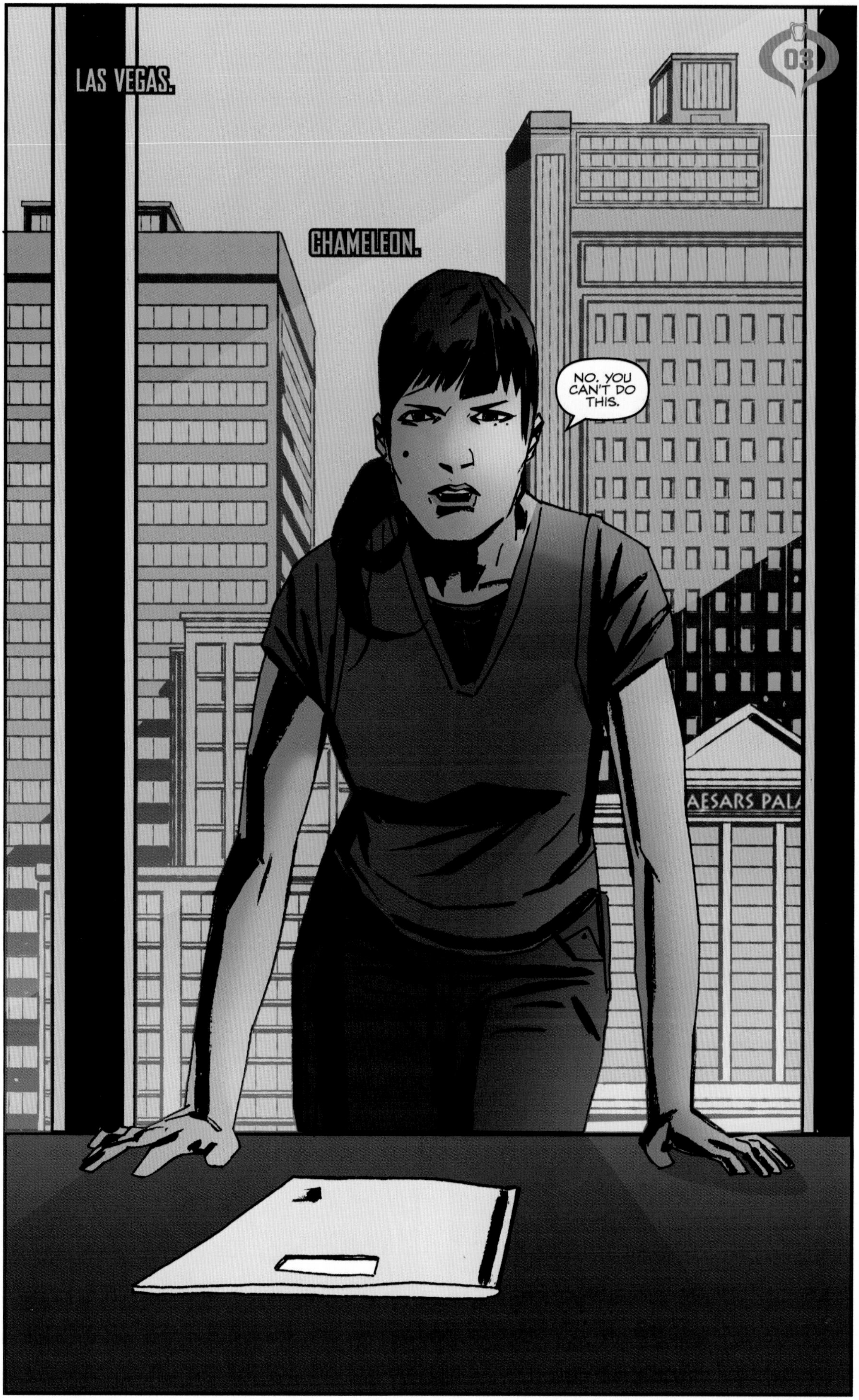
03
LAS VEGAS.
CHAMELEON.
NO. YOU CAN'T DO THIS.
AESARS PALA

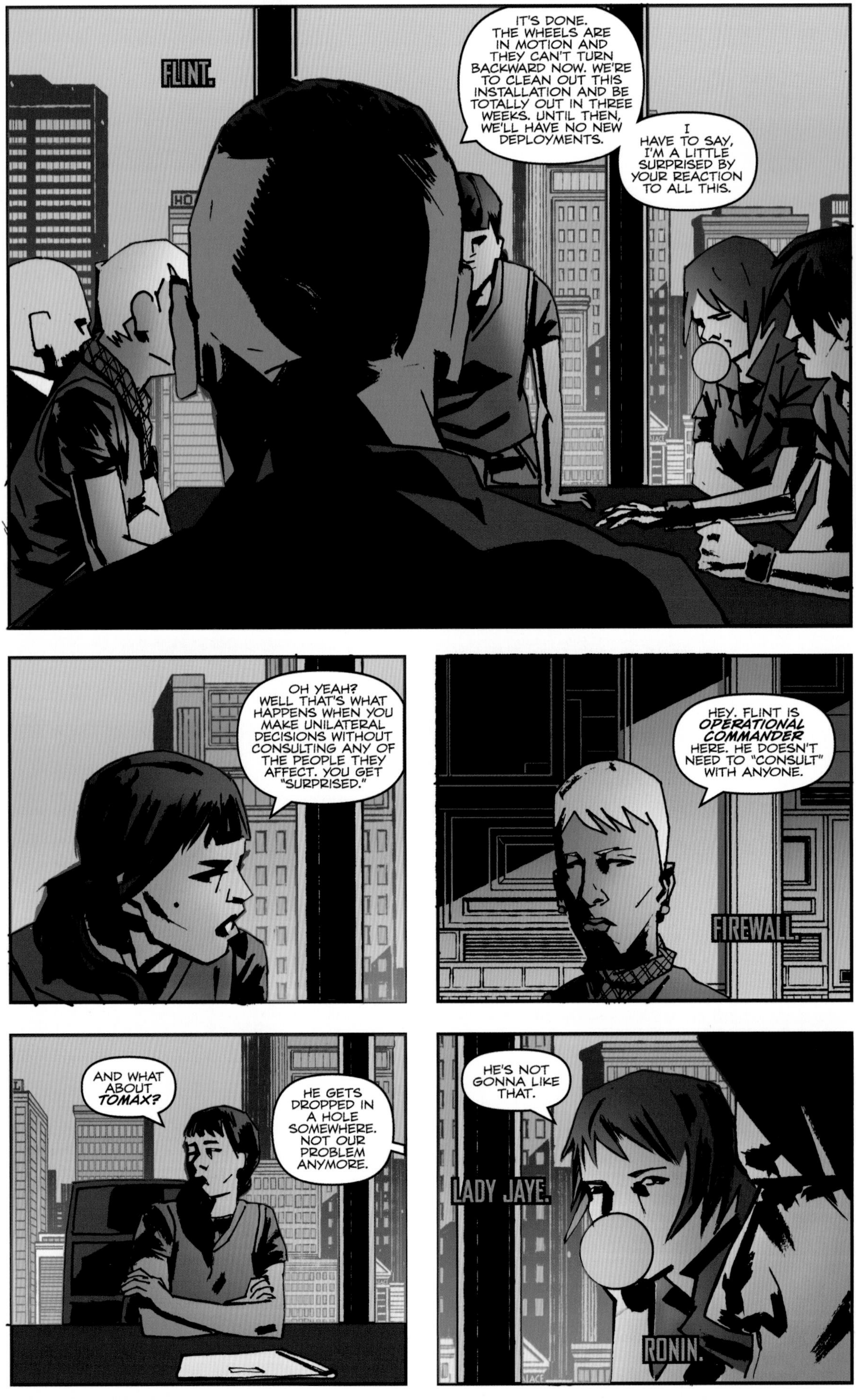
FLINT.
IT'S DONE. THE WHEELS ARE IN MOTION AND THEY CAN'T TURN BACKWARD NOW. WE'RE TO CLEAN OUT THIS INSTALLATION AND BE TOTALLY OUT IN THREE WEEKS. UNTIL THEN, WE'LL HAVE NO NEW DEPLOYMENTS.
I HAVE TO SAY, I'M A LITTLE SURPRISED BY YOUR REACTION TO ALL THIS.
OH YEAH? WELL THAT'S WHAT HAPPENS WHEN YOU MAKE UNILATERAL DECISIONS WITHOUT CONSULTING ANY OF THE PEOPLE THEY AFFECT. YOU GET "SURPRISED."
HEY. FLINT IS *OPERATIONAL COMMANDER* HERE. HE DOESN'T NEED TO "CONSULT" WITH ANYONE.
FIREWALL.
AND WHAT ABOUT *TOMAX?*
HE GETS DROPPED IN A HOLE SOMEWHERE. NOT OUR PROBLEM ANYMORE.
HE'S NOT GONNA LIKE THAT.
LADY JAYE.
RONIN.

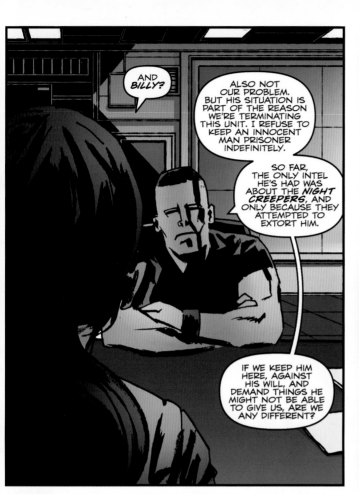

AND *BILLY?*

ALSO NOT OUR PROBLEM. BUT HIS SITUATION IS PART OF THE REASON WE'RE TERMINATING THIS UNIT. I REFUSE TO KEEP AN INNOCENT MAN PRISONER INDEFINITELY.

SO FAR, THE ONLY INTEL HE'S HAD WAS ABOUT THE *NIGHT CREEPERS*, AND ONLY BECAUSE THEY ATTEMPTED TO EXTORT HIM.

IF WE KEEP HIM HERE, AGAINST HIS WILL, AND DEMAND THINGS HE MIGHT NOT BE ABLE TO GIVE US, ARE WE ANY DIFFERENT?

CHAMELEON IS RIGHT. YOU *CAN'T* DO THIS.

CLOCKSPRING.

WHAT YOU'RE SAYING IS, YOU CAN NO LONGER MAKE THE *HARD CALLS* THAT THIS UNIT WAS SPECIFICALLY *ASSEMBLED* TO MAKE.

AND SO, BECAUSE OF *THAT*, WHAT HAPPENS? WHAT'S GOING TO HAPPEN TO FIREWALL? SHE GOES BACK INTO THE ADMINISTRATIVE POOL. MAYBE SHE PUSHES PAPERS AROUND ON ELLIS ISLAND TO MAKE *DUKE'S* TEAM LOOK MORE DIVERSE.

WHAT'S GOING TO HAPPEN TO *ME?* I WAS RUNNING COMMUNICATIONS FOR ONE OF THE MOST SOPHISTICATED COUNTER-TERROR UNITS IN THE WORLD. BUT NOW I'LL BE SENT BACK TO SOME FOBBIT-HOLE HELPING TEST THAT INVISIBILITY CLOAK THEY'RE NEVER GOING TO FIGURE OUT.

AND WHAT'S GOING TO HAPPEN TO *CHAMELEON?*

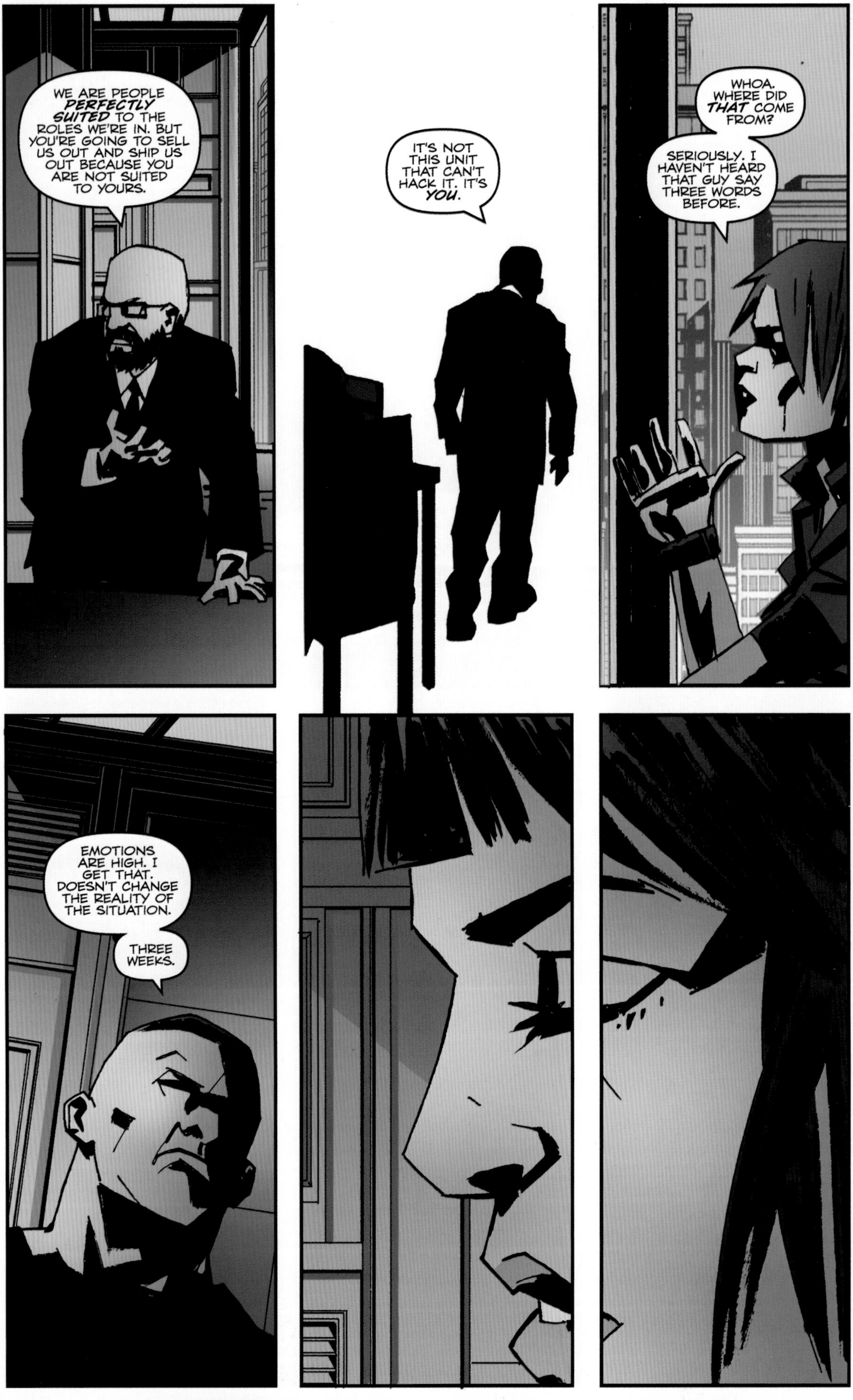
WE ARE PEOPLE PERFECTLY SUITED TO THE ROLES WE'RE IN. BUT YOU'RE GOING TO SELL US OUT AND SHIP US OUT BECAUSE YOU ARE NOT SUITED TO YOURS.
IT'S NOT THIS UNIT THAT CAN'T HACK IT. IT'S YOU.
WHOA. WHERE DID THAT COME FROM?
SERIOUSLY. I HAVEN'T HEARD THAT GUY SAY THREE WORDS BEFORE.
EMOTIONS ARE HIGH. I GET THAT. DOESN'T CHANGE THE REALITY OF THE SITUATION.
THREE WEEKS.

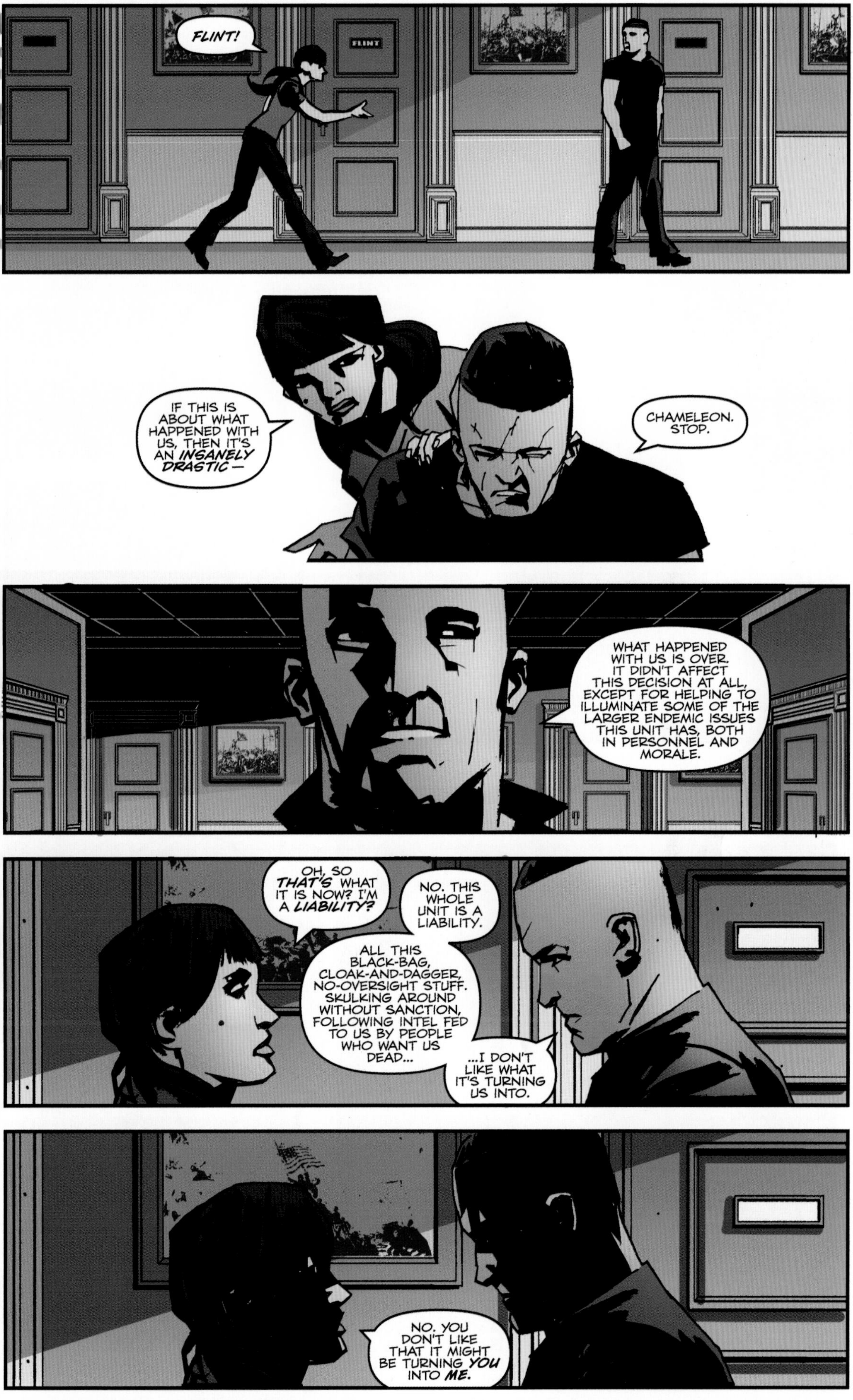
FLINT!
FLINT
IF THIS IS ABOUT WHAT HAPPENED WITH US, THEN IT'S AN INSANELY DRASTIC—
CHAMELEON. STOP.
WHAT HAPPENED WITH US IS OVER. IT DIDN'T AFFECT THIS DECISION AT ALL, EXCEPT FOR HELPING TO ILLUMINATE SOME OF THE LARGER ENDEMIC ISSUES THIS UNIT HAS, BOTH IN PERSONNEL AND MORALE.
OH, SO THAT'S WHAT IT IS NOW? I'M A LIABILITY?
NO. THIS WHOLE UNIT IS A LIABILITY.
ALL THIS BLACK-BAG, CLOAK-AND-DAGGER, NO-OVERSIGHT STUFF. SKULKING AROUND WITHOUT SANCTION, FOLLOWING INTEL FED TO US BY PEOPLE WHO WANT US DEAD...
...I DON'T LIKE WHAT IT'S TURNING US INTO.
NO. YOU DON'T LIKE THAT IT MIGHT BE TURNING YOU INTO ME.

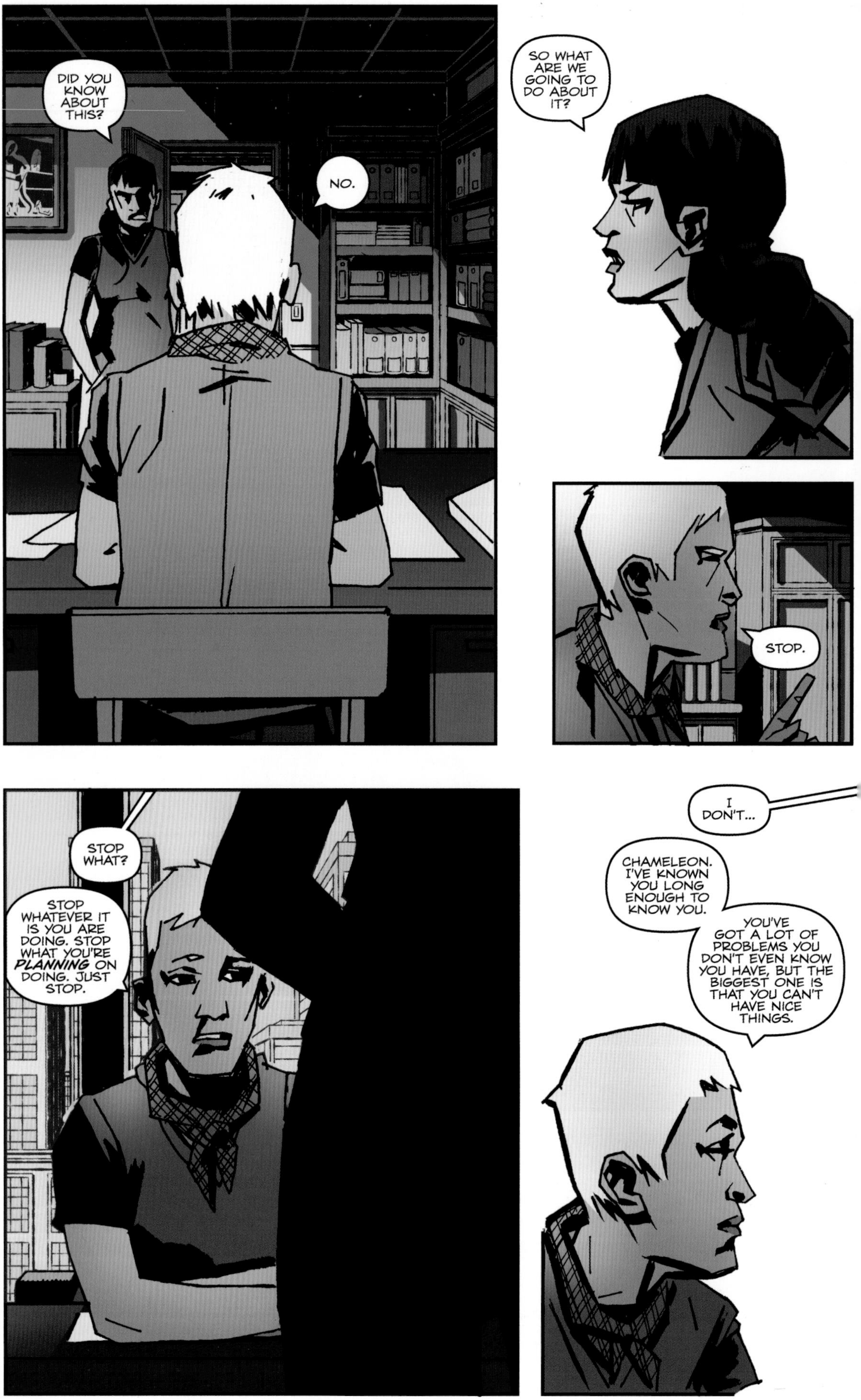
DID YOU KNOW ABOUT THIS?
NO.
SO WHAT ARE WE GOING TO DO ABOUT IT?
STOP.
STOP WHAT?
STOP WHATEVER IT IS YOU ARE DOING. STOP WHAT YOU'RE *PLANNING* ON DOING. JUST STOP.
I DON'T...
CHAMELEON. I'VE KNOWN YOU LONG ENOUGH TO KNOW YOU.
YOU'VE GOT A LOT OF PROBLEMS YOU DON'T EVEN KNOW YOU HAVE, BUT THE BIGGEST ONE IS THAT YOU CAN'T HAVE NICE THINGS.

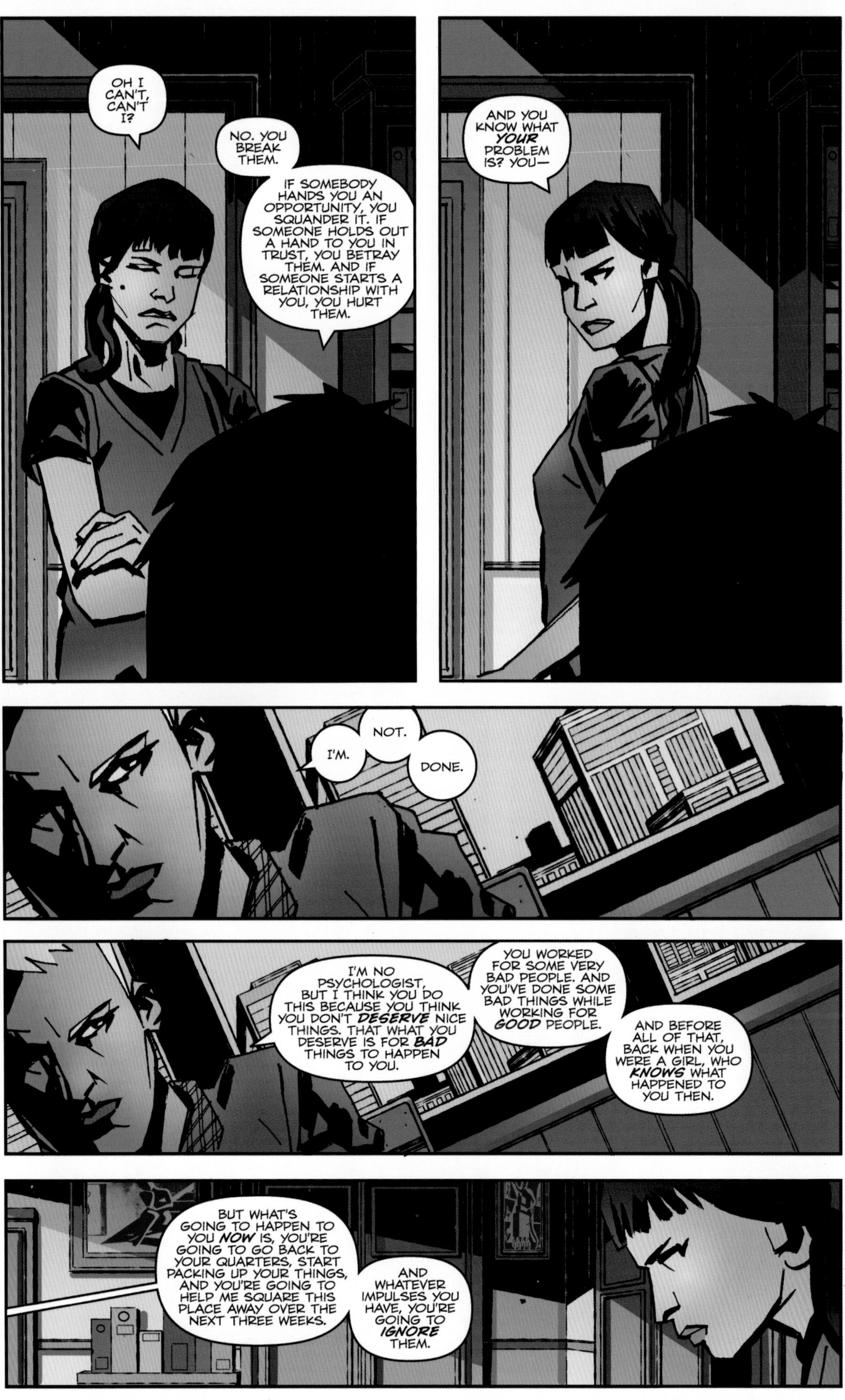
OH I CAN'T, CAN'T I?
NO. YOU BREAK THEM.
IF SOMEBODY HANDS YOU AN OPPORTUNITY, YOU SQUANDER IT. IF SOMEONE HOLDS OUT A HAND TO YOU IN TRUST, YOU BETRAY THEM. AND IF SOMEONE STARTS A RELATIONSHIP WITH YOU, YOU HURT THEM.
AND YOU KNOW WHAT *YOUR* PROBLEM IS? YOU—
I'M.
NOT.
DONE.
I'M NO PSYCHOLOGIST, BUT I THINK YOU DO THIS BECAUSE YOU THINK YOU DON'T *DESERVE* NICE THINGS. THAT WHAT YOU DESERVE IS FOR *BAD* THINGS TO HAPPEN TO YOU.
YOU WORKED FOR SOME VERY BAD PEOPLE. AND YOU'VE DONE SOME BAD THINGS WHILE WORKING FOR *GOOD* PEOPLE.
AND BEFORE ALL OF THAT, BACK WHEN YOU WERE A GIRL, WHO *KNOWS* WHAT HAPPENED TO YOU THEN.
BUT WHAT'S GOING TO HAPPEN TO YOU *NOW* IS, YOU'RE GOING TO GO BACK TO YOUR QUARTERS, START PACKING UP YOUR THINGS, AND YOU'RE GOING TO HELP ME SQUARE THIS PLACE AWAY OVER THE NEXT THREE WEEKS.
AND WHATEVER IMPULSES YOU HAVE, YOU'RE GOING TO *IGNORE* THEM.

CARRYING ON WITH FLINT? THAT WAS JUST STUPID. HOW LONG DID YOU REALLY THINK THAT WAS GOING TO LAST? THE MAN IS MORE WHITE-BREAD THAN THE PILLSBURY DOUGH BOY.

BUT YOU GOT YOUR FINGERS RIGHT INTO HIS CRACKS AND NOW HIS HEAD'S ALL SPUN AROUND BECAUSE HE THINKS *HE* DID SOMETHING WRONG.

I HAVE TO VERBALLY FENCE WITH A PSYCHOPATH EVERY DAY, AND THE MAN WHO FIXES MY INTERNET IS HAVING SOME KIND OF SLOW-MOTION BREAKDOWN AND I WON'T HAVE ANY MORE CHAOS IN THIS UNIT. I WON'T HAVE IT.

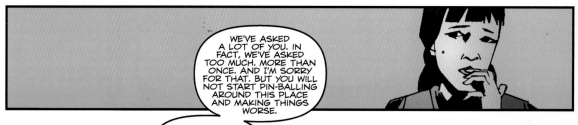

WE'VE ASKED A LOT OF YOU. IN FACT, WE'VE ASKED TOO MUCH. MORE THAN ONCE. AND I'M SORRY FOR THAT. BUT YOU WILL NOT START PIN-BALLING AROUND THIS PLACE AND MAKING THINGS WORSE.

BECAUSE YOU ARE *STRONG*. AND I *BELIEVE* IN YOU. AND THAT MEANS YOU CAN DO IT, BECAUSE I'M NEVER WRONG. THAT'S WHY I HAVE THIS JOB.

I... I DON'T KNOW WHAT TO—

GET OUT OF MY OFFICE.

AND STAY AWAY FROM FLINT.

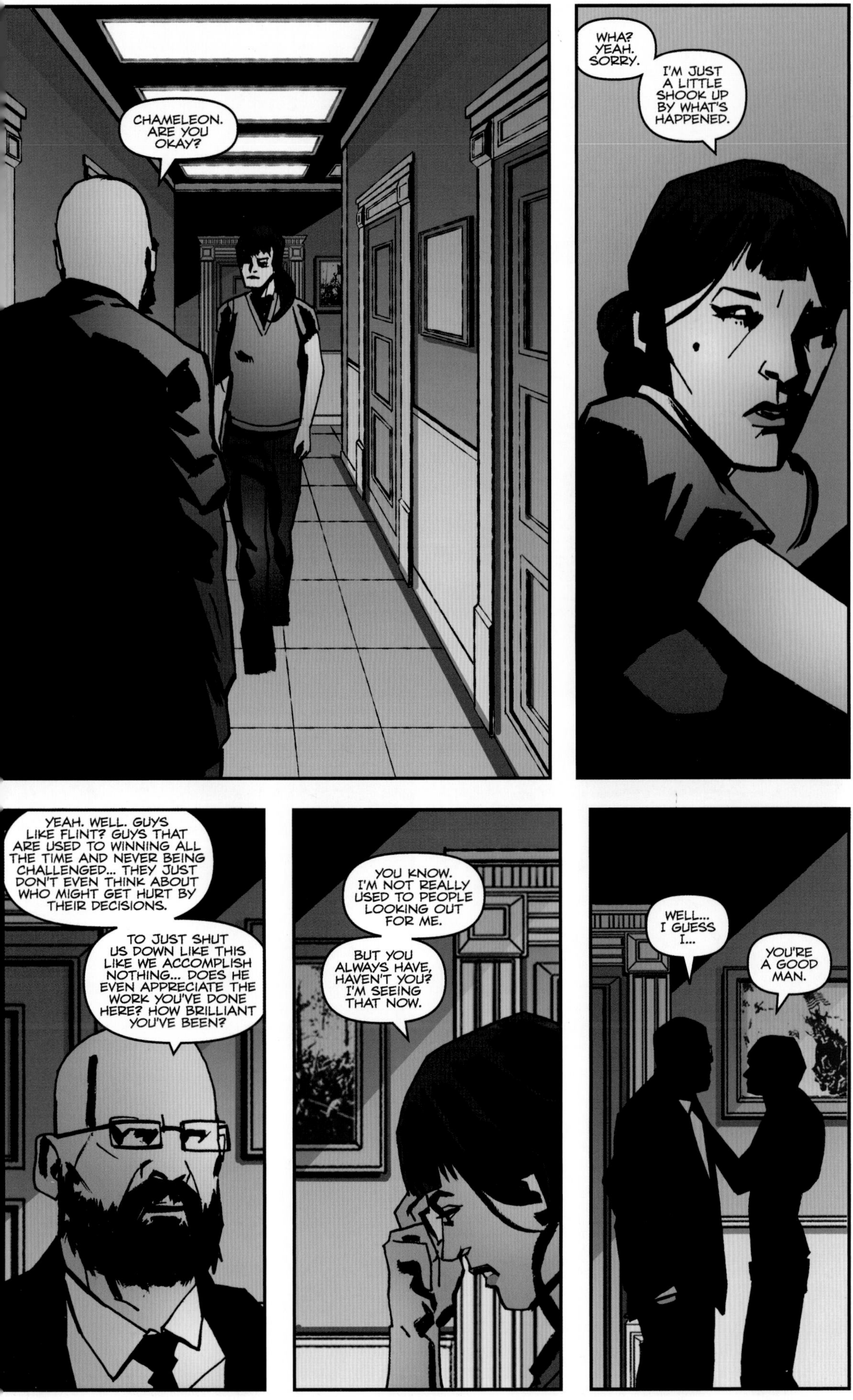
CHAMELEON. ARE YOU OKAY?
WHA? YEAH. SORRY.
I'M JUST A LITTLE SHOOK UP BY WHAT'S HAPPENED.
YEAH. WELL. GUYS LIKE FLINT? GUYS THAT ARE USED TO WINNING ALL THE TIME AND NEVER BEING CHALLENGED... THEY JUST DON'T EVEN THINK ABOUT WHO MIGHT GET HURT BY THEIR DECISIONS.
TO JUST SHUT US DOWN LIKE THIS LIKE WE ACCOMPLISH NOTHING... DOES HE EVEN APPRECIATE THE WORK YOU'VE DONE HERE? HOW BRILLIANT YOU'VE BEEN?
YOU KNOW. I'M NOT REALLY USED TO PEOPLE LOOKING OUT FOR ME.
BUT YOU ALWAYS HAVE, HAVEN'T YOU? I'M SEEING THAT NOW.
WELL... I GUESS I...
YOU'RE A GOOD MAN.

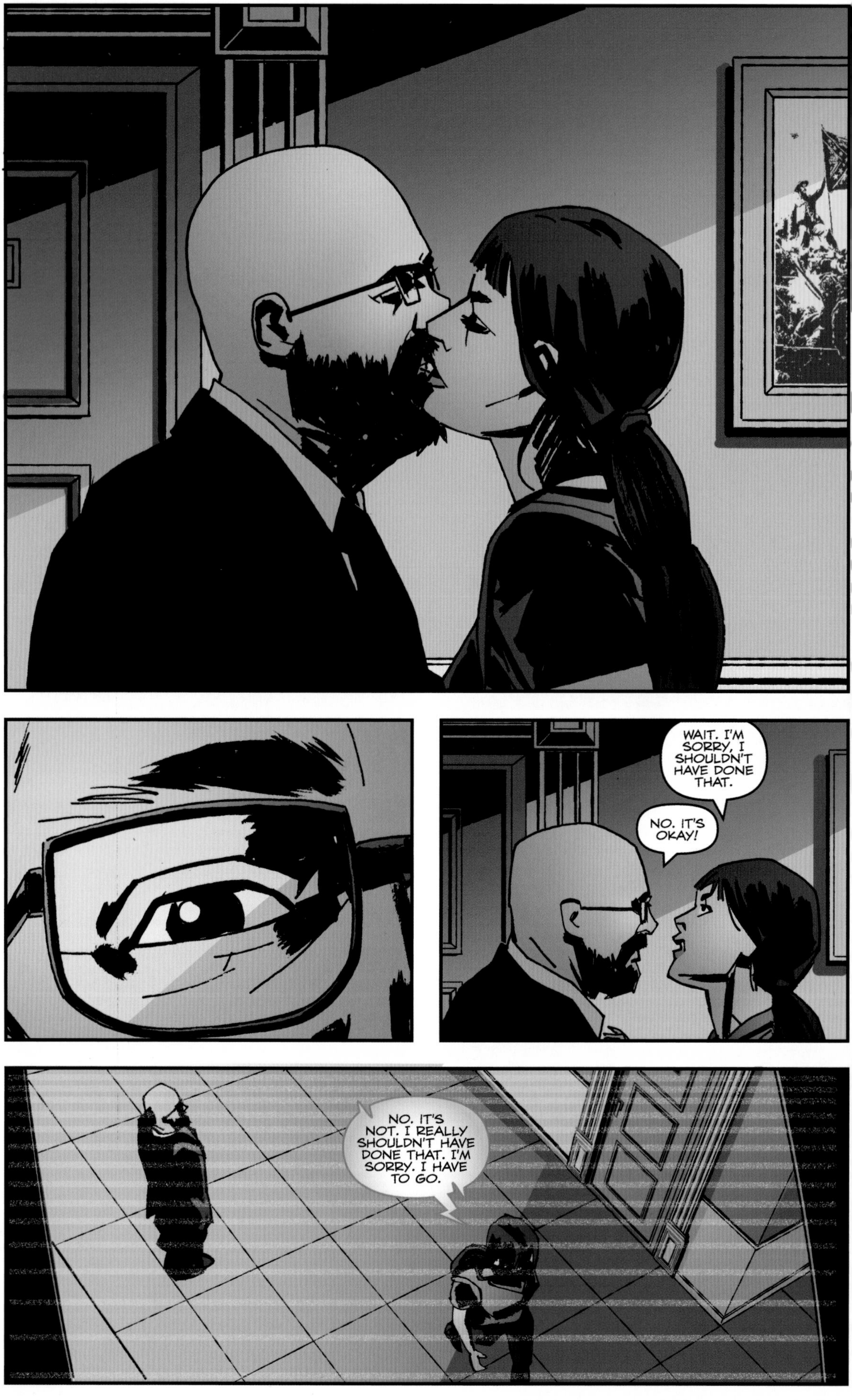

WAIT. I'M SORRY, I SHOULDN'T HAVE DONE THAT.
NO. IT'S OKAY!
NO. IT'S NOT. I REALLY SHOULDN'T HAVE DONE THAT. I'M SORRY. I HAVE TO GO.

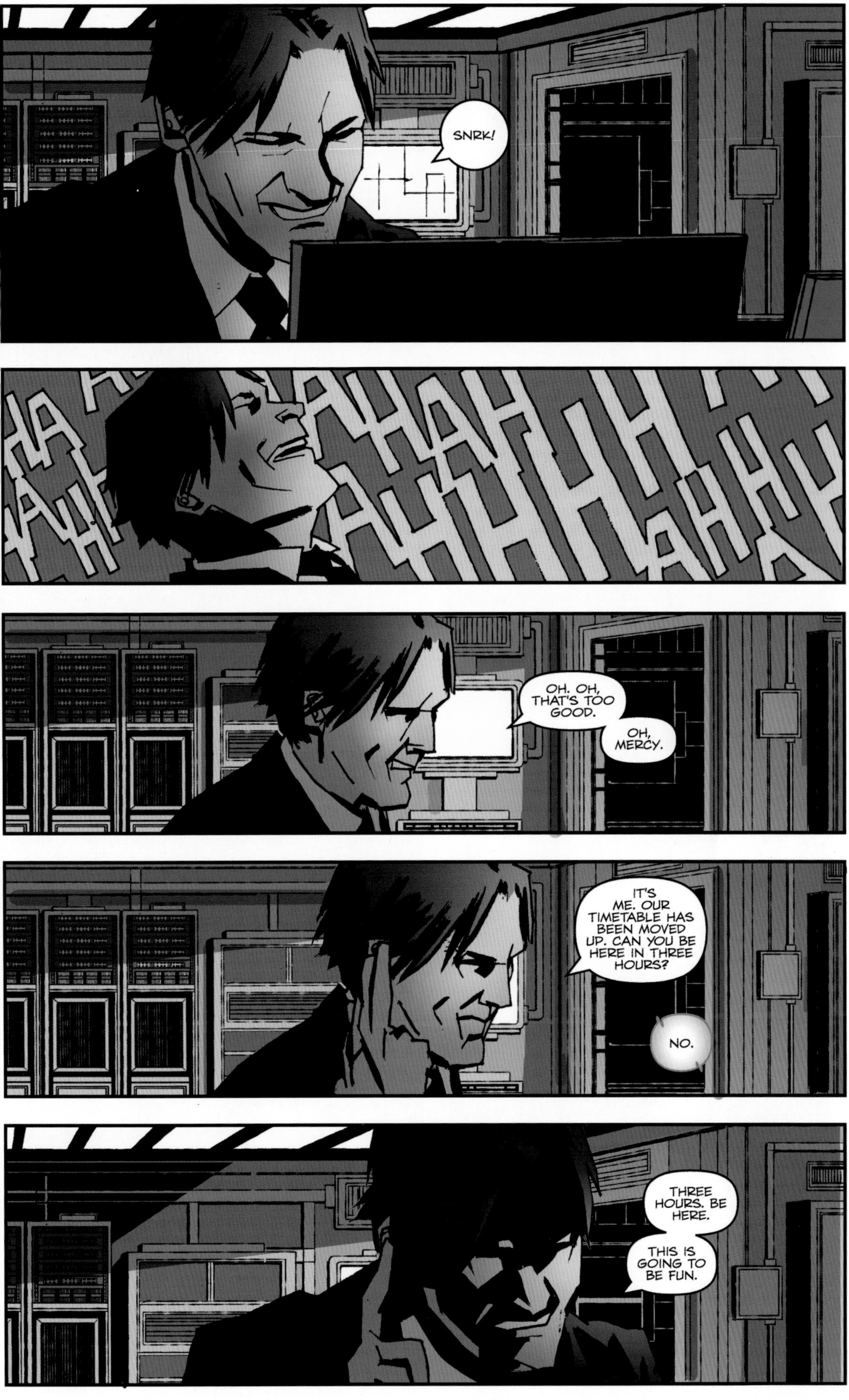
SNRK!
HAHAHAHAHAHAHAHA
OH. OH, THAT'S TOO GOOD.
OH, MERCY.
IT'S ME. OUR TIMETABLE HAS BEEN MOVED UP. CAN YOU BE HERE IN THREE HOURS?
NO.
THREE HOURS. BE HERE.
THIS IS GOING TO BE FUN.

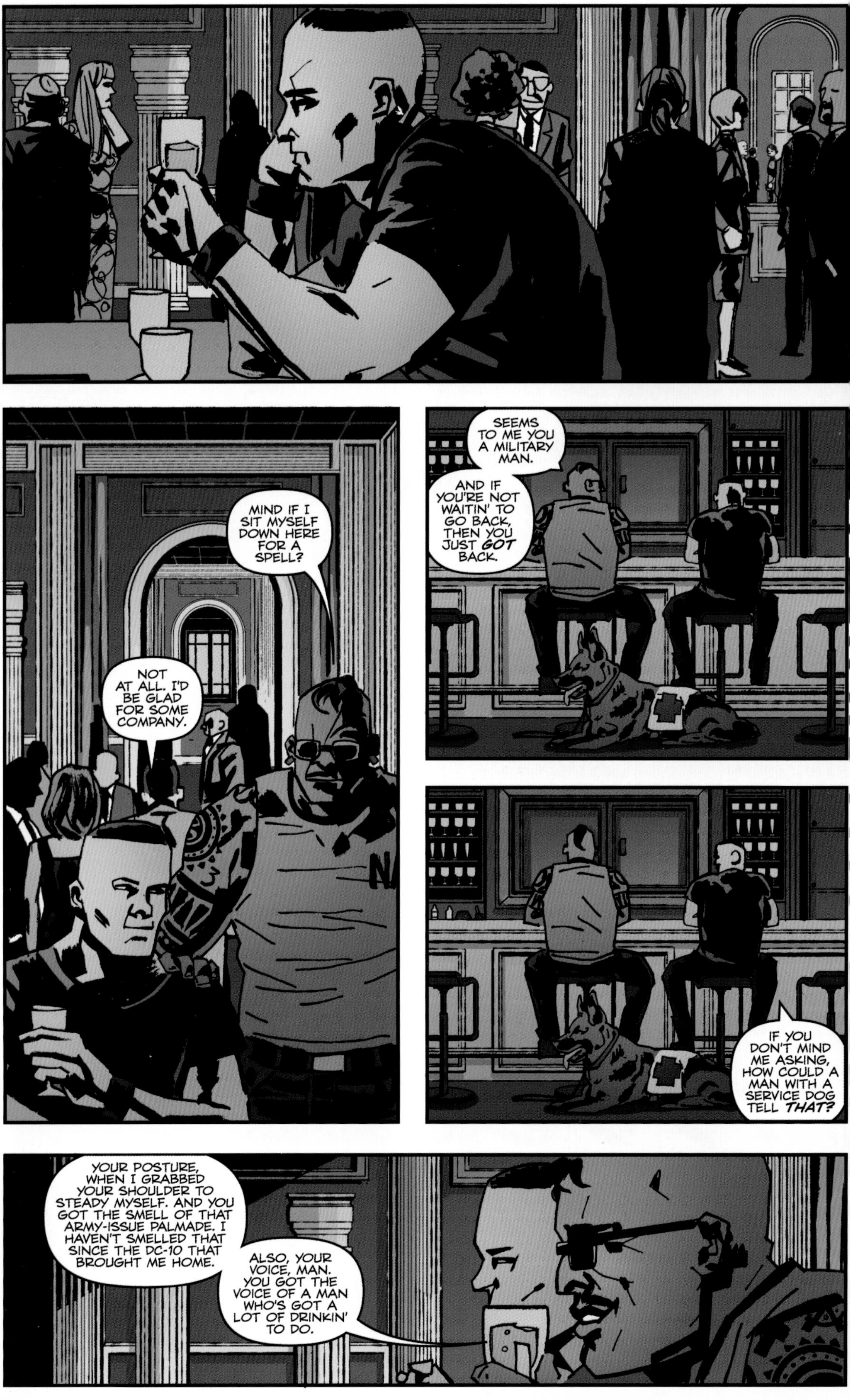
MIND IF I SIT MYSELF DOWN HERE FOR A SPELL?
NOT AT ALL. I'D BE GLAD FOR SOME COMPANY.
SEEMS TO ME YOU A MILITARY MAN.
AND IF YOU'RE NOT WAITIN' TO GO BACK, THEN YOU JUST *GOT* BACK.
IF YOU DON'T MIND ME ASKING, HOW COULD A MAN WITH A SERVICE DOG TELL *THAT?*
YOUR POSTURE, WHEN I GRABBED YOUR SHOULDER TO STEADY MYSELF. AND YOU GOT THE SMELL OF THAT ARMY-ISSUE PALMADE. I HAVEN'T SMELLED THAT SINCE THE DC-10 THAT BROUGHT ME HOME.
ALSO, YOUR VOICE, MAN. YOU GOT THE VOICE OF A MAN WHO'S GOT A LOT OF DRINKIN' TO DO.

I MEAN, IT WAS JUST LIKE I *DREAMED* IT WOULD BE. IT'S LIKE SHE *SAW* ME FOR THE FIRST TIME, YOU KNOW?

AND THEN... THEN IT WAS LIKE I WOKE UP. BECAUSE SHE TOOK IT ALL *BACK*.

SHE DIDN'T TAKE IT *BACK*, CLOCKSPRING. SHE DIDN'T EVEN GIVE IT TO YOU IN THE *FIRST PLACE*.

SHE KISSED YOU FOR TWO REASONS: *ONE*, BECAUSE YOU STOOD UP AND LOOKED LIKE A MAN IN THAT MEETING. AND *TWO*— AND THIS IS THE MOST IMPORTANT ONE—TO *GET BACK AT FLINT*.

SEE, THAT'S HOW WOMEN ARE. THEY'RE MOTIVATED BY THEIR *EMOTIONS*. IT'S WHAT MAKES THEM *WEAK*, AND EASY TO MANIPULATE.

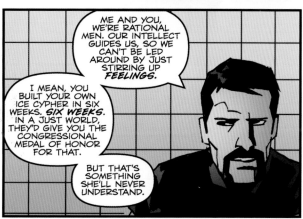

ME AND YOU, WE'RE RATIONAL MEN. OUR INTELLECT GUIDES US, SO WE CAN'T BE LED AROUND BY JUST STIRRING UP *FEELINGS*.

I MEAN, YOU BUILT YOUR OWN ICE CYPHER IN SIX WEEKS. *SIX WEEKS*. IN A JUST WORLD, THEY'D GIVE YOU THE CONGRESSIONAL MEDAL OF HONOR FOR THAT.

BUT THAT'S SOMETHING SHE'LL NEVER UNDERSTAND.

HOW DO YOU EVEN DISGUISE THE POWER THIS SYSTEM MUST DRAW?

WELL, THAT PART'S *EASY*, ACTUALLY...

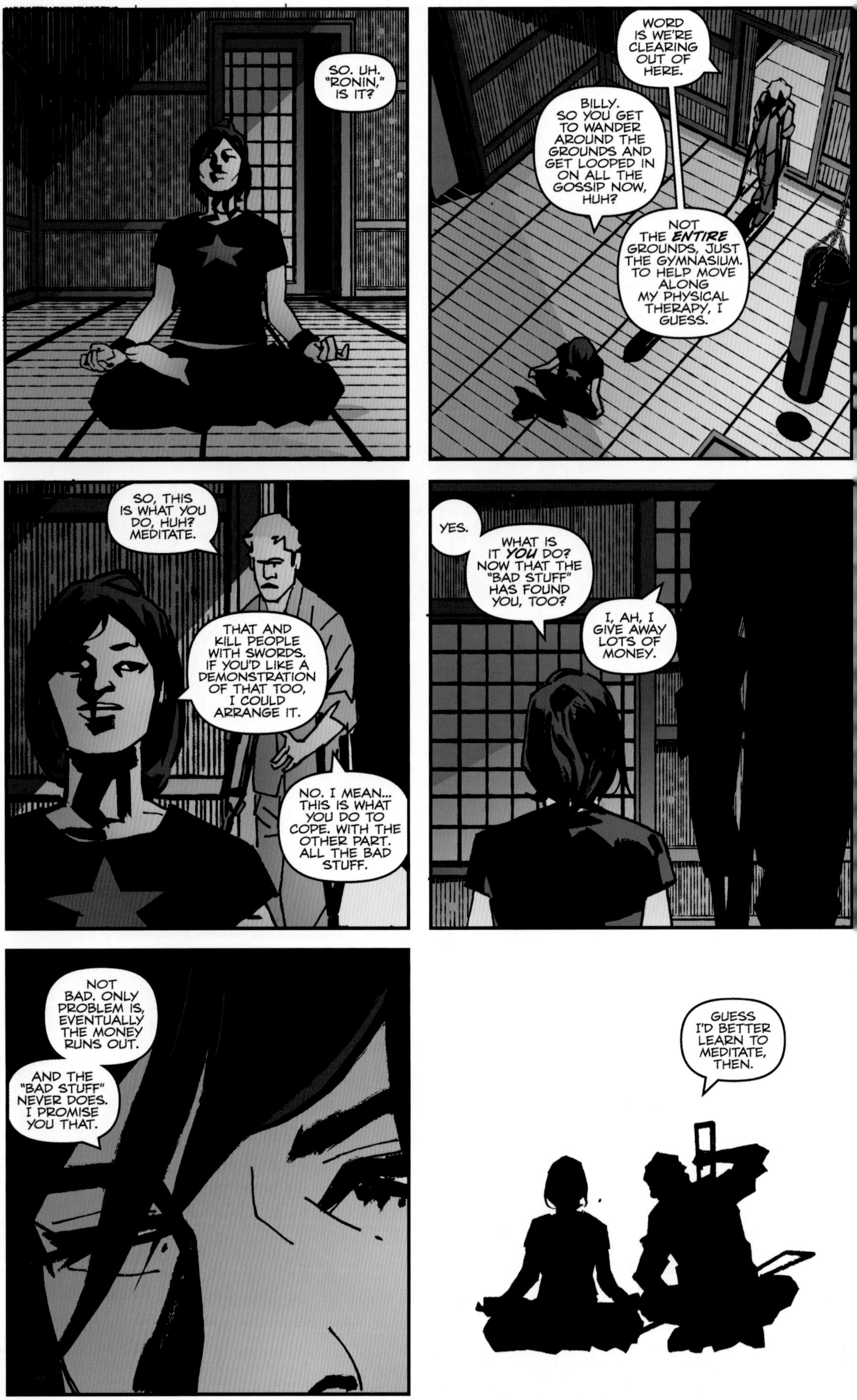
SO. UH. "RONIN," IS IT?
WORD IS WE'RE CLEARING OUT OF HERE.
BILLY. SO YOU GET TO WANDER AROUND THE GROUNDS AND GET LOOPED IN ON ALL THE GOSSIP NOW, HUH?
NOT THE ENTIRE GROUNDS, JUST THE GYMNASIUM. TO HELP MOVE ALONG MY PHYSICAL THERAPY, I GUESS.
SO, THIS IS WHAT YOU DO, HUH? MEDITATE.
THAT AND KILL PEOPLE WITH SWORDS. IF YOU'D LIKE A DEMONSTRATION OF THAT TOO, I COULD ARRANGE IT.
NO. I MEAN... THIS IS WHAT YOU DO TO COPE. WITH THE OTHER PART. ALL THE BAD STUFF.
YES.
WHAT IS IT YOU DO? NOW THAT THE "BAD STUFF" HAS FOUND YOU, TOO?
I, AH, I GIVE AWAY LOTS OF MONEY.
NOT BAD. ONLY PROBLEM IS, EVENTUALLY THE MONEY RUNS OUT.
AND THE "BAD STUFF" NEVER DOES. I PROMISE YOU THAT.
GUESS I'D BETTER LEARN TO MEDITATE, THEN.

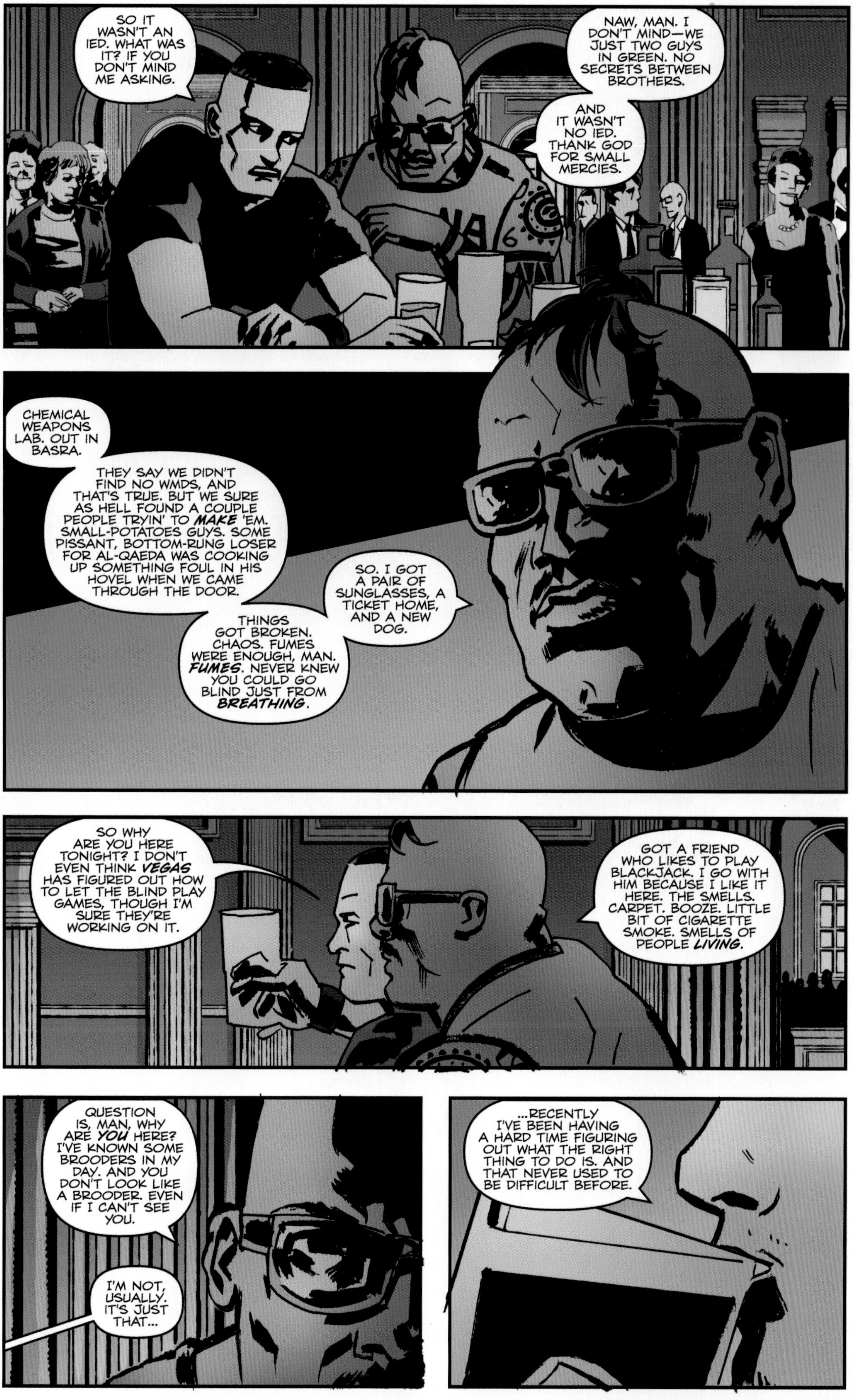
SO IT WASN'T AN IED. WHAT WAS IT? IF YOU DON'T MIND ME ASKING.
NAW, MAN. I DON'T MIND—WE JUST TWO GUYS IN GREEN. NO SECRETS BETWEEN BROTHERS.
AND IT WASN'T NO IED. THANK GOD FOR SMALL MERCIES.
CHEMICAL WEAPONS LAB. OUT IN BASRA.
THEY SAY WE DIDN'T FIND NO WMDS, AND THAT'S TRUE. BUT WE SURE AS HELL FOUND A COUPLE PEOPLE TRYIN' TO *MAKE* 'EM. SMALL-POTATOES GUYS. SOME PISSANT, BOTTOM-RUNG LOSER FOR AL-QAEDA WAS COOKING UP SOMETHING FOUL IN HIS HOVEL WHEN WE CAME THROUGH THE DOOR.
THINGS GOT BROKEN. CHAOS. FUMES WERE ENOUGH, MAN. *FUMES*. NEVER KNEW YOU COULD GO BLIND JUST FROM *BREATHING*.
SO. I GOT A PAIR OF SUNGLASSES, A TICKET HOME, AND A NEW DOG.
SO WHY ARE YOU HERE TONIGHT? I DON'T EVEN THINK *VEGAS* HAS FIGURED OUT HOW TO LET THE BLIND PLAY GAMES, THOUGH I'M SURE THEY'RE WORKING ON IT.
GOT A FRIEND WHO LIKES TO PLAY BLACKJACK. I GO WITH HIM BECAUSE I LIKE IT HERE. THE SMELLS. CARPET. BOOZE. LITTLE BIT OF CIGARETTE SMOKE. SMELLS OF PEOPLE *LIVING*.
QUESTION IS, MAN, WHY ARE *YOU* HERE? I'VE KNOWN SOME BROODERS IN MY DAY. AND YOU DON'T LOOK LIKE A BROODER. EVEN IF I CAN'T SEE YOU.
I'M NOT, USUALLY. IT'S JUST THAT...
...RECENTLY I'VE BEEN HAVING A HARD TIME FIGURING OUT WHAT THE RIGHT THING TO DO IS. AND THAT NEVER USED TO BE DIFFICULT BEFORE.

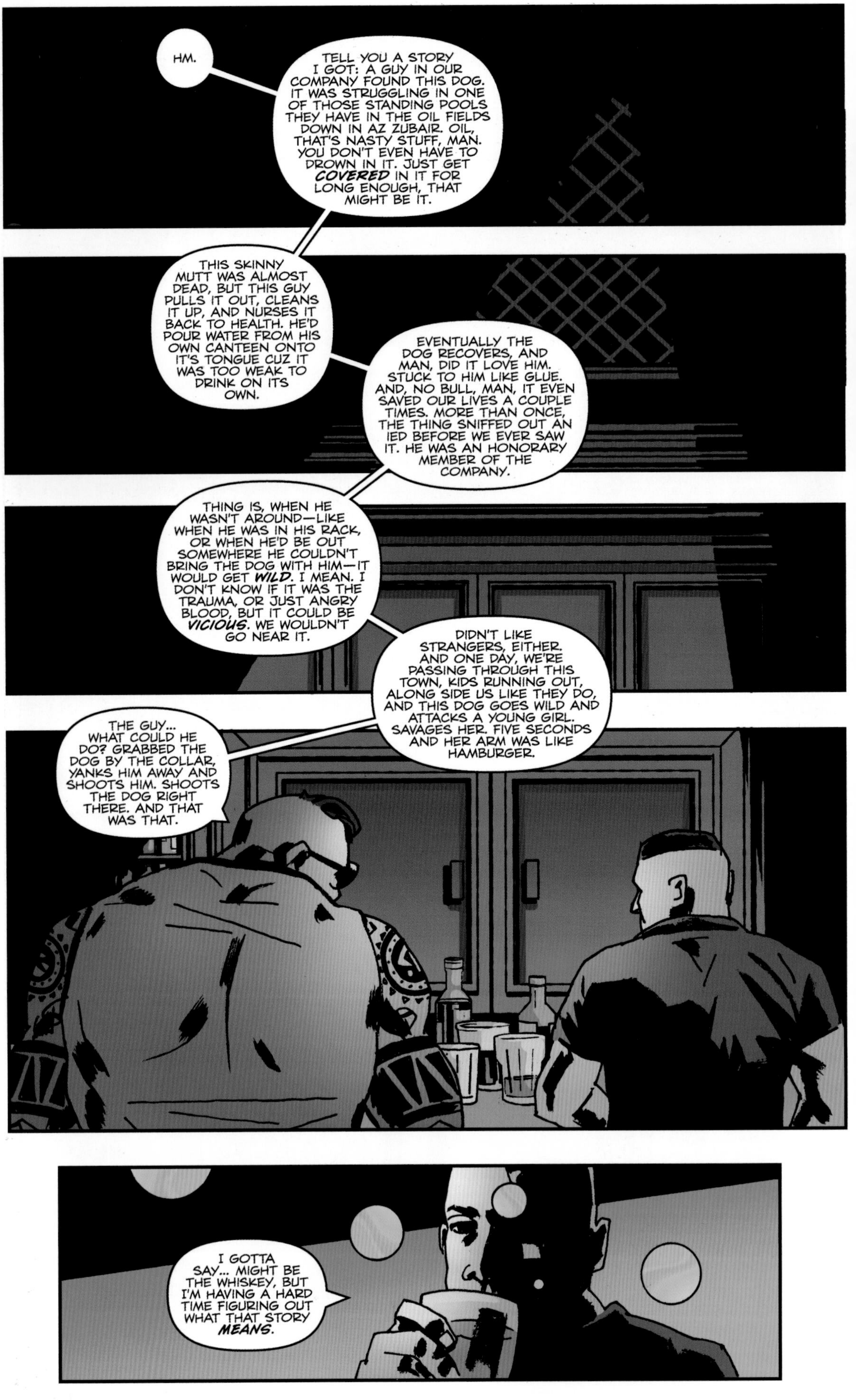
HM.
TELL YOU A STORY I GOT: A GUY IN OUR COMPANY FOUND THIS DOG. IT WAS STRUGGLING IN ONE OF THOSE STANDING POOLS THEY HAVE IN THE OIL FIELDS DOWN IN AZ ZUBAIR. OIL, THAT'S NASTY STUFF, MAN. YOU DON'T EVEN HAVE TO DROWN IN IT. JUST GET COVERED IN IT FOR LONG ENOUGH, THAT MIGHT BE IT.
THIS SKINNY MUTT WAS ALMOST DEAD, BUT THIS GUY PULLS IT OUT, CLEANS IT UP, AND NURSES IT BACK TO HEALTH. HE'D POUR WATER FROM HIS OWN CANTEEN ONTO IT'S TONGUE CUZ IT WAS TOO WEAK TO DRINK ON ITS OWN.
EVENTUALLY THE DOG RECOVERS, AND MAN, DID IT LOVE HIM. STUCK TO HIM LIKE GLUE. AND, NO BULL, MAN, IT EVEN SAVED OUR LIVES A COUPLE TIMES. MORE THAN ONCE, THE THING SNIFFED OUT AN IED BEFORE WE EVER SAW IT. HE WAS AN HONORARY MEMBER OF THE COMPANY.
THING IS, WHEN HE WASN'T AROUND—LIKE WHEN HE WAS IN HIS RACK, OR WHEN HE'D BE OUT SOMEWHERE HE COULDN'T BRING THE DOG WITH HIM—IT WOULD GET WILD. I MEAN. I DON'T KNOW IF IT WAS THE TRAUMA, OR JUST ANGRY BLOOD, BUT IT COULD BE VICIOUS. WE WOULDN'T GO NEAR IT.
DIDN'T LIKE STRANGERS, EITHER. AND ONE DAY, WE'RE PASSING THROUGH THIS TOWN, KIDS RUNNING OUT, ALONG SIDE US LIKE THEY DO, AND THIS DOG GOES WILD AND ATTACKS A YOUNG GIRL. SAVAGES HER. FIVE SECONDS AND HER ARM WAS LIKE HAMBURGER.
THE GUY... WHAT COULD HE DO? GRABBED THE DOG BY THE COLLAR, YANKS HIM AWAY AND SHOOTS HIM. SHOOTS THE DOG RIGHT THERE. AND THAT WAS THAT.
I GOTTA SAY... MIGHT BE THE WHISKEY, BUT I'M HAVING A HARD TIME FIGURING OUT WHAT THAT STORY MEANS.

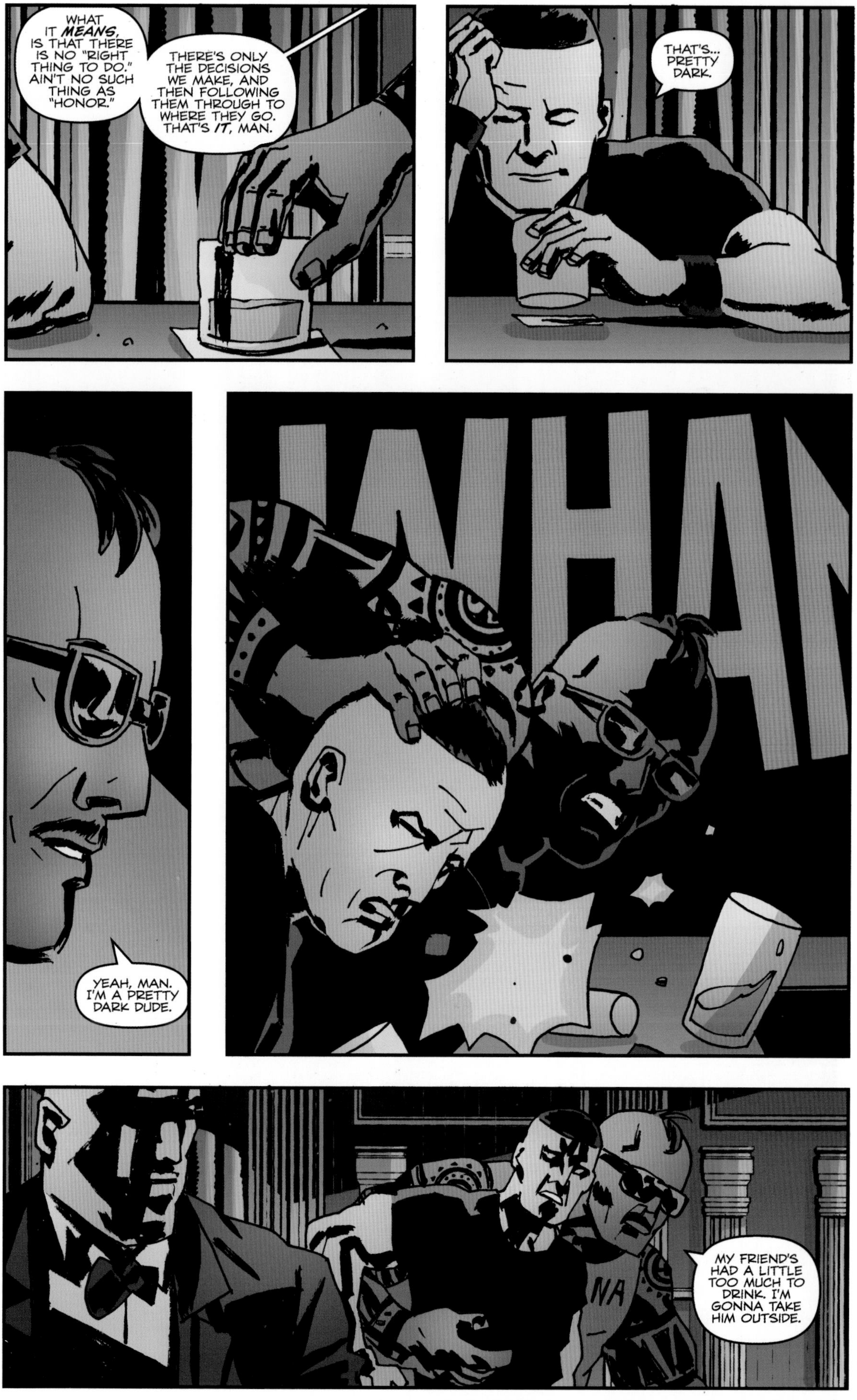
WHAT IT MEANS, IS THAT THERE IS NO "RIGHT THING TO DO." AIN'T NO SUCH THING AS "HONOR."
THERE'S ONLY THE DECISIONS WE MAKE, AND THEN FOLLOWING THEM THROUGH TO WHERE THEY GO. THAT'S IT, MAN.
THAT'S... PRETTY DARK.
YEAH, MAN. I'M A PRETTY DARK DUDE.
WHAN
MY FRIEND'S HAD A LITTLE TOO MUCH TO DRINK. I'M GONNA TAKE HIM OUTSIDE.

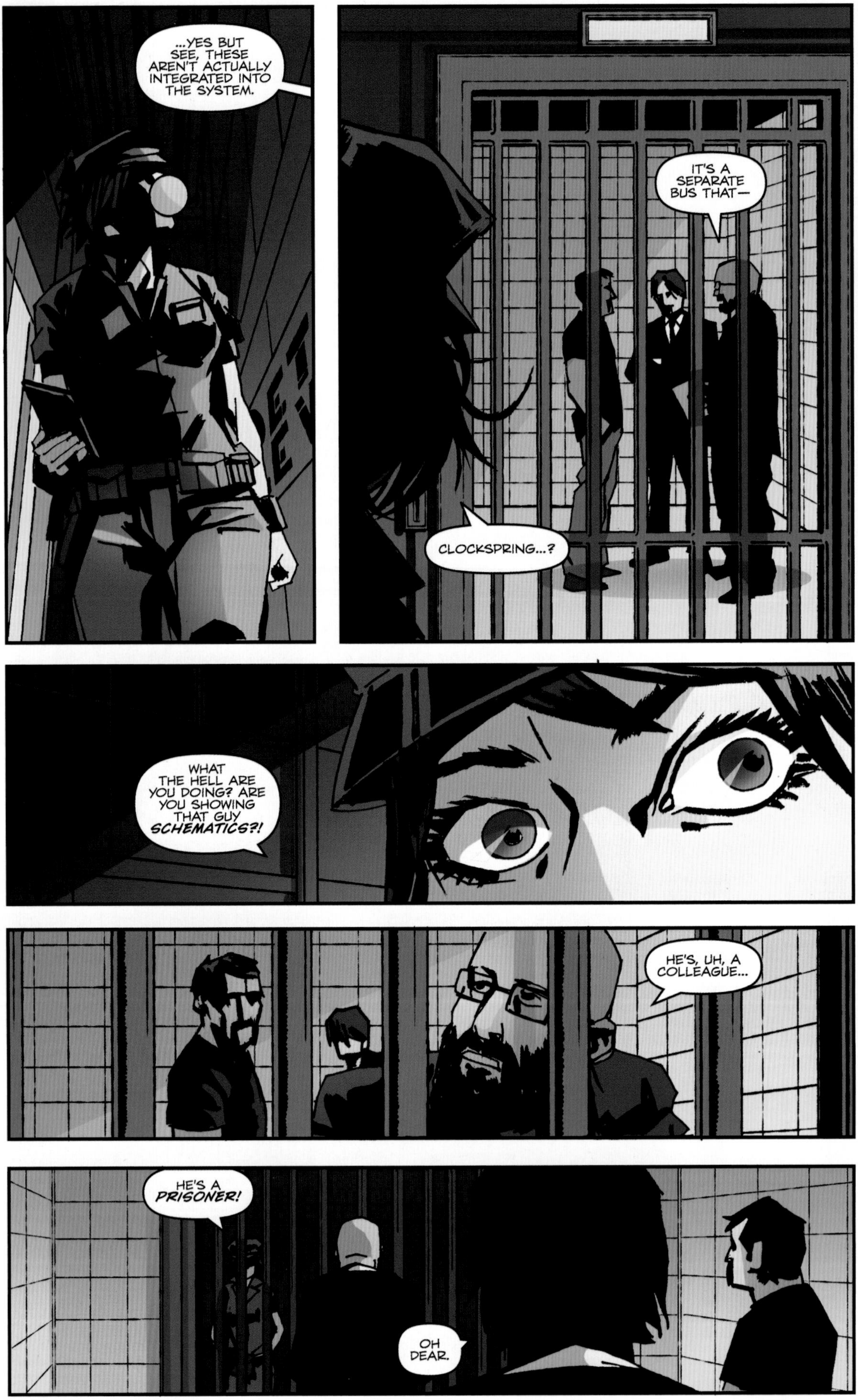
...YES BUT SEE, THESE AREN'T ACTUALLY INTEGRATED INTO THE SYSTEM.
IT'S A SEPARATE BUS THAT—
CLOCKSPRING...?
WHAT THE HELL ARE YOU DOING? ARE YOU SHOWING THAT GUY *SCHEMATICS*?!
HE'S, UH, A COLLEAGUE...
HE'S A *PRISONER*!
OH DEAR.

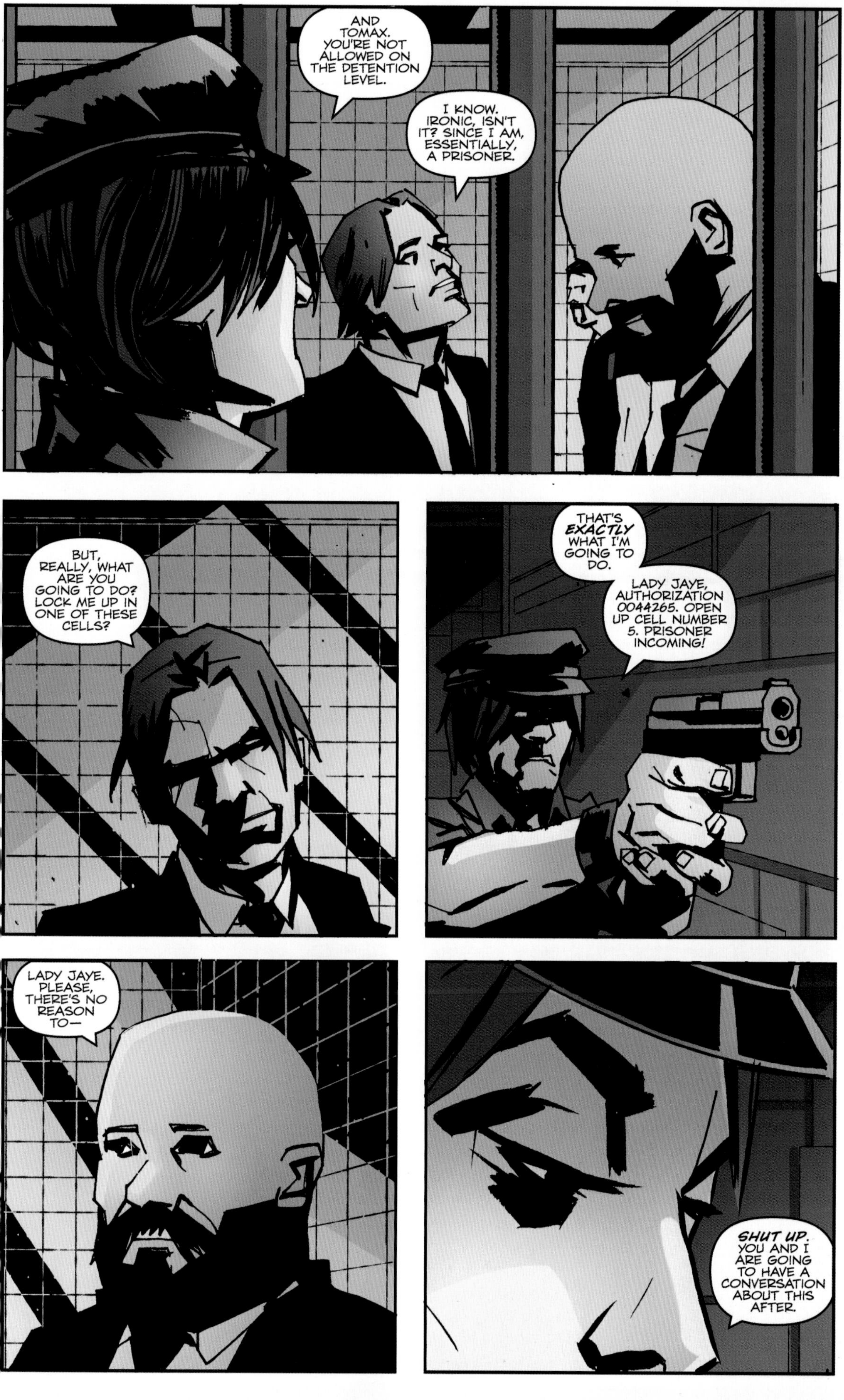
AND TOMAX. YOU'RE NOT ALLOWED ON THE DETENTION LEVEL.
I KNOW. IRONIC, ISN'T IT? SINCE I AM, ESSENTIALLY, A PRISONER.
BUT, REALLY, WHAT ARE YOU GOING TO DO? LOCK ME UP IN ONE OF THESE CELLS?
THAT'S *EXACTLY* WHAT I'M GOING TO DO.
LADY JAYE, AUTHORIZATION 0044265. OPEN UP CELL NUMBER 5. PRISONER INCOMING!
LADY JAYE. PLEASE, THERE'S NO REASON TO—
SHUT UP. YOU AND I ARE GOING TO HAVE A CONVERSATION ABOUT THIS AFTER.

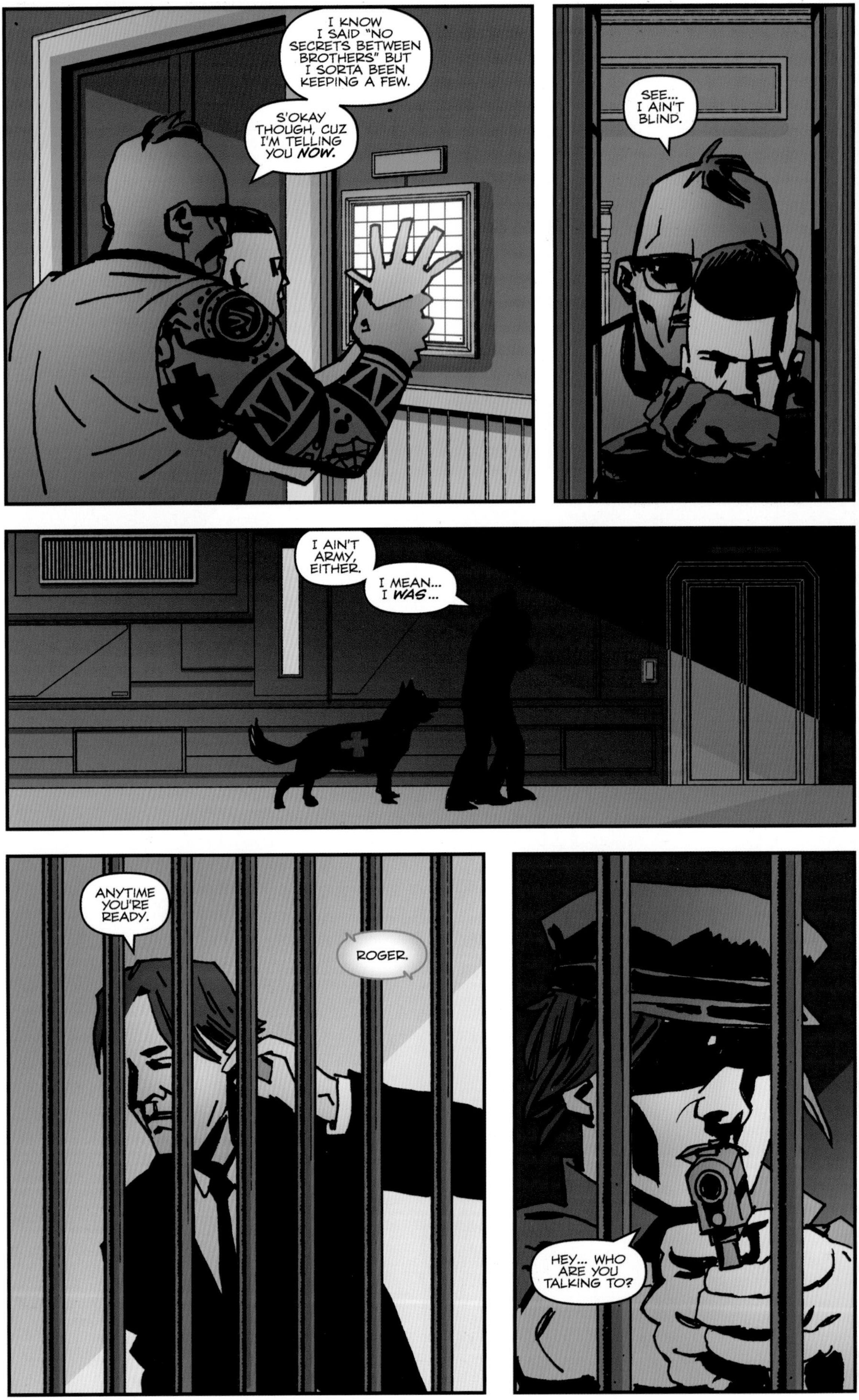
I KNOW I SAID "NO SECRETS BETWEEN BROTHERS" BUT I SORTA BEEN KEEPING A FEW.
S'OKAY THOUGH, CUZ I'M TELLING YOU **NOW.**
SEE... I AIN'T BLIND.
I AIN'T ARMY, EITHER.
I MEAN... I **WAS**...
ANYTIME YOU'RE READY.
ROGER.
HEY... WHO ARE YOU TALKING TO?

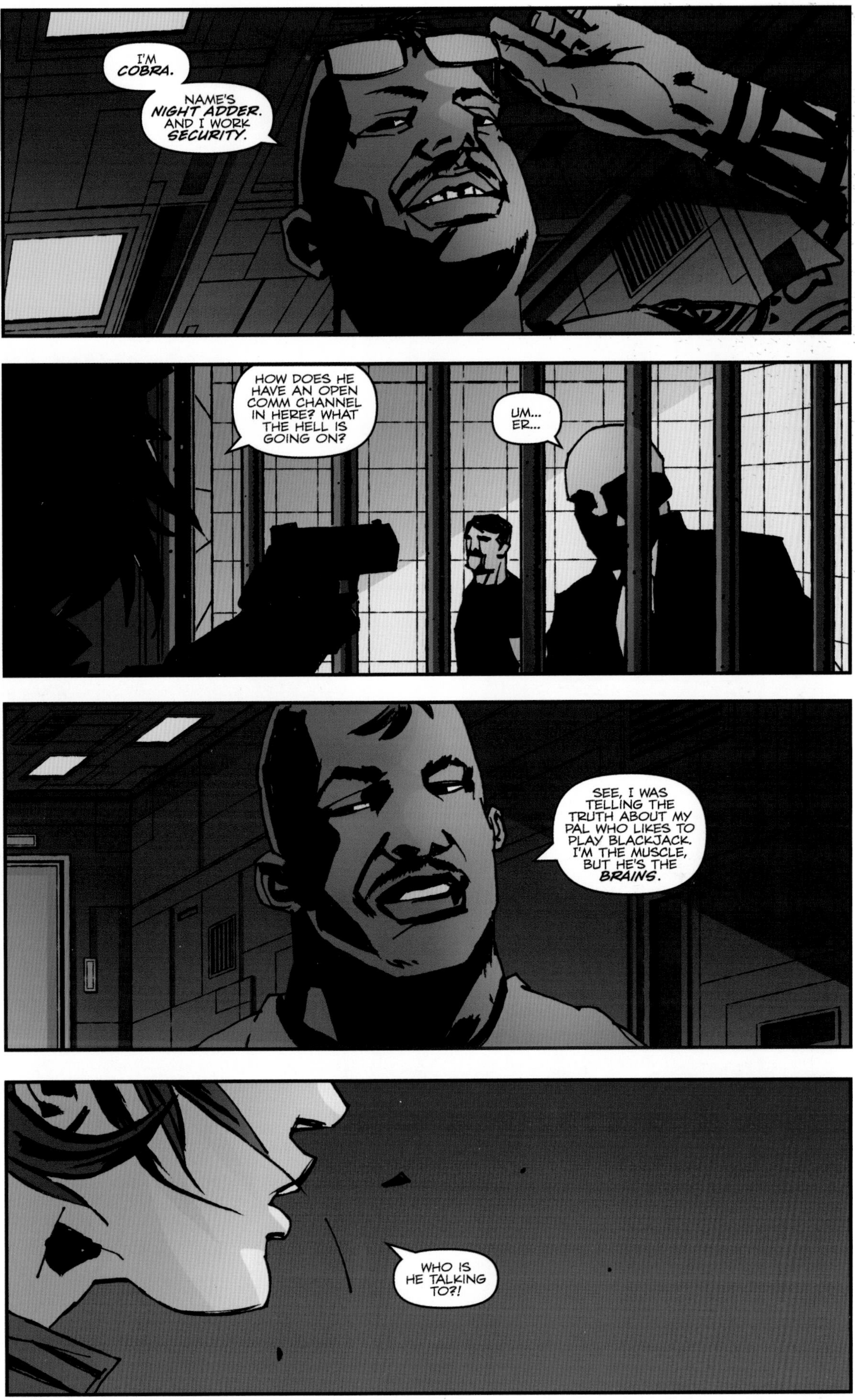
I'M COBRA.
NAME'S NIGHT ADDER. AND I WORK SECURITY.
HOW DOES HE HAVE AN OPEN COMM CHANNEL IN HERE? WHAT THE HELL IS GOING ON?
UM... ER...
SEE, I WAS TELLING THE TRUTH ABOUT MY PAL WHO LIKES TO PLAY BLACKJACK. I'M THE MUSCLE, BUT HE'S THE BRAINS.
WHO IS HE TALKING TO?!

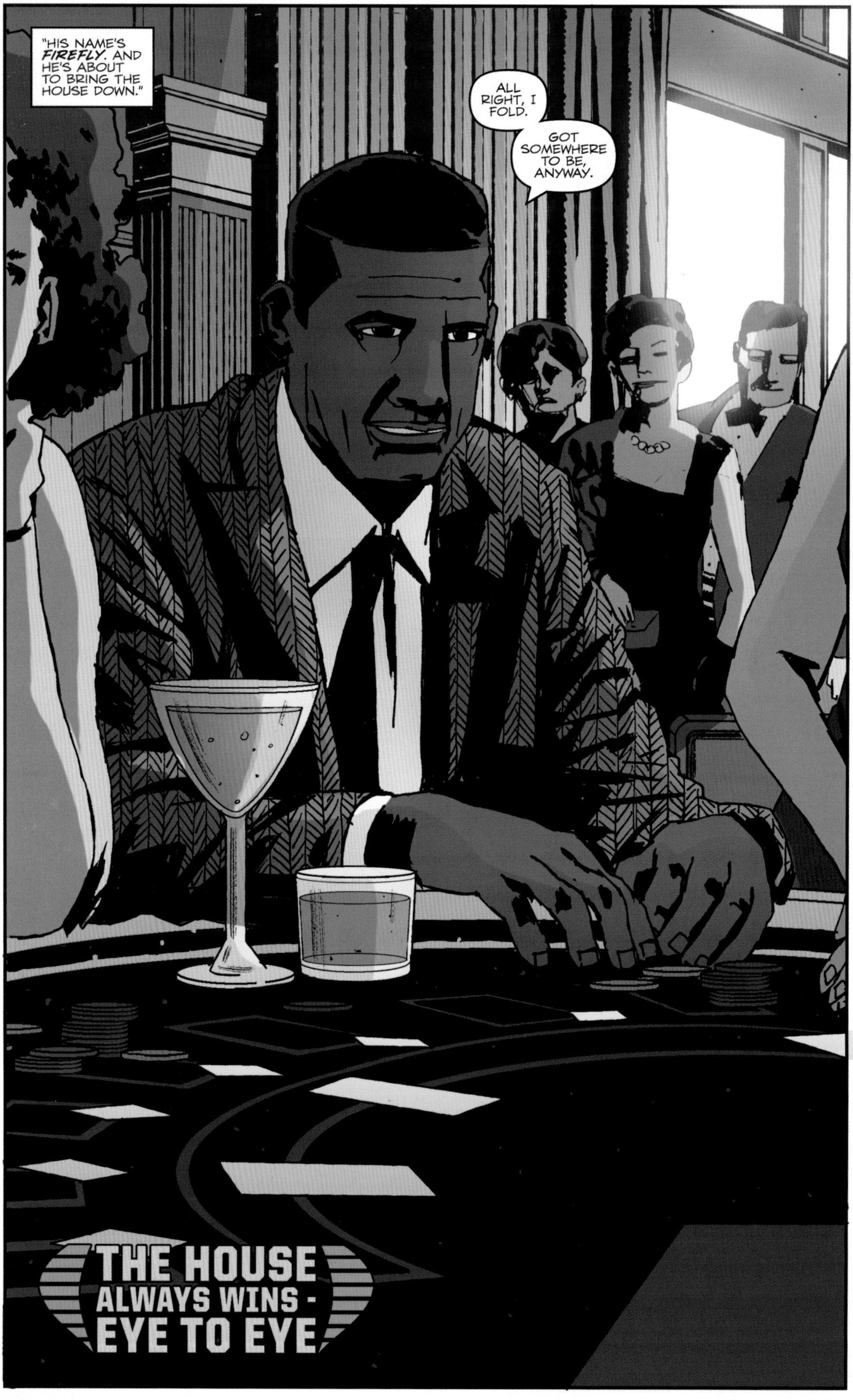
"HIS NAME'S FIREFLY. AND HE'S ABOUT TO BRING THE HOUSE DOWN."
ALL RIGHT, I FOLD.
GOT SOMEWHERE TO BE, ANYWAY.
THE HOUSE ALWAYS WINS - EYE TO EYE

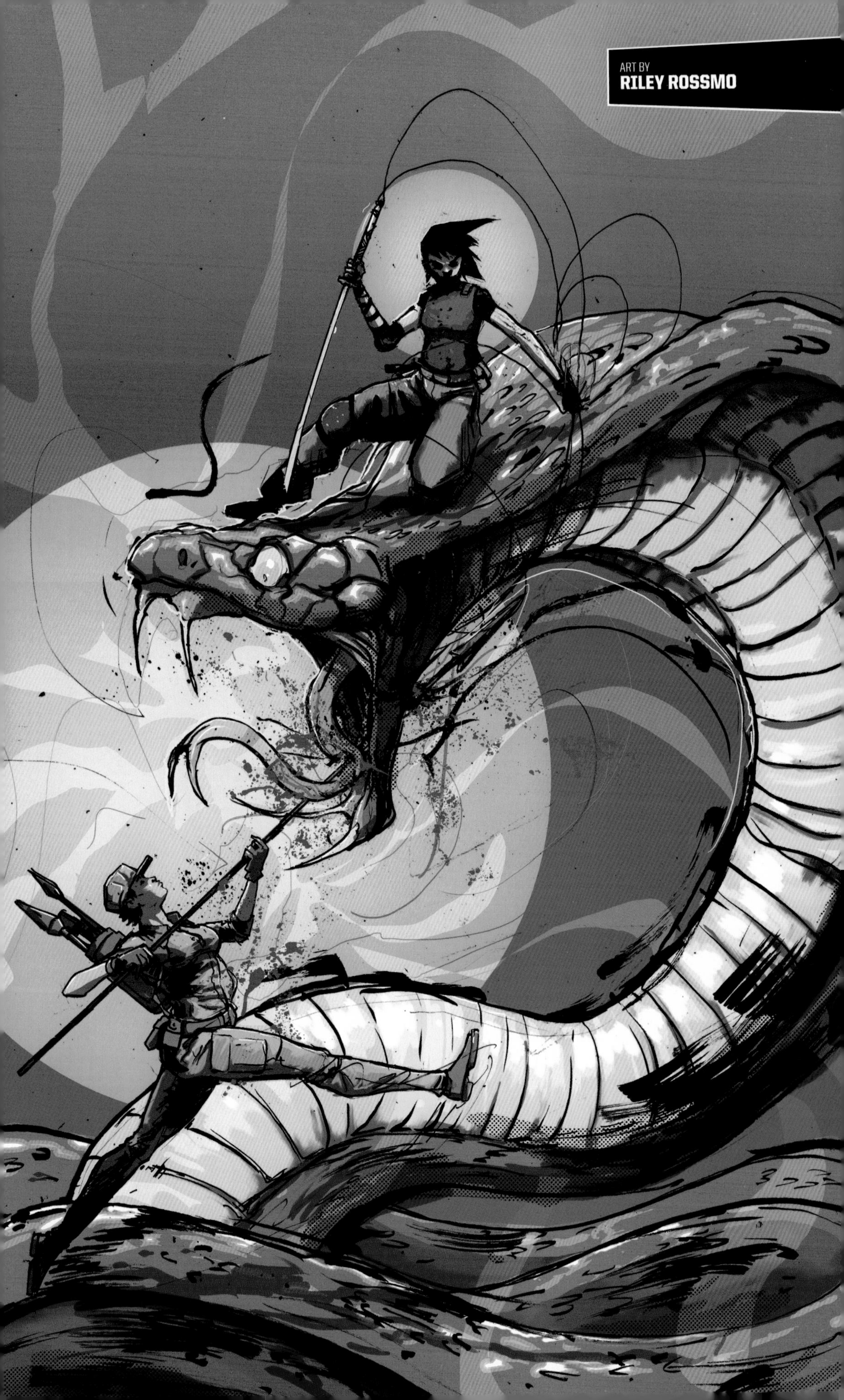

ART BY
RILEY ROSSMO

ART BY
ANTONIO FUSO
COLORS BY
STEFANO SIMEONE

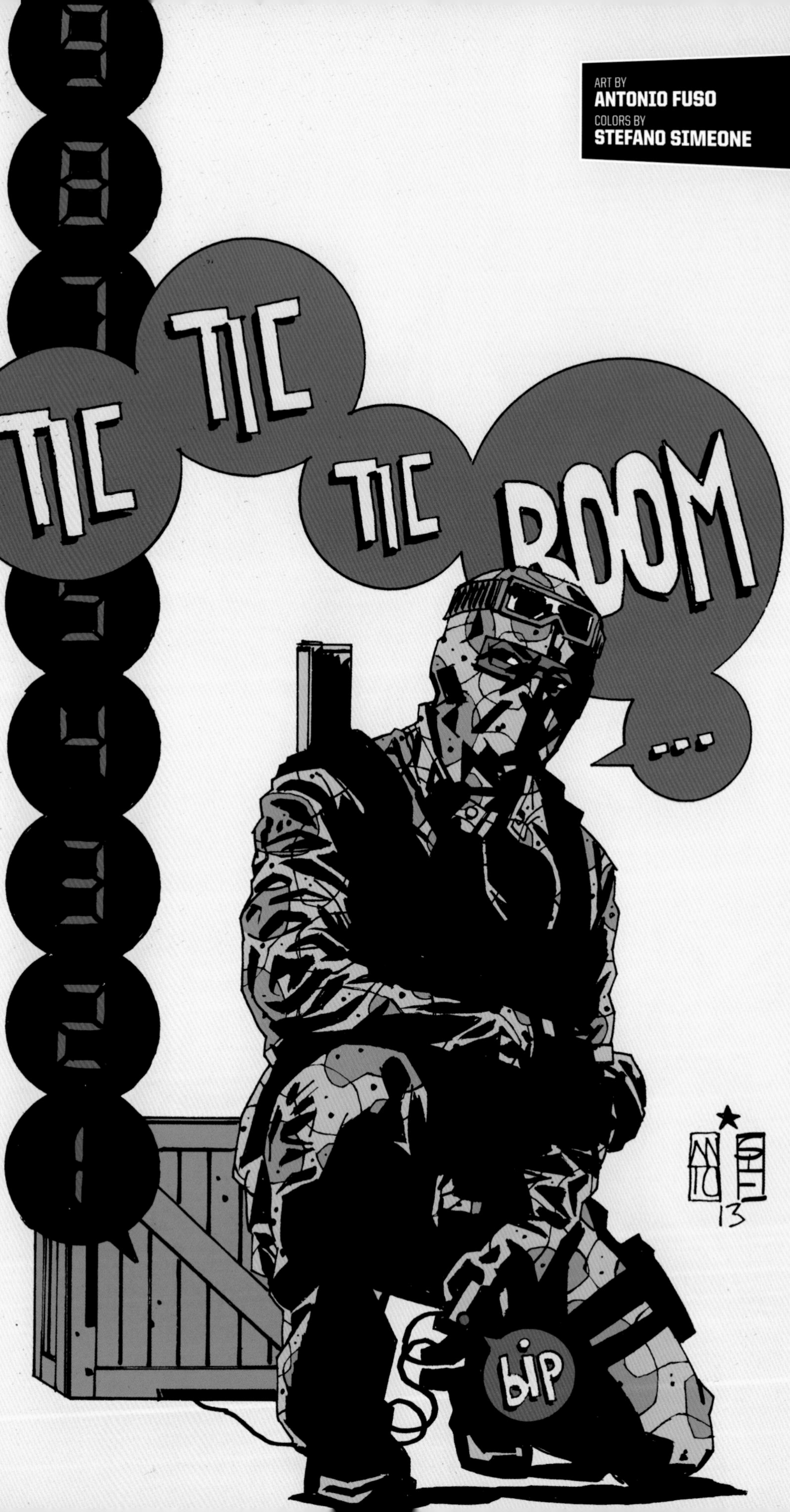

TIC
TIC
TIC
BOOM
...
bip

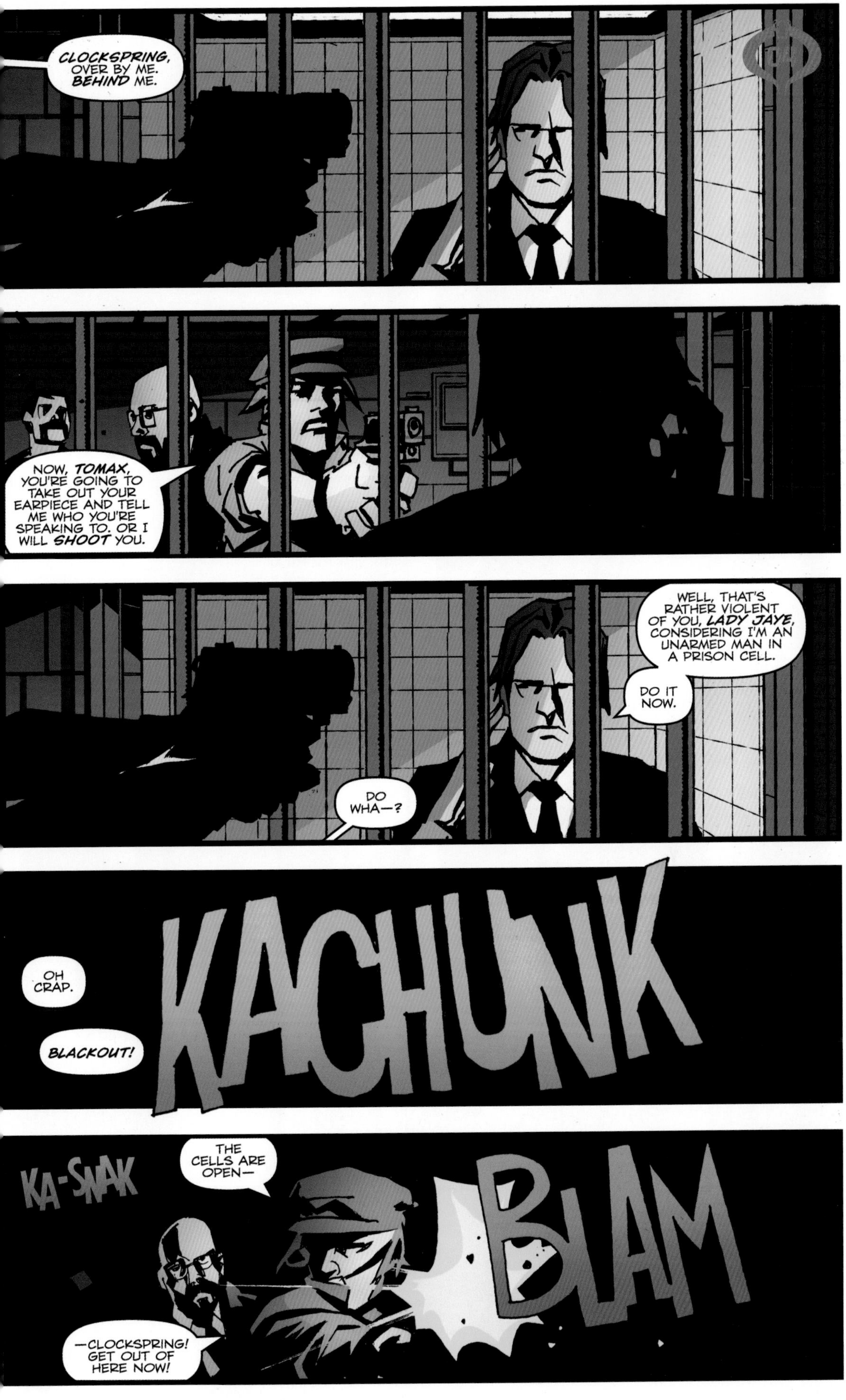

CLOCKSPRING, OVER BY ME. BEHIND ME.
NOW, TOMAX, YOU'RE GOING TO TAKE OUT YOUR EARPIECE AND TELL ME WHO YOU'RE SPEAKING TO. OR I WILL SHOOT YOU.
WELL, THAT'S RATHER VIOLENT OF YOU, LADY JAYE, CONSIDERING I'M AN UNARMED MAN IN A PRISON CELL.
DO IT NOW.
DO WHA—?
KACHUNK
OH CRAP.
BLACKOUT!
KA-SNAK
THE CELLS ARE OPEN—
BLAM
—CLOCKSPRING! GET OUT OF HERE NOW!

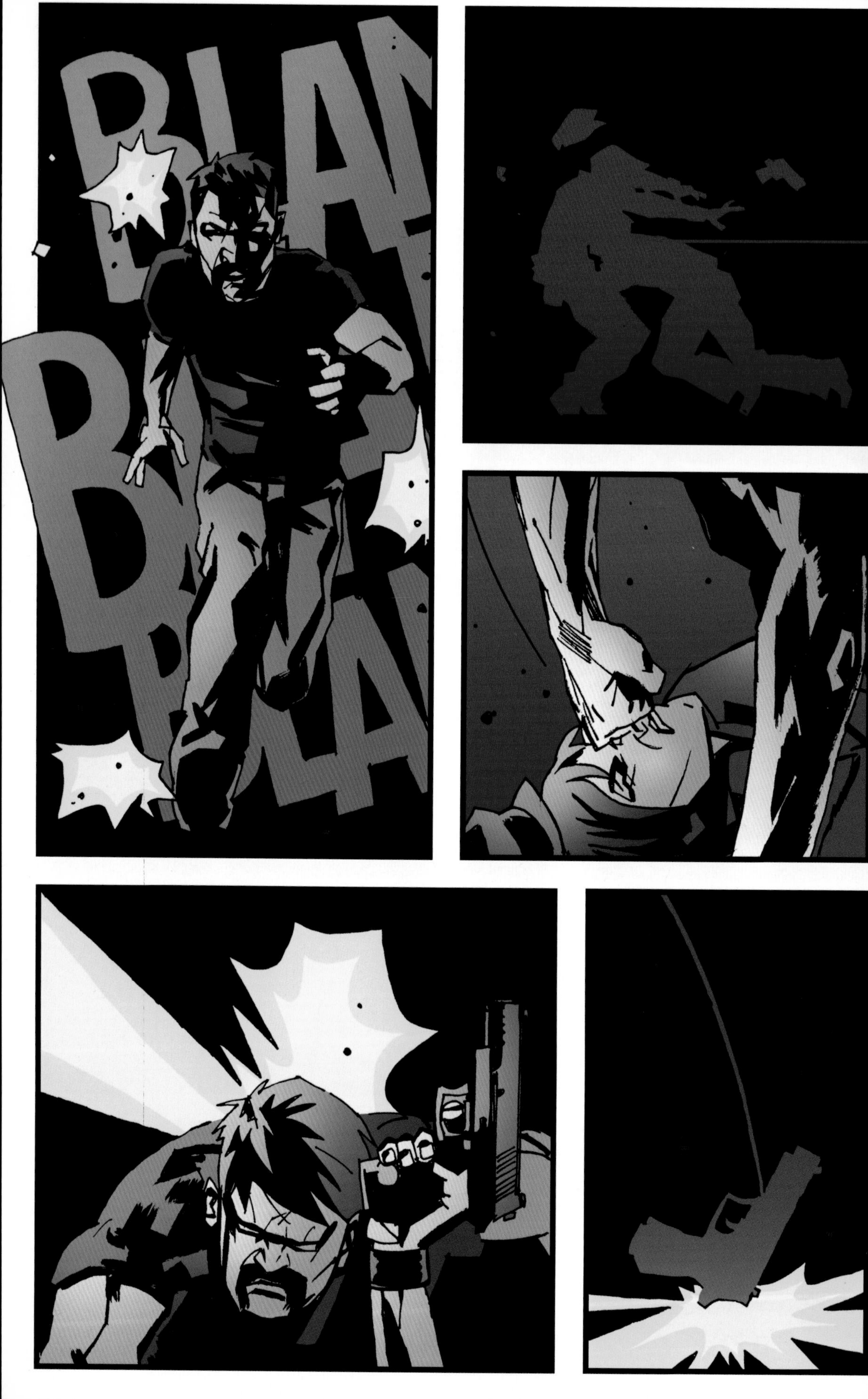

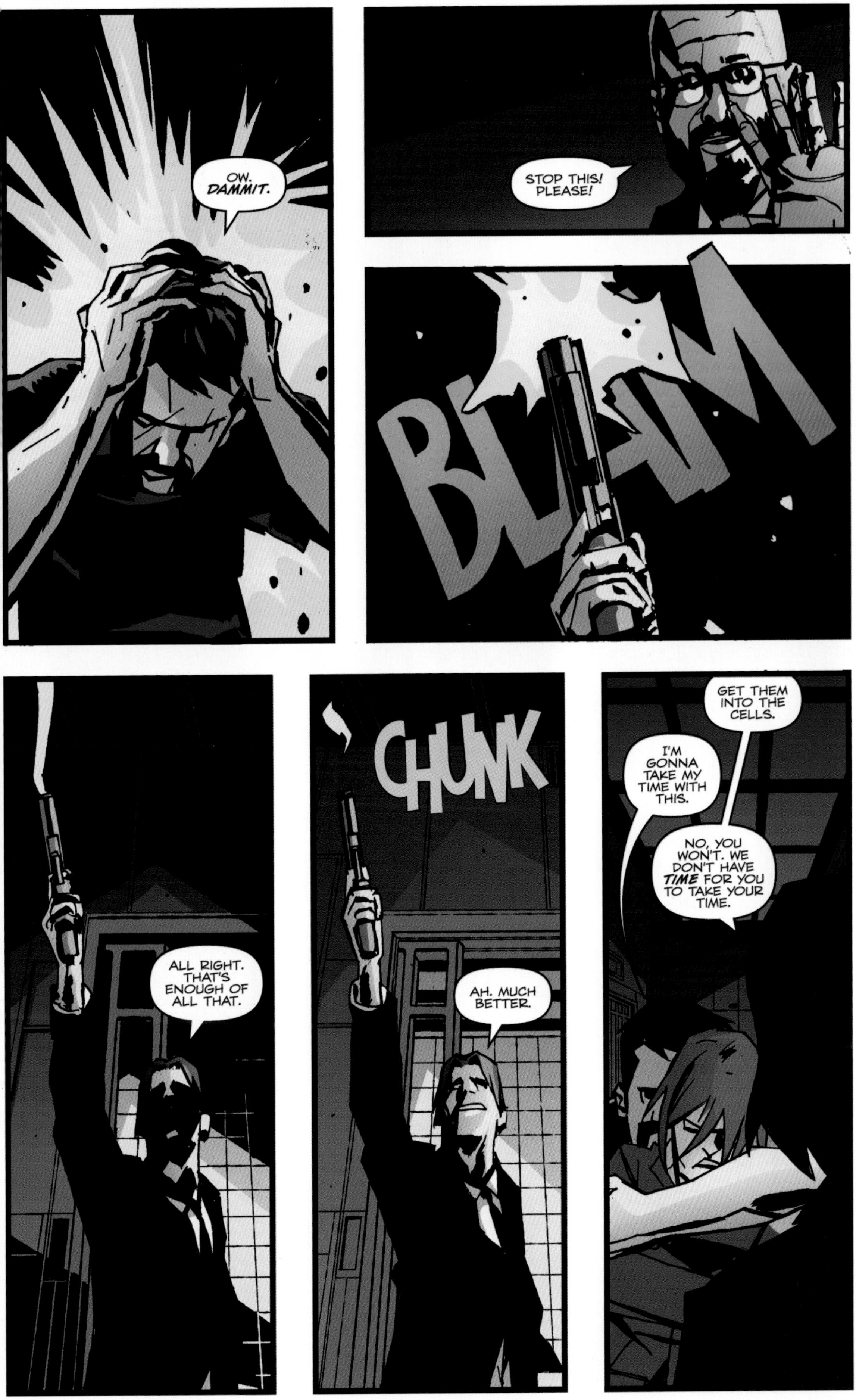
OW. DAMMIT.
STOP THIS! PLEASE!
BLAM
ALL RIGHT. THAT'S ENOUGH OF ALL THAT.
CHUNK
AH. MUCH BETTER.
GET THEM INTO THE CELLS.
I'M GONNA TAKE MY TIME WITH THIS.
NO, YOU WON'T. WE DON'T HAVE TIME FOR YOU TO TAKE YOUR TIME.

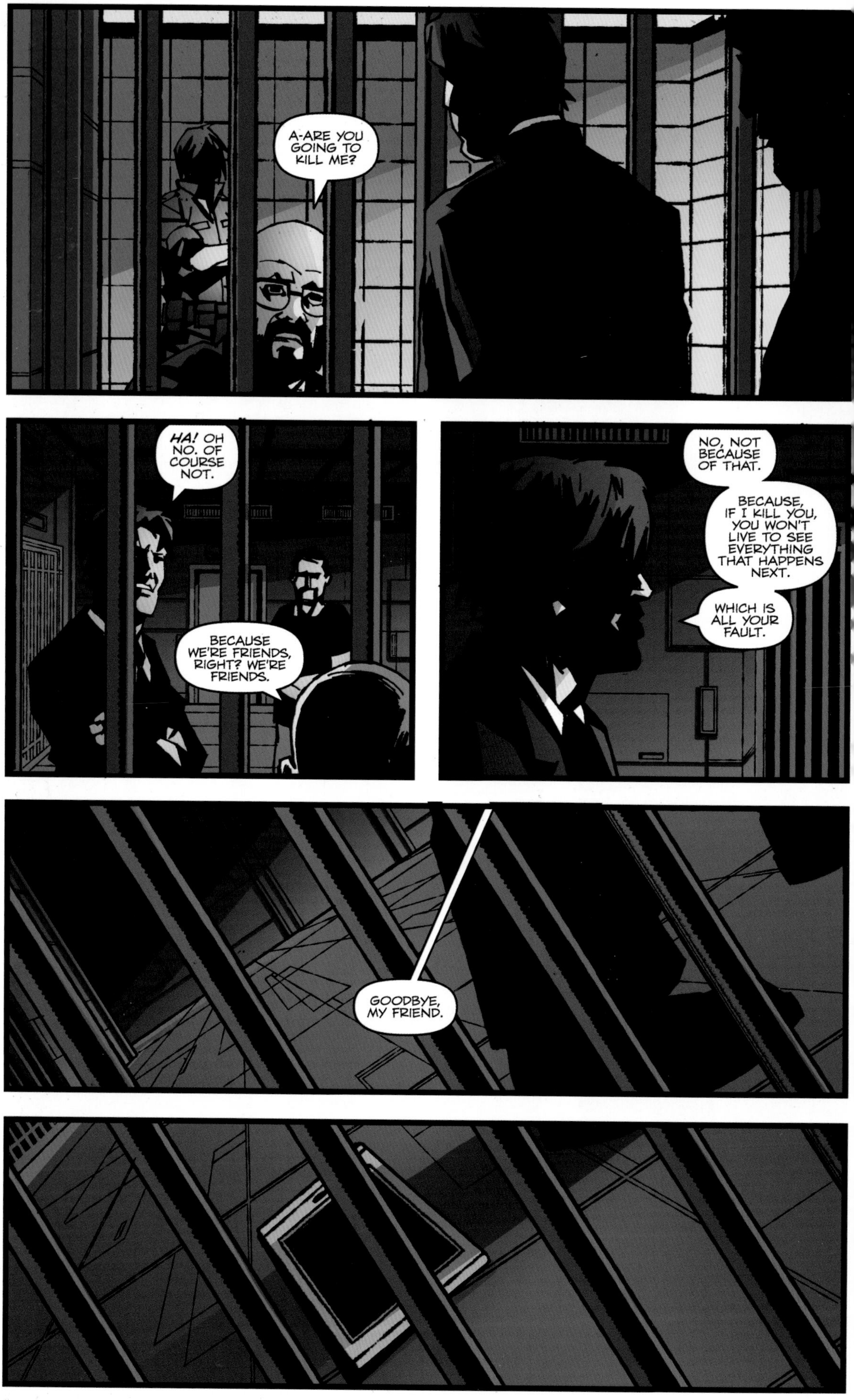
A-ARE YOU GOING TO KILL ME?
HA! OH NO. OF COURSE NOT.
BECAUSE WE'RE FRIENDS, RIGHT? WE'RE FRIENDS.
NO, NOT BECAUSE OF THAT.
BECAUSE, IF I KILL YOU, YOU WON'T LIVE TO SEE EVERYTHING THAT HAPPENS NEXT.
WHICH IS ALL YOUR FAULT.
GOODBYE, MY FRIEND.

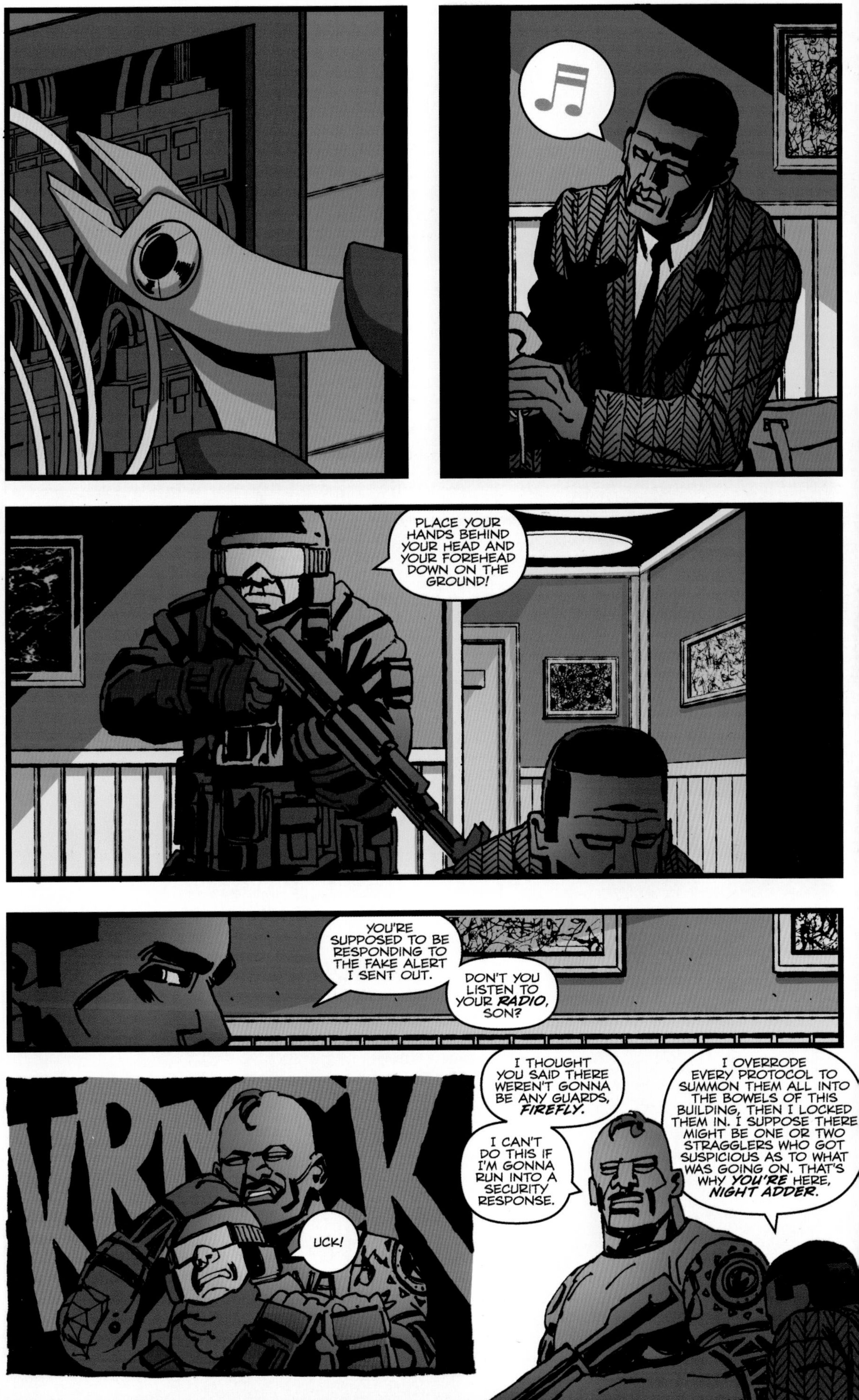
PLACE YOUR HANDS BEHIND YOUR HEAD AND YOUR FOREHEAD DOWN ON THE GROUND!
YOU'RE SUPPOSED TO BE RESPONDING TO THE FAKE ALERT I SENT OUT.
DON'T YOU LISTEN TO YOUR *RADIO*, SON?
UCK!
I THOUGHT YOU SAID THERE WEREN'T GONNA BE ANY GUARDS, *FIREFLY*.
I CAN'T DO THIS IF I'M GONNA RUN INTO A SECURITY RESPONSE.
I OVERRODE EVERY PROTOCOL TO SUMMON THEM ALL INTO THE BOWELS OF THIS BUILDING, THEN I LOCKED THEM IN. I SUPPOSE THERE MIGHT BE ONE OR TWO STRAGGLERS WHO GOT SUSPICIOUS AS TO WHAT WAS GOING ON. THAT'S WHY *YOU'RE* HERE, *NIGHT ADDER*.

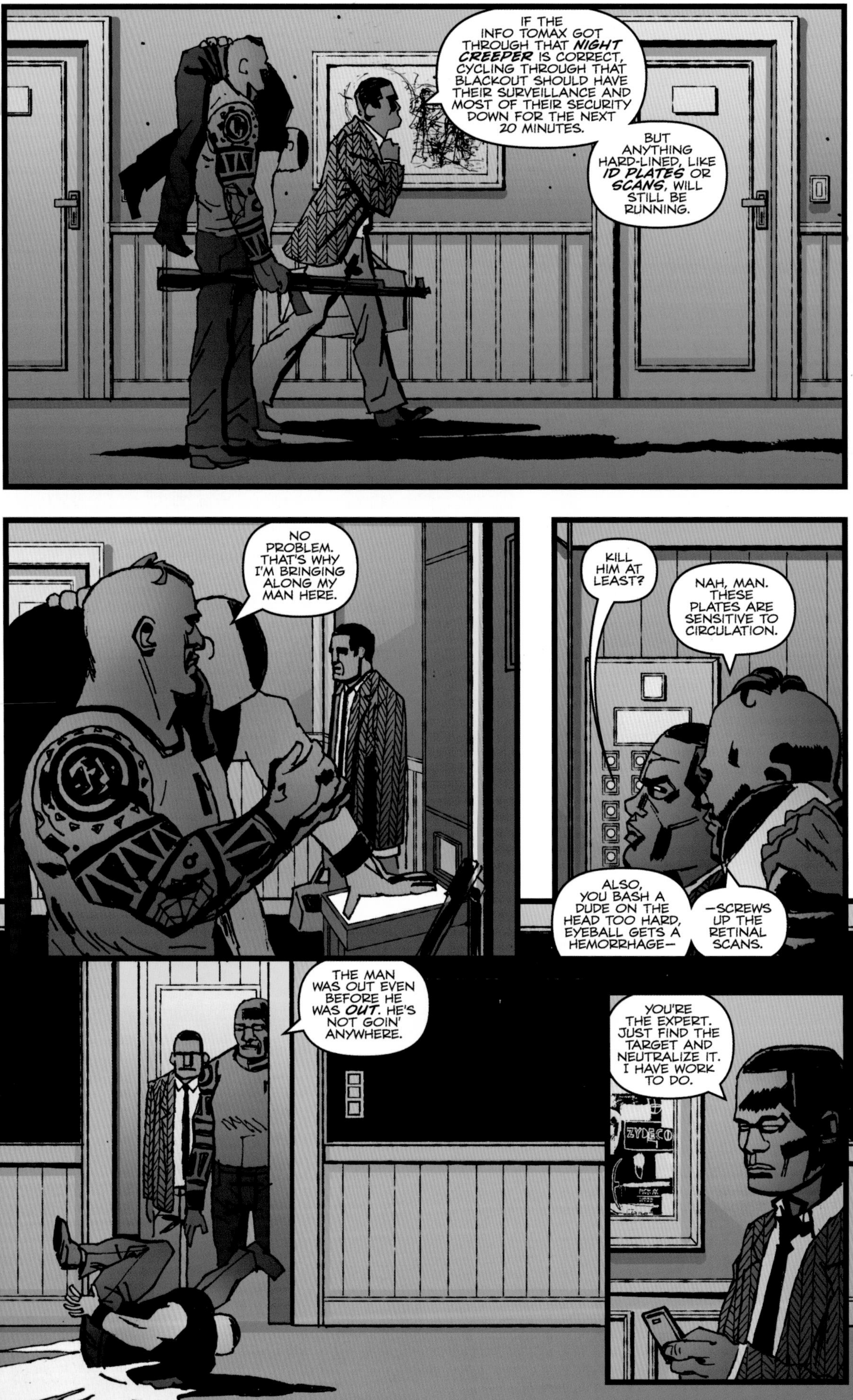

IF THE INFO TOMAX GOT THROUGH THAT **NIGHT CREEPER** IS CORRECT, CYCLING THROUGH THAT BLACKOUT SHOULD HAVE THEIR SURVEILLANCE AND MOST OF THEIR SECURITY DOWN FOR THE NEXT 20 MINUTES.
BUT ANYTHING HARD-LINED, LIKE ***ID PLATES*** OR ***SCANS***, WILL STILL BE RUNNING.
NO PROBLEM. THAT'S WHY I'M BRINGING ALONG MY MAN HERE.
KILL HIM AT LEAST?
NAH, MAN. THESE PLATES ARE SENSITIVE TO CIRCULATION.
ALSO, YOU BASH A DUDE ON THE HEAD TOO HARD, EYEBALL GETS A HEMORRHAGE—
—SCREWS UP THE RETINAL SCANS.
THE MAN WAS OUT EVEN BEFORE HE WAS ***OUT***. HE'S NOT GOIN' ANYWHERE.
YOU'RE THE EXPERT. JUST FIND THE TARGET AND NEUTRALIZE IT. I HAVE WORK TO DO.
ZYDECO

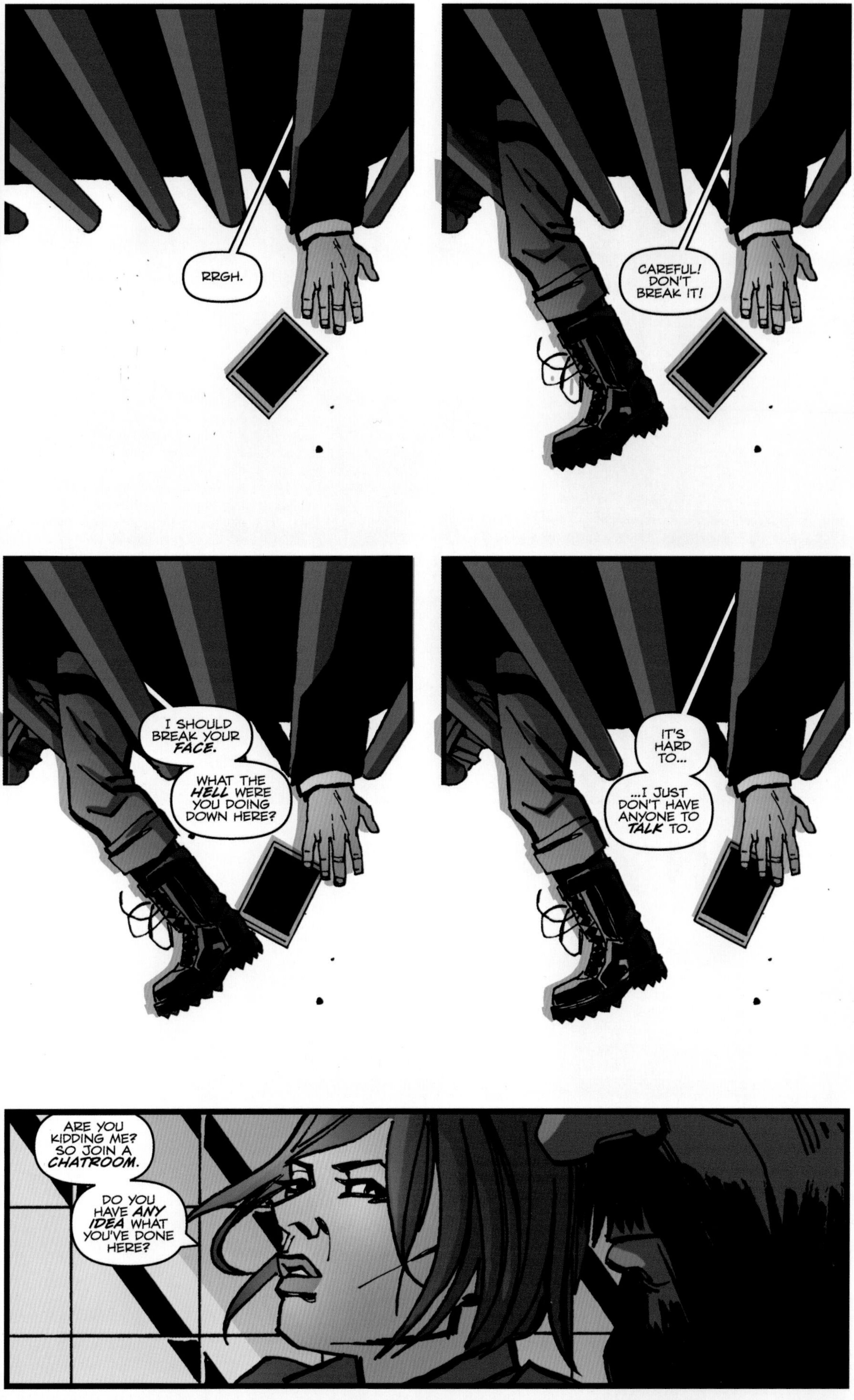
RRGH.
CAREFUL! DON'T BREAK IT!
I SHOULD BREAK YOUR FACE.
WHAT THE HELL WERE YOU DOING DOWN HERE?
IT'S HARD TO...
...I JUST DON'T HAVE ANYONE TO TALK TO.
ARE YOU KIDDING ME? SO JOIN A CHATROOM.
DO YOU HAVE ANY IDEA WHAT YOU'VE DONE HERE?

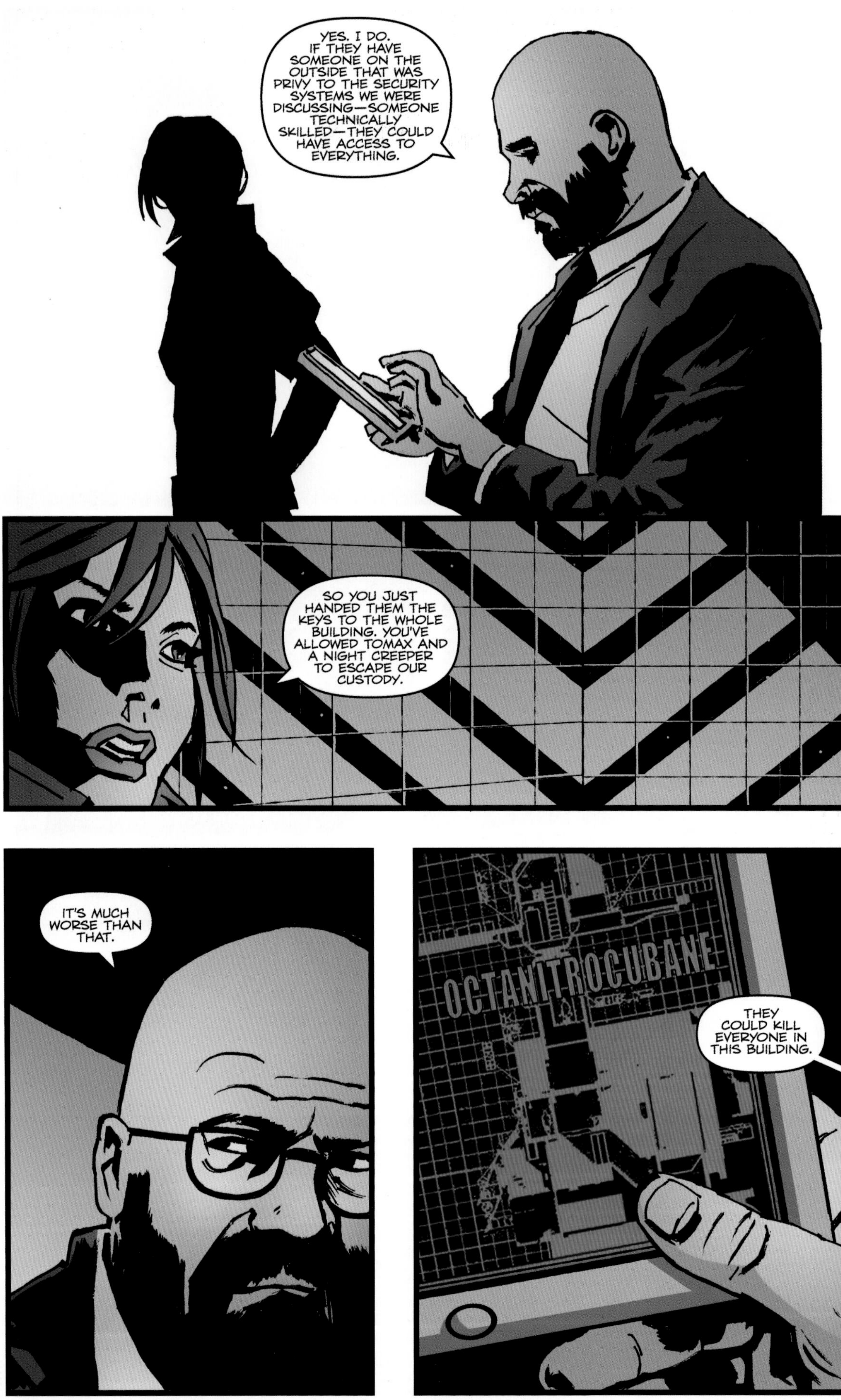
YES. I DO. IF THEY HAVE SOMEONE ON THE OUTSIDE THAT WAS PRIVY TO THE SECURITY SYSTEMS WE WERE DISCUSSING—SOMEONE TECHNICALLY SKILLED—THEY COULD HAVE ACCESS TO EVERYTHING.
SO YOU JUST HANDED THEM THE KEYS TO THE WHOLE BUILDING. YOU'VE ALLOWED TOMAX AND A NIGHT CREEPER TO ESCAPE OUR CUSTODY.
IT'S MUCH WORSE THAN THAT.
OCTANITROCUBANE
THEY COULD KILL EVERYONE IN THIS BUILDING.

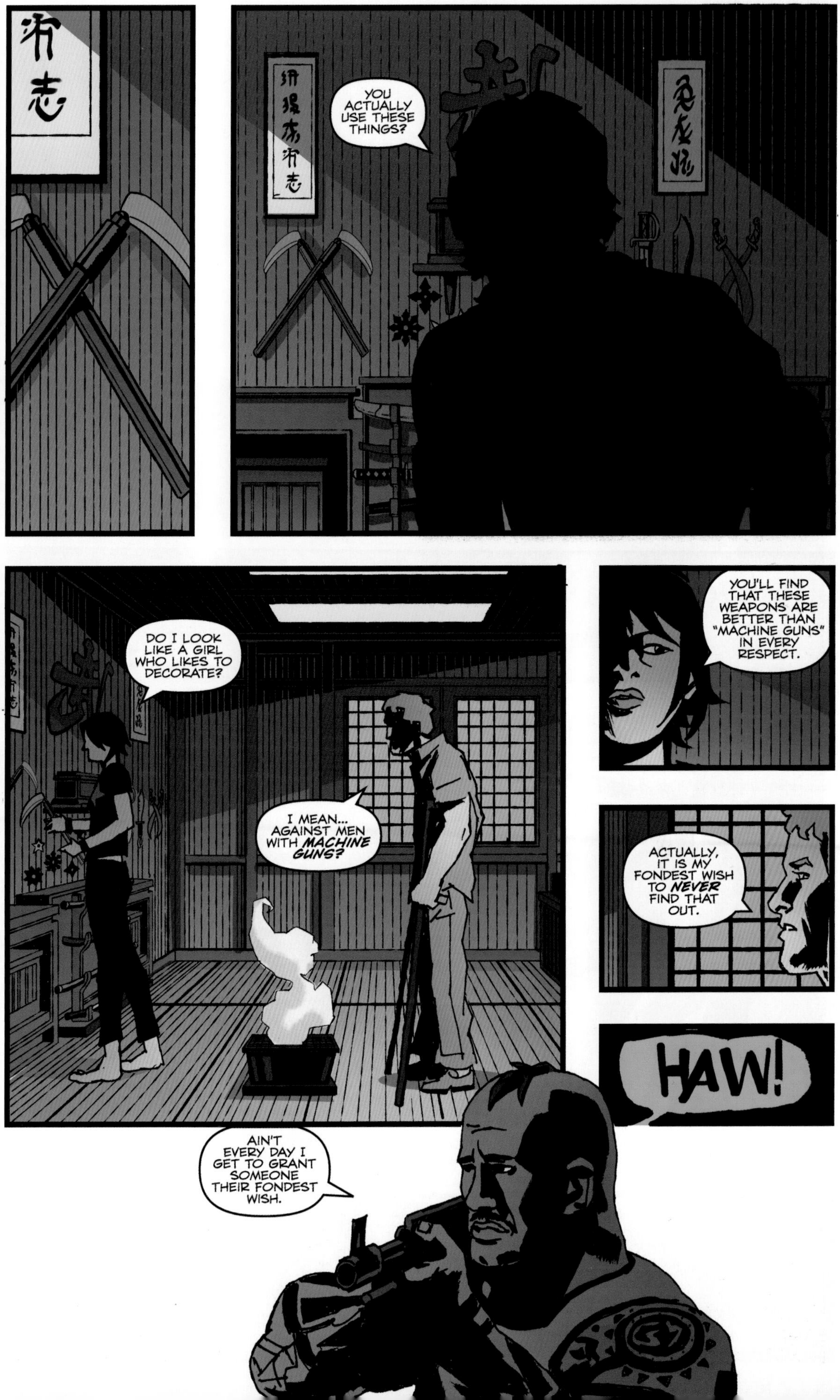
YOU ACTUALLY USE THESE THINGS?
DO I LOOK LIKE A GIRL WHO LIKES TO DECORATE?
I MEAN... AGAINST MEN WITH *MACHINE GUNS?*
YOU'LL FIND THAT THESE WEAPONS ARE BETTER THAN "MACHINE GUNS" IN EVERY RESPECT.
ACTUALLY, IT IS MY FONDEST WISH TO *NEVER* FIND THAT OUT.
HAW!
AIN'T EVERY DAY I GET TO GRANT SOMEONE THEIR FONDEST WISH.

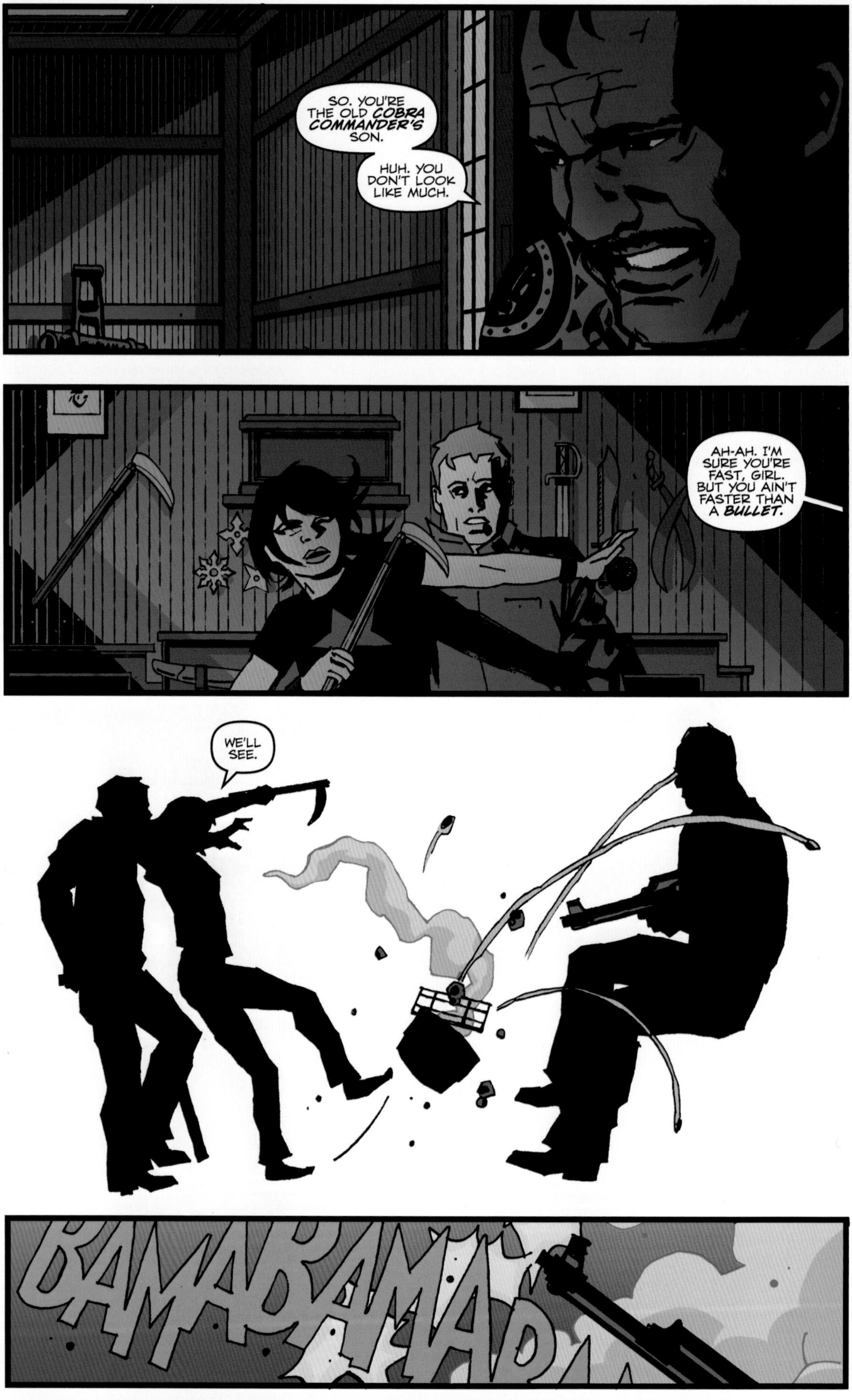
SO. YOU'RE THE OLD COBRA COMMANDER'S SON.
HUH. YOU DON'T LOOK LIKE MUCH.
AH-AH. I'M SURE YOU'RE FAST, GIRL. BUT YOU AIN'T FASTER THAN A BULLET.
WE'LL SEE.
BAMABAMABAMA

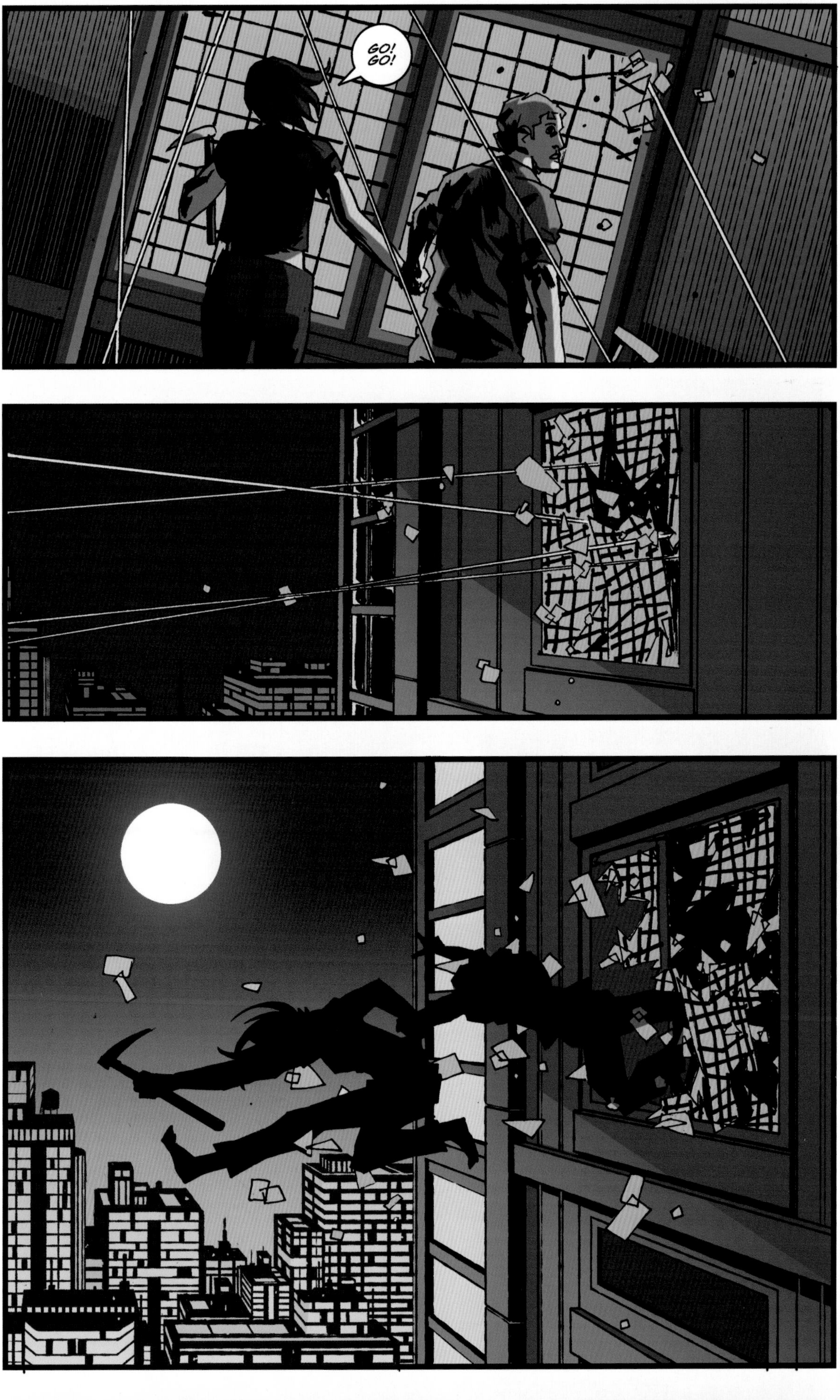
GO! GO!

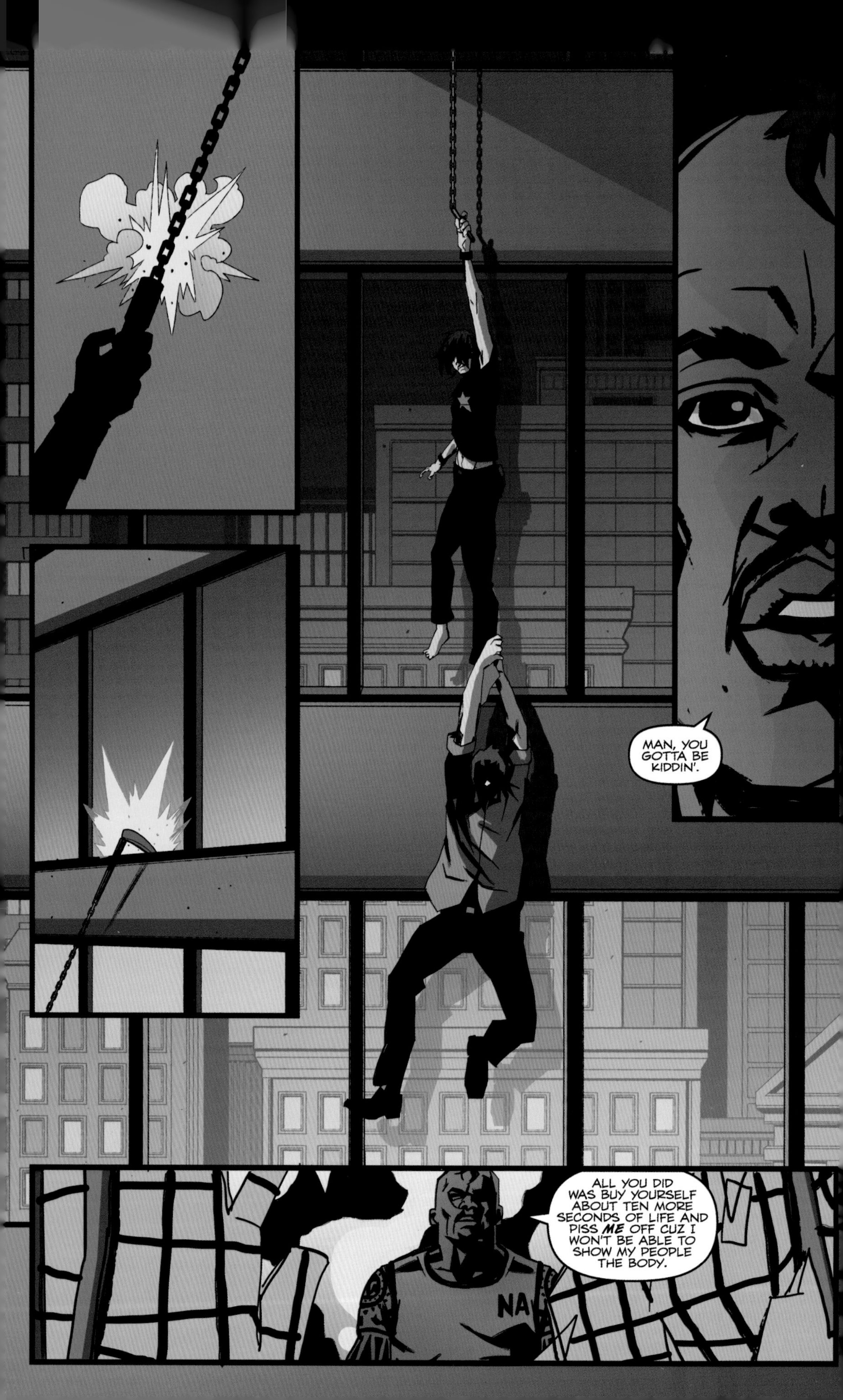
MAN, YOU GOTTA BE KIDDIN'.
ALL YOU DID WAS BUY YOURSELF ABOUT TEN MORE SECONDS OF LIFE AND PISS *ME* OFF CUZ I WON'T BE ABLE TO SHOW MY PEOPLE THE BODY.

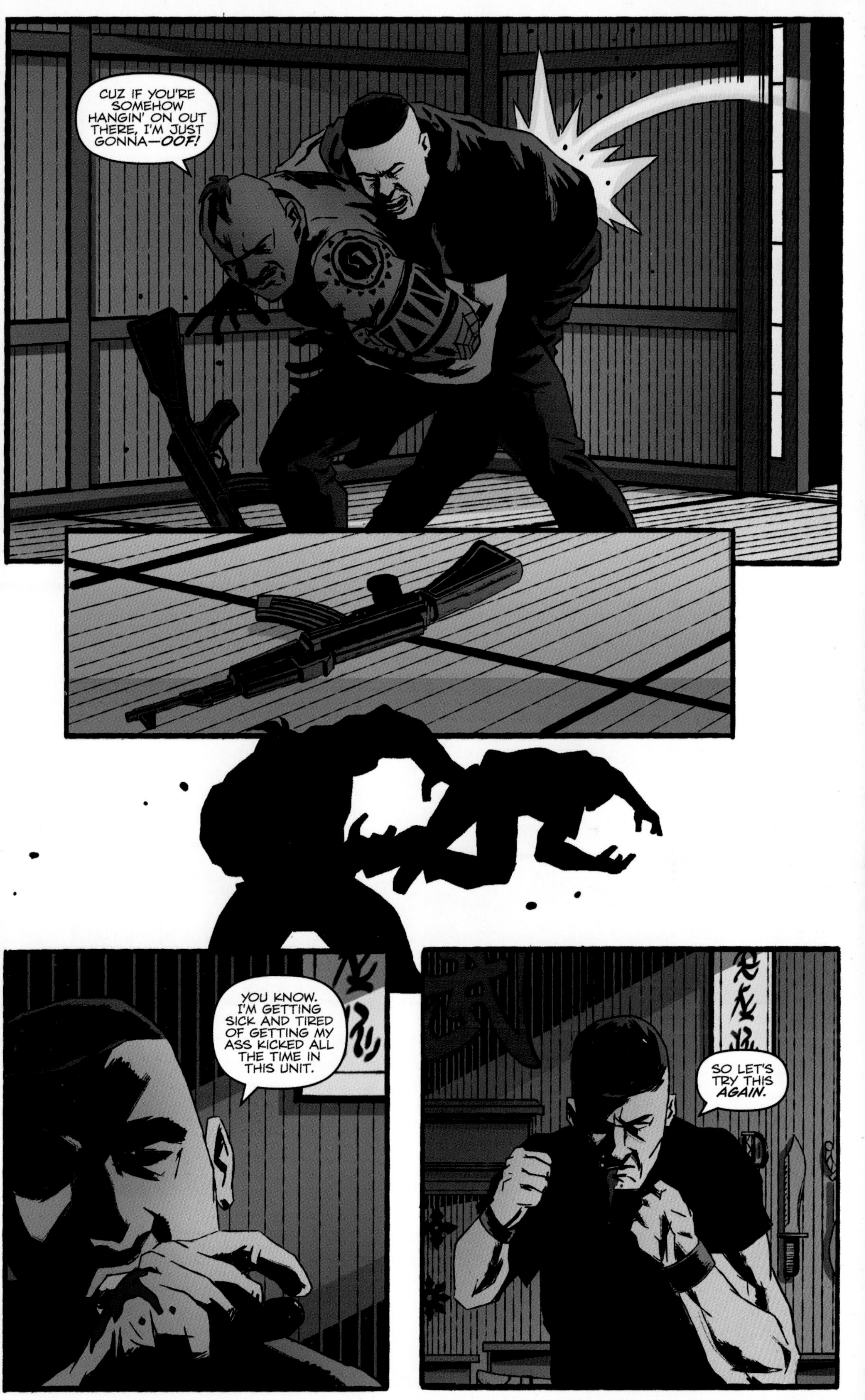
CUZ IF YOU'RE SOMEHOW HANGIN' ON OUT THERE, I'M JUST GONNA—*OOF!*
YOU KNOW. I'M GETTING SICK AND TIRED OF GETTING MY ASS KICKED ALL THE TIME IN THIS UNIT.
SO LET'S TRY THIS *AGAIN*.

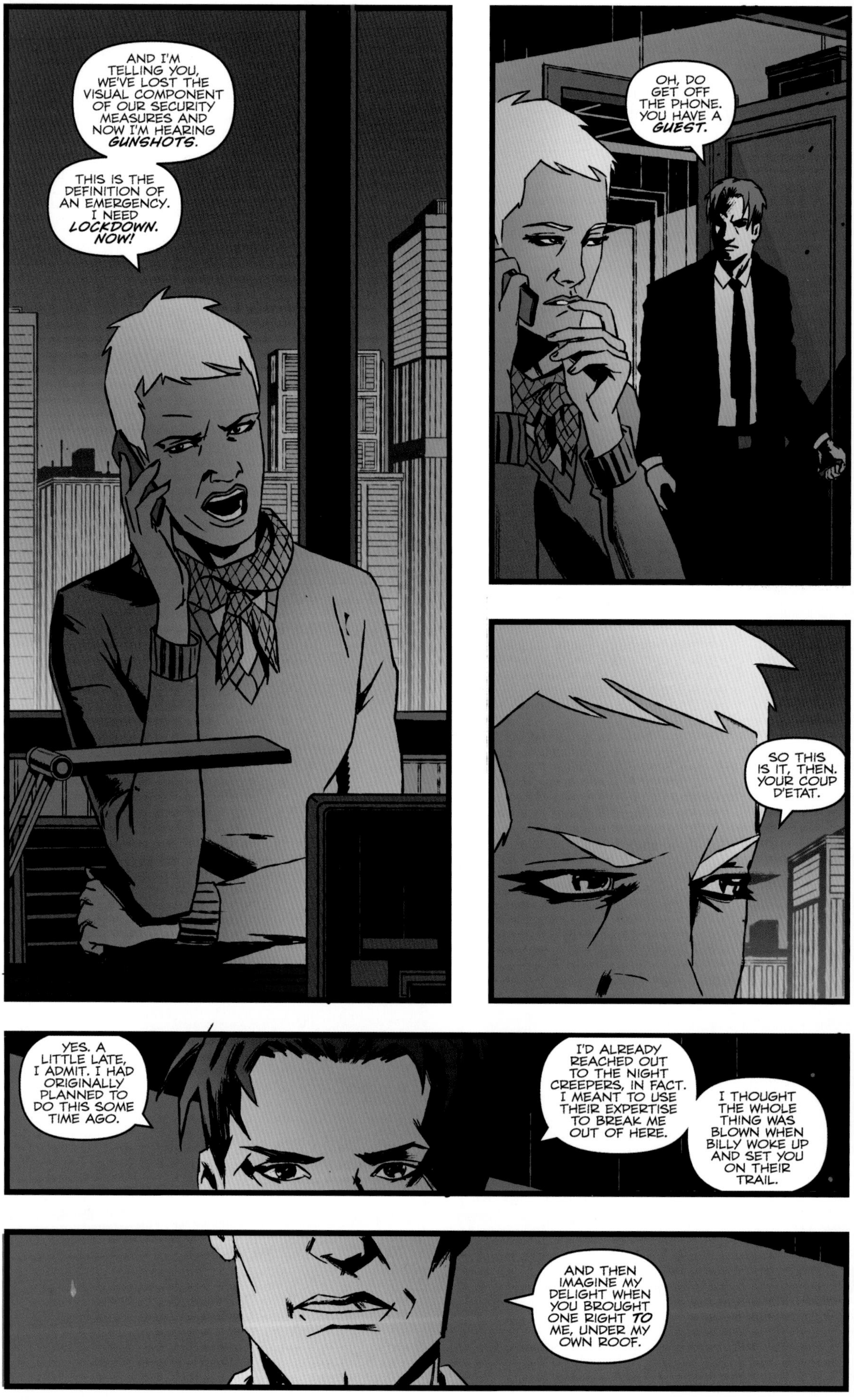
AND I'M TELLING YOU, WE'VE LOST THE VISUAL COMPONENT OF OUR SECURITY MEASURES AND NOW I'M HEARING ***GUNSHOTS***.
THIS IS THE DEFINITION OF AN EMERGENCY. I NEED ***LOCKDOWN. NOW!***
OH, DO GET OFF THE PHONE. YOU HAVE A ***GUEST***.
SO THIS IS IT, THEN. YOUR COUP D'ETAT.
YES. A LITTLE LATE, I ADMIT. I HAD ORIGINALLY PLANNED TO DO THIS SOME TIME AGO.
I'D ALREADY REACHED OUT TO THE NIGHT CREEPERS, IN FACT. I MEANT TO USE THEIR EXPERTISE TO BREAK ME OUT OF HERE.
I THOUGHT THE WHOLE THING WAS BLOWN WHEN BILLY WOKE UP AND SET YOU ON THEIR TRAIL.
AND THEN IMAGINE MY DELIGHT WHEN YOU BROUGHT ONE RIGHT ***TO*** ME, UNDER MY OWN ROOF.

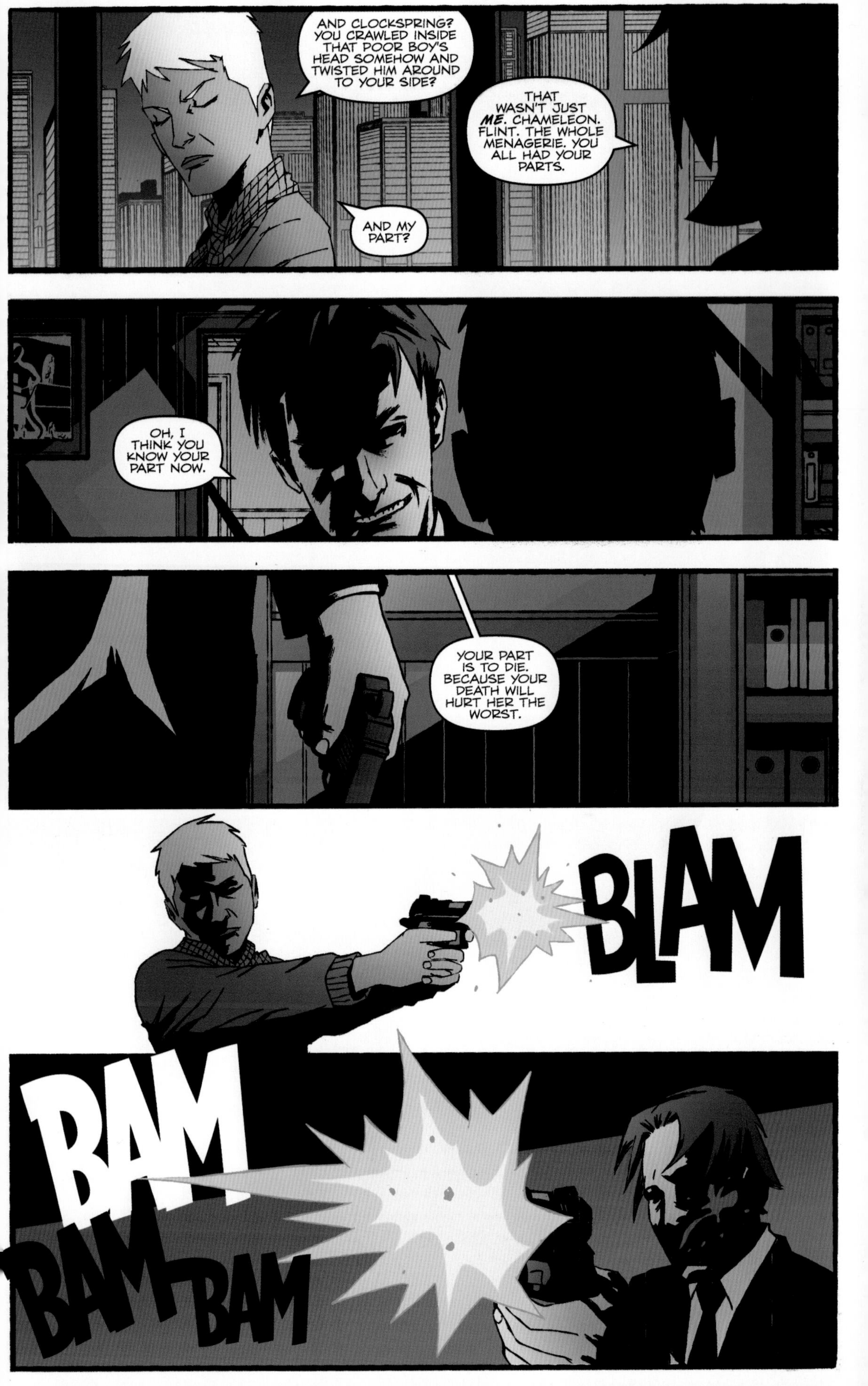
AND CLOCKSPRING? YOU CRAWLED INSIDE THAT POOR BOY'S HEAD SOMEHOW AND TWISTED HIM AROUND TO YOUR SIDE?
THAT WASN'T JUST *ME*. CHAMELEON. FLINT. THE WHOLE MENAGERIE. YOU ALL HAD YOUR PARTS.
AND MY PART?
OH, I THINK YOU KNOW YOUR PART NOW.
YOUR PART IS TO DIE. BECAUSE YOUR DEATH WILL HURT HER THE WORST.
BLAM
BAM
BAM BAM

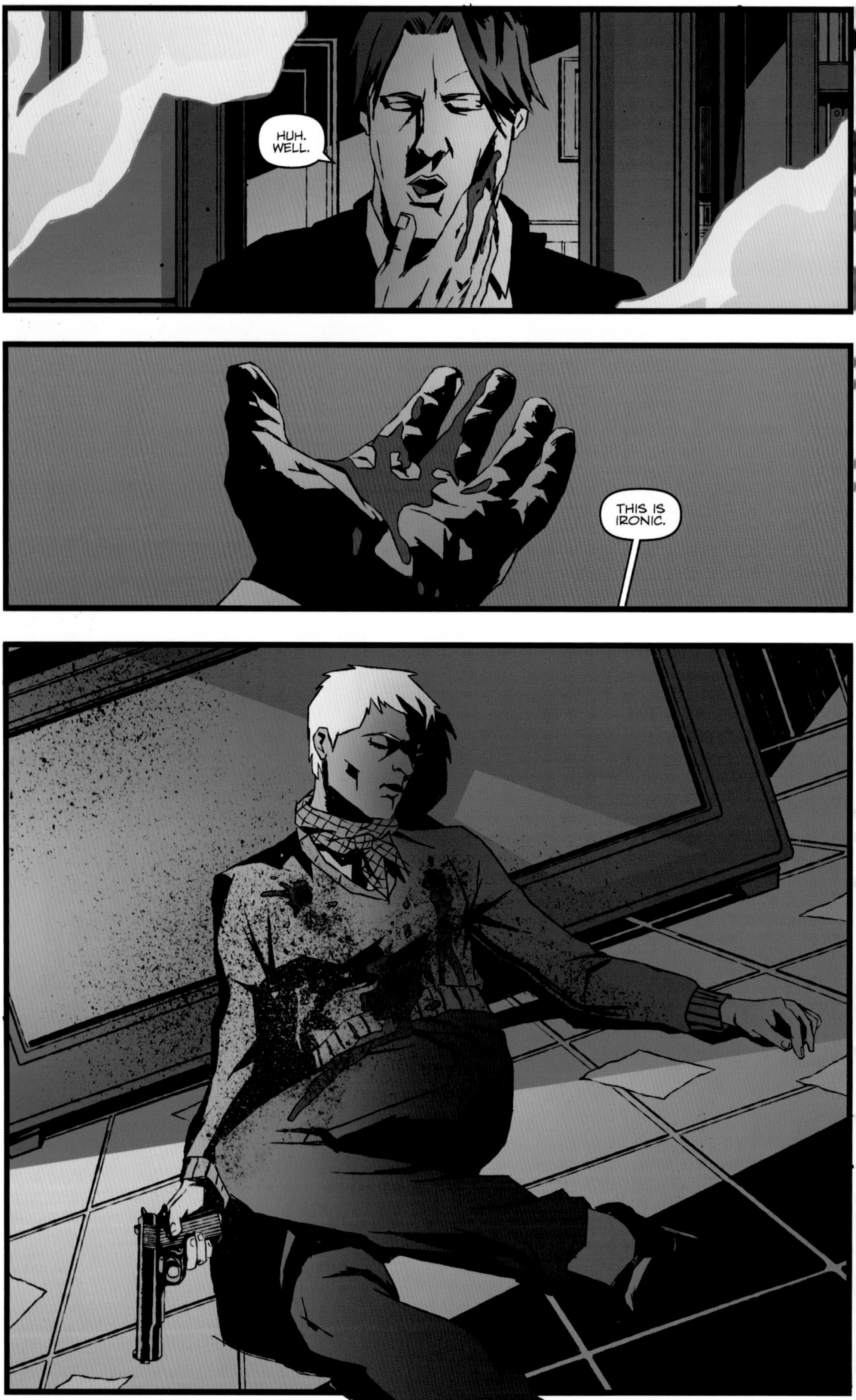
HUH. WELL.
THIS IS IRONIC.

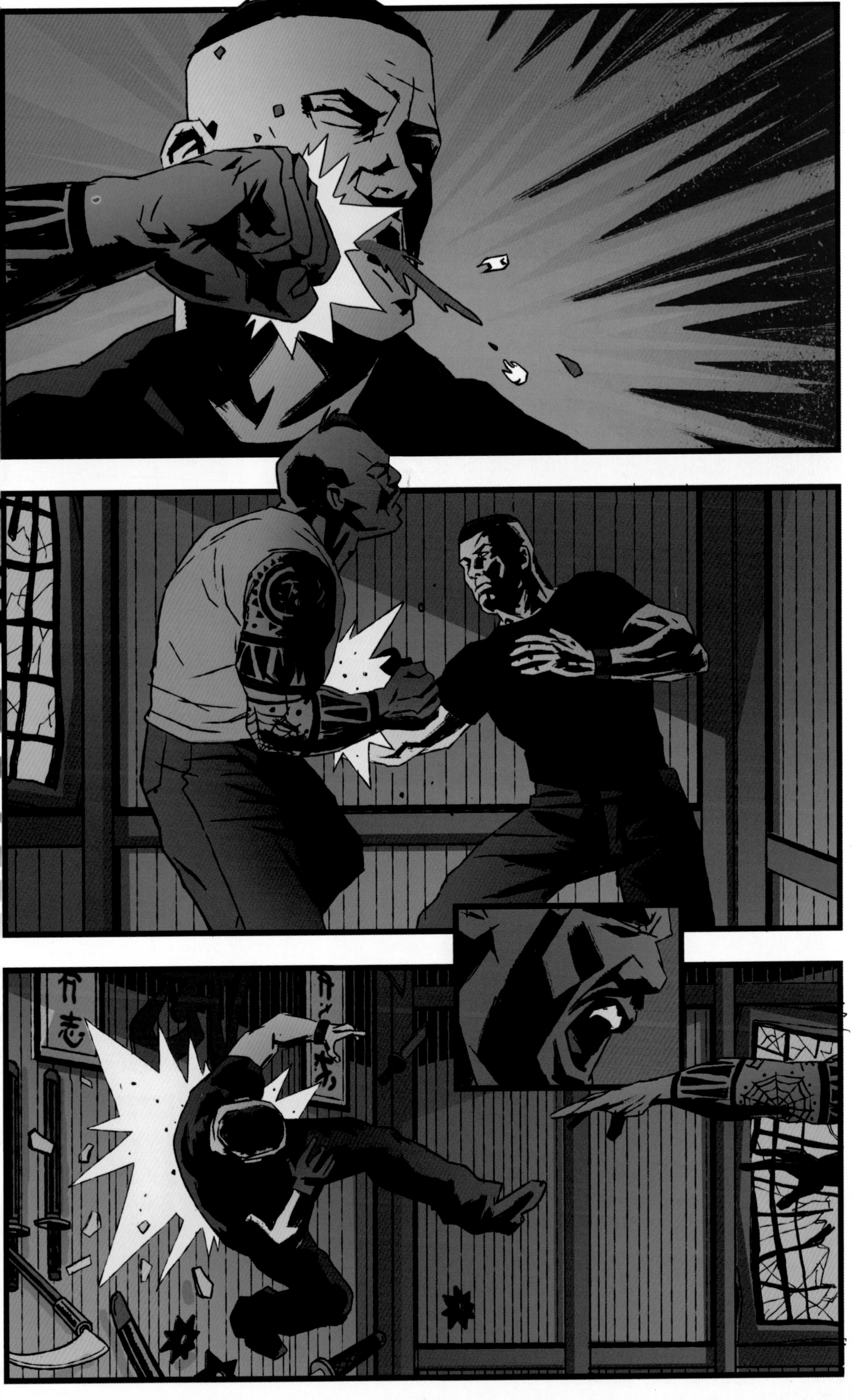

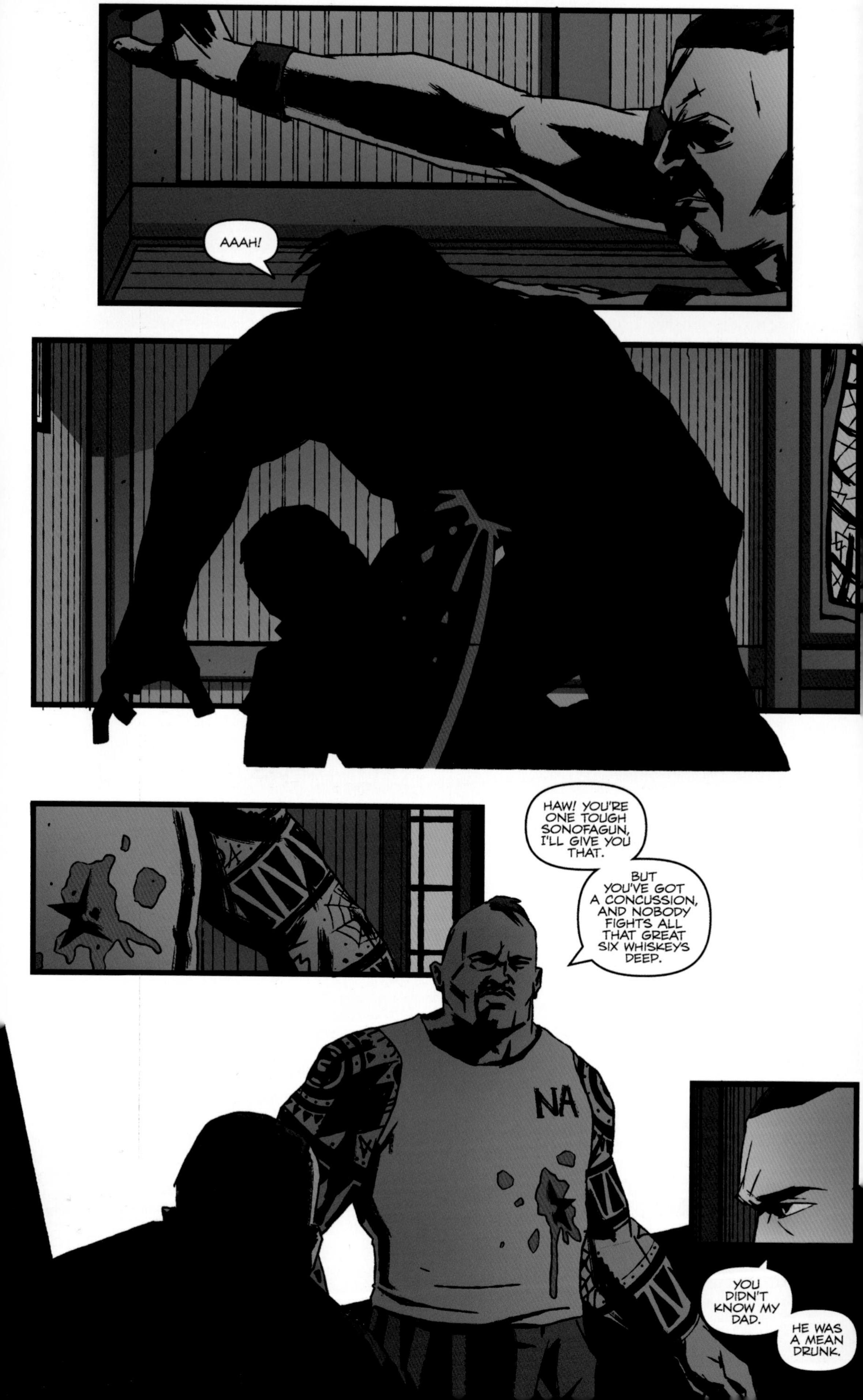
AAAH!
HAW! YOU'RE ONE TOUGH SONOFAGUN, I'LL GIVE YOU THAT.
BUT YOU'VE GOT A CONCUSSION, AND NOBODY FIGHTS ALL THAT GREAT SIX WHISKEYS DEEP.
NA
YOU DIDN'T KNOW MY DAD.
HE WAS A MEAN DRUNK.

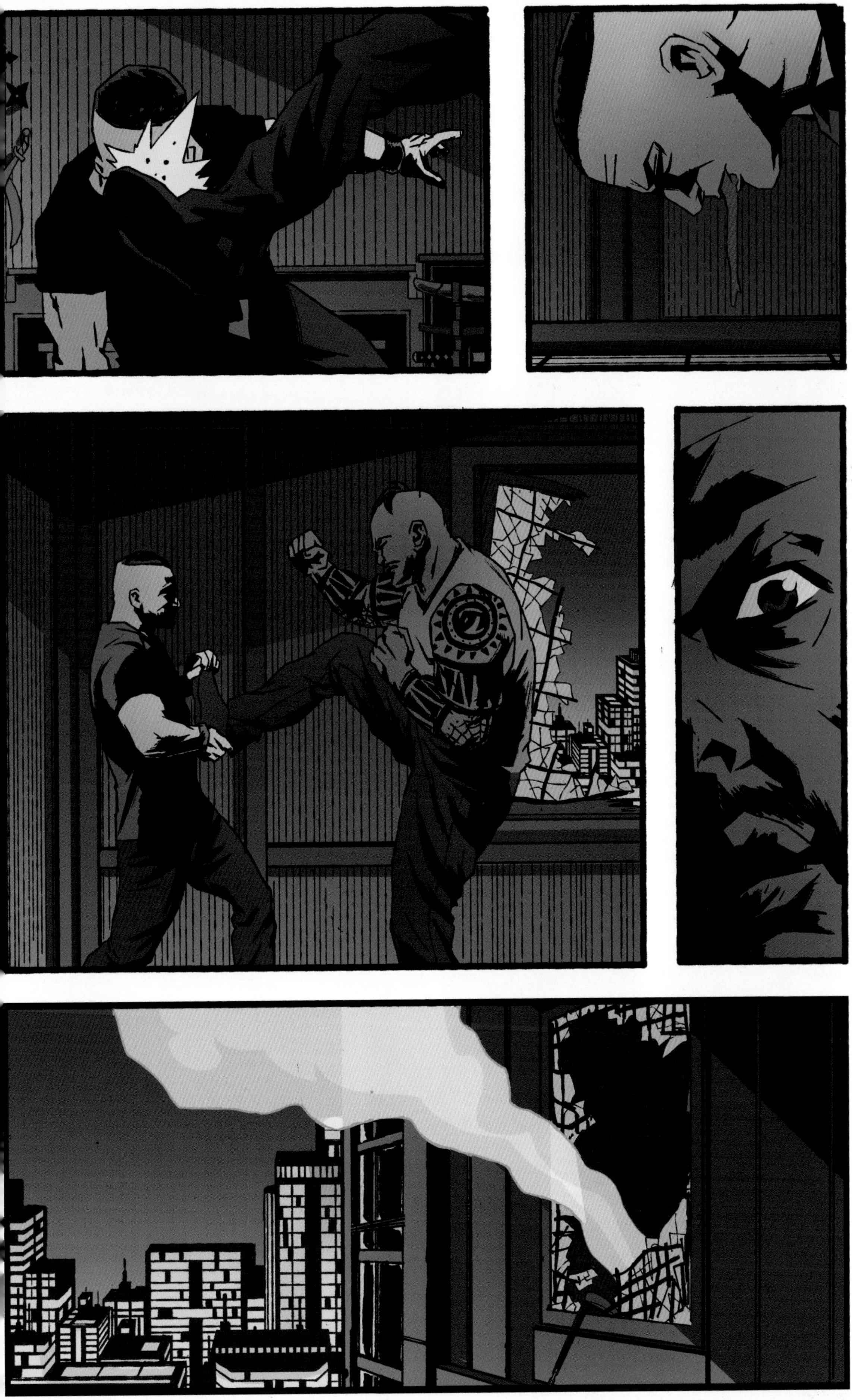

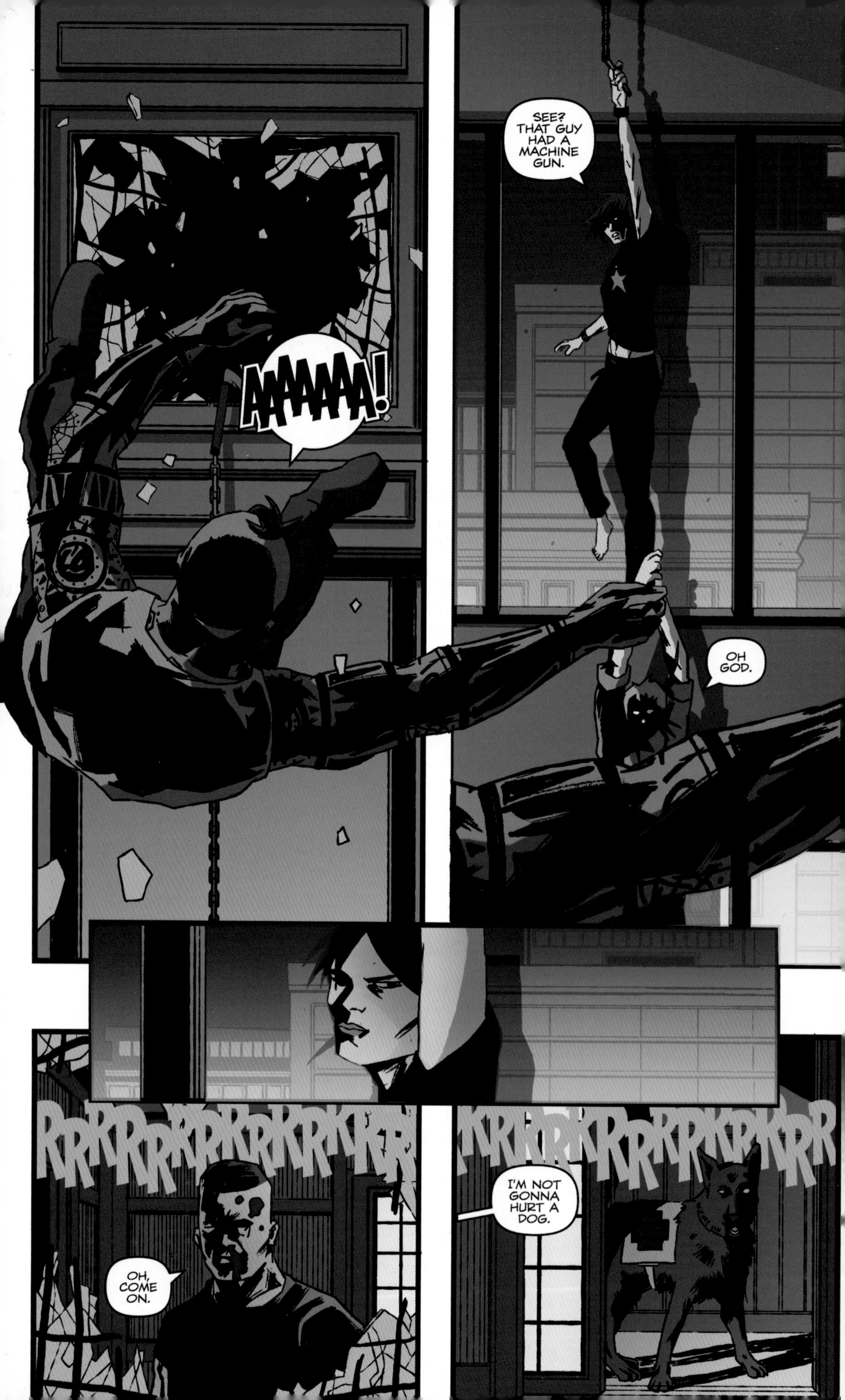
AAAAAA!
SEE? THAT GUY HAD A MACHINE GUN.
OH GOD.
RRRRRRRRRRRRRRRR
OH, COME ON.
KRRRKRRRRRRRRRRR
I'M NOT GONNA HURT A DOG.

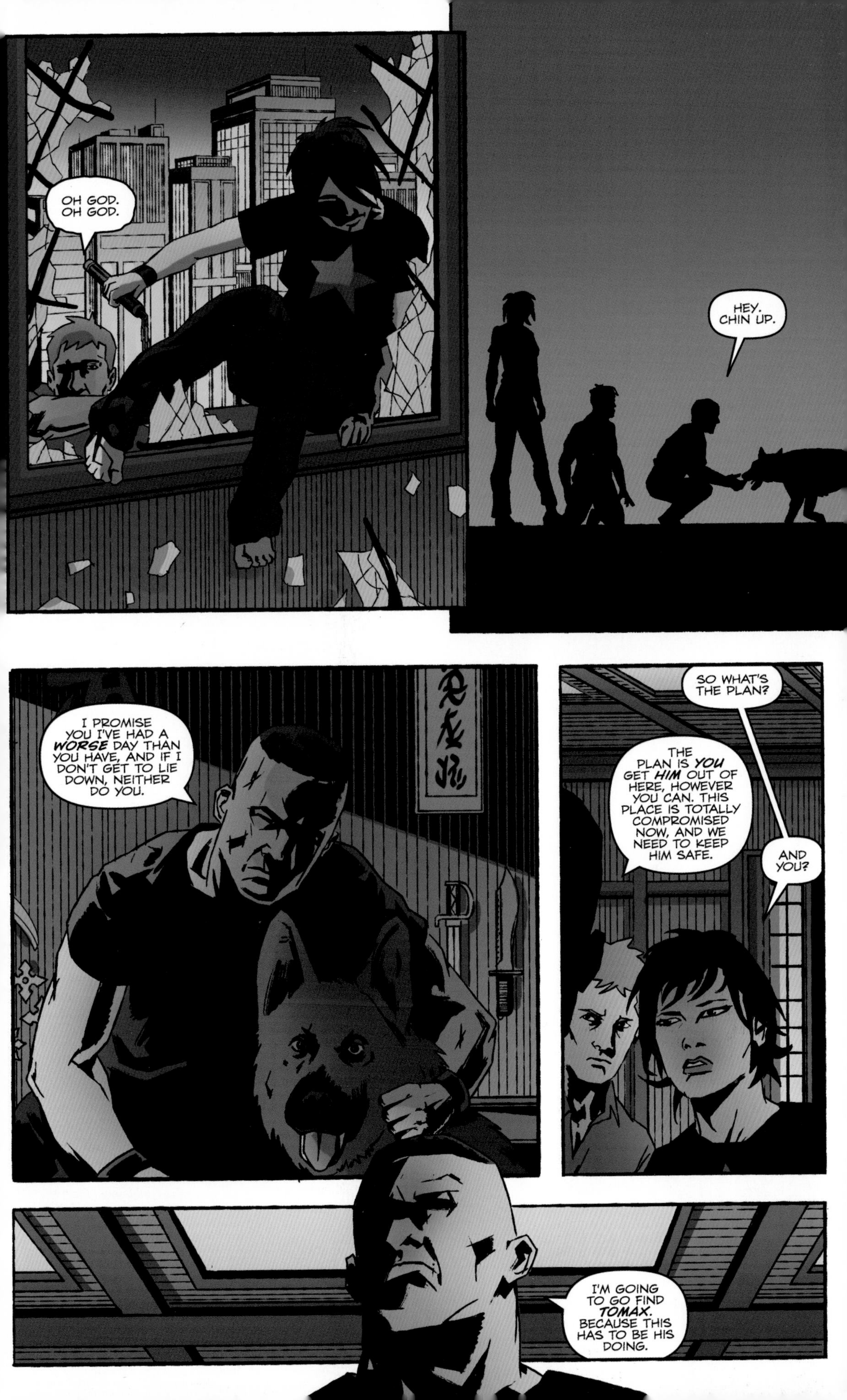

OH GOD. OH GOD.
HEY. CHIN UP.
I PROMISE YOU I'VE HAD A **WORSE** DAY THAN YOU HAVE, AND IF I DON'T GET TO LIE DOWN, NEITHER DO YOU.
SO WHAT'S THE PLAN?
THE PLAN IS **YOU** GET **HIM** OUT OF HERE, HOWEVER YOU CAN. THIS PLACE IS TOTALLY COMPROMISED NOW, AND WE NEED TO KEEP HIM SAFE.
AND YOU?
I'M GOING TO GO FIND **TOMAX**. BECAUSE THIS HAS TO BE HIS DOING.

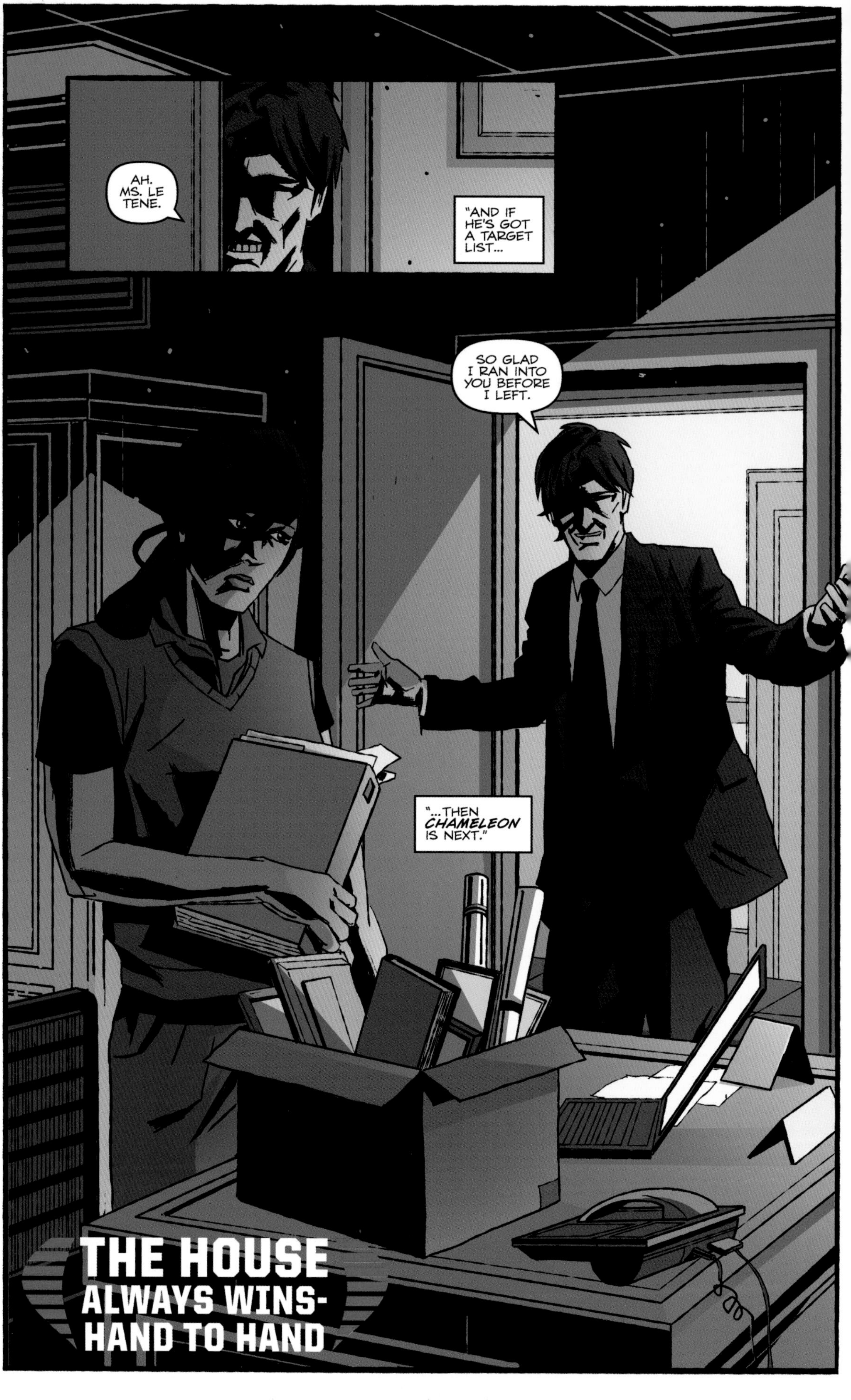
AH. MS. LE TENE.
"AND IF HE'S GOT A TARGET LIST...
SO GLAD I RAN INTO YOU BEFORE I LEFT.
"...THEN CHAMELEON IS NEXT."
THE HOUSE ALWAYS WINS- HAND TO HAND

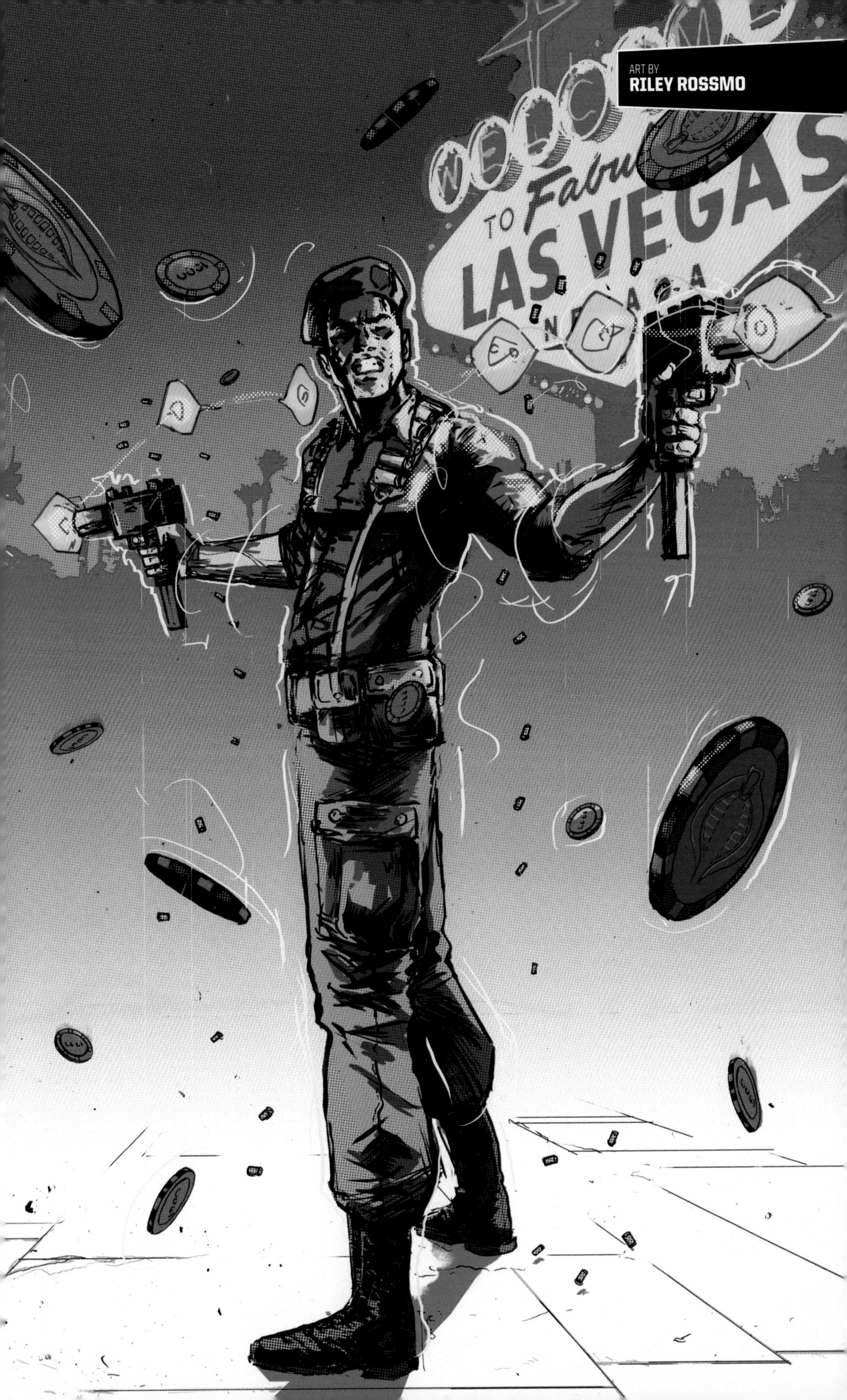
TO
LAS VEGAS

ART BY
RILEY ROSSMO

ART BY
ANTONIO FUSO

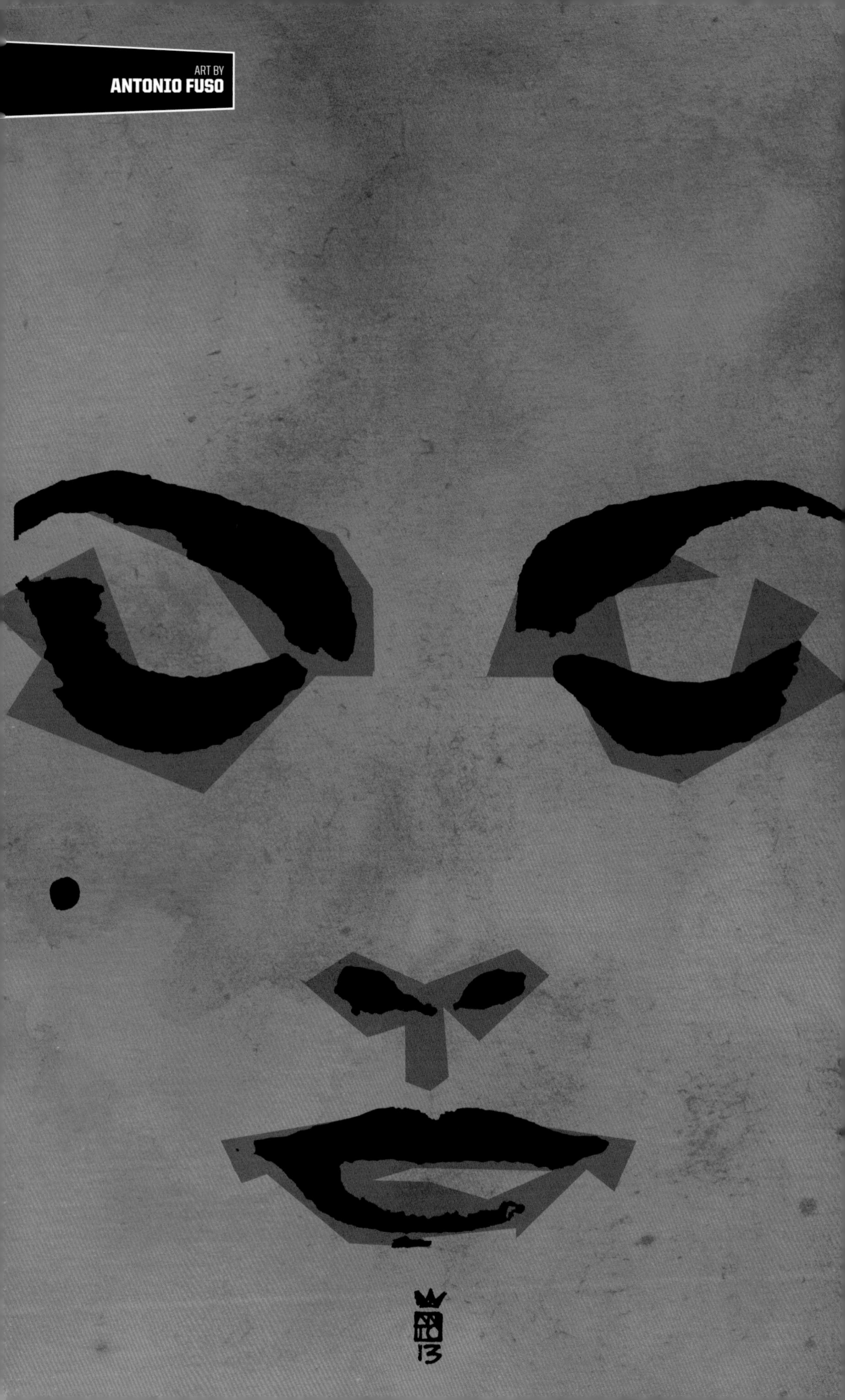

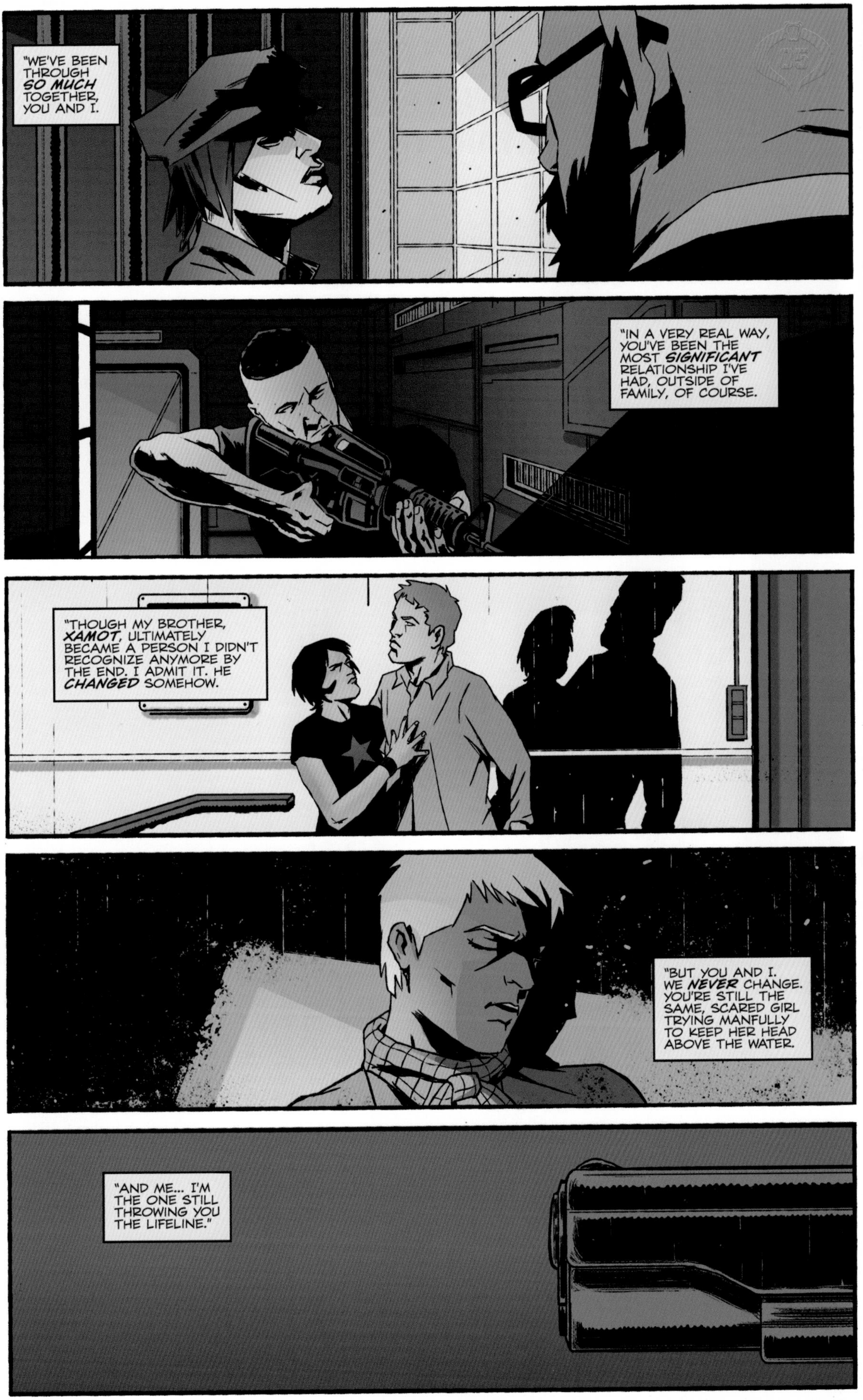
"WE'VE BEEN THROUGH SO MUCH TOGETHER, YOU AND I.
"IN A VERY REAL WAY, YOU'VE BEEN THE MOST SIGNIFICANT RELATIONSHIP I'VE HAD, OUTSIDE OF FAMILY, OF COURSE.
"THOUGH MY BROTHER, XAMOT, ULTIMATELY BECAME A PERSON I DIDN'T RECOGNIZE ANYMORE BY THE END. I ADMIT IT. HE CHANGED SOMEHOW.
"BUT YOU AND I. WE NEVER CHANGE. YOU'RE STILL THE SAME, SCARED GIRL TRYING MANFULLY TO KEEP HER HEAD ABOVE THE WATER.
"AND ME... I'M THE ONE STILL THROWING YOU THE LIFELINE."

THE HOUSE ALWAYS WINS- HEART TO HEART

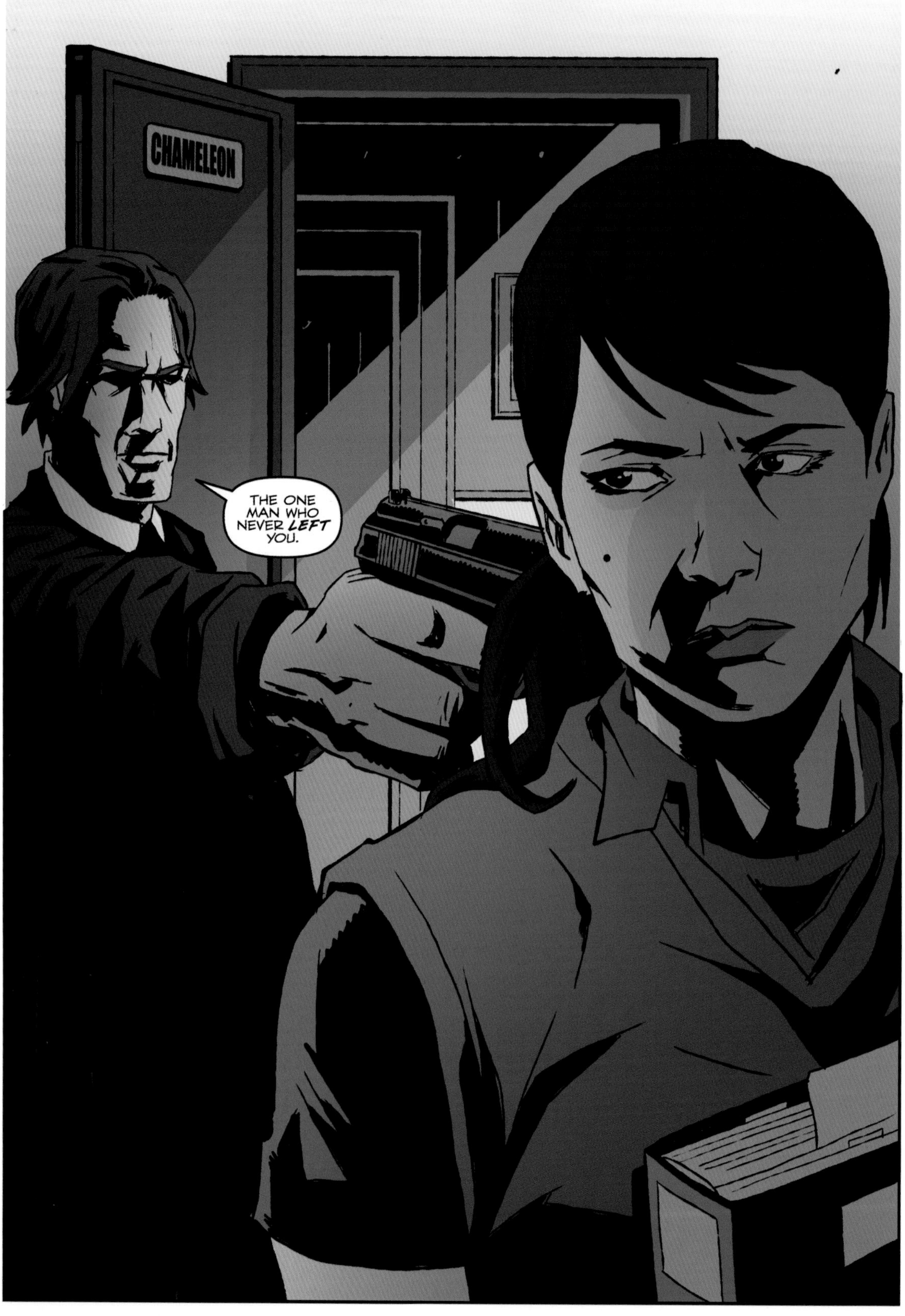
CHAMELEON
THE ONE MAN WHO NEVER LEFT YOU.

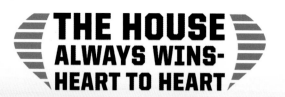

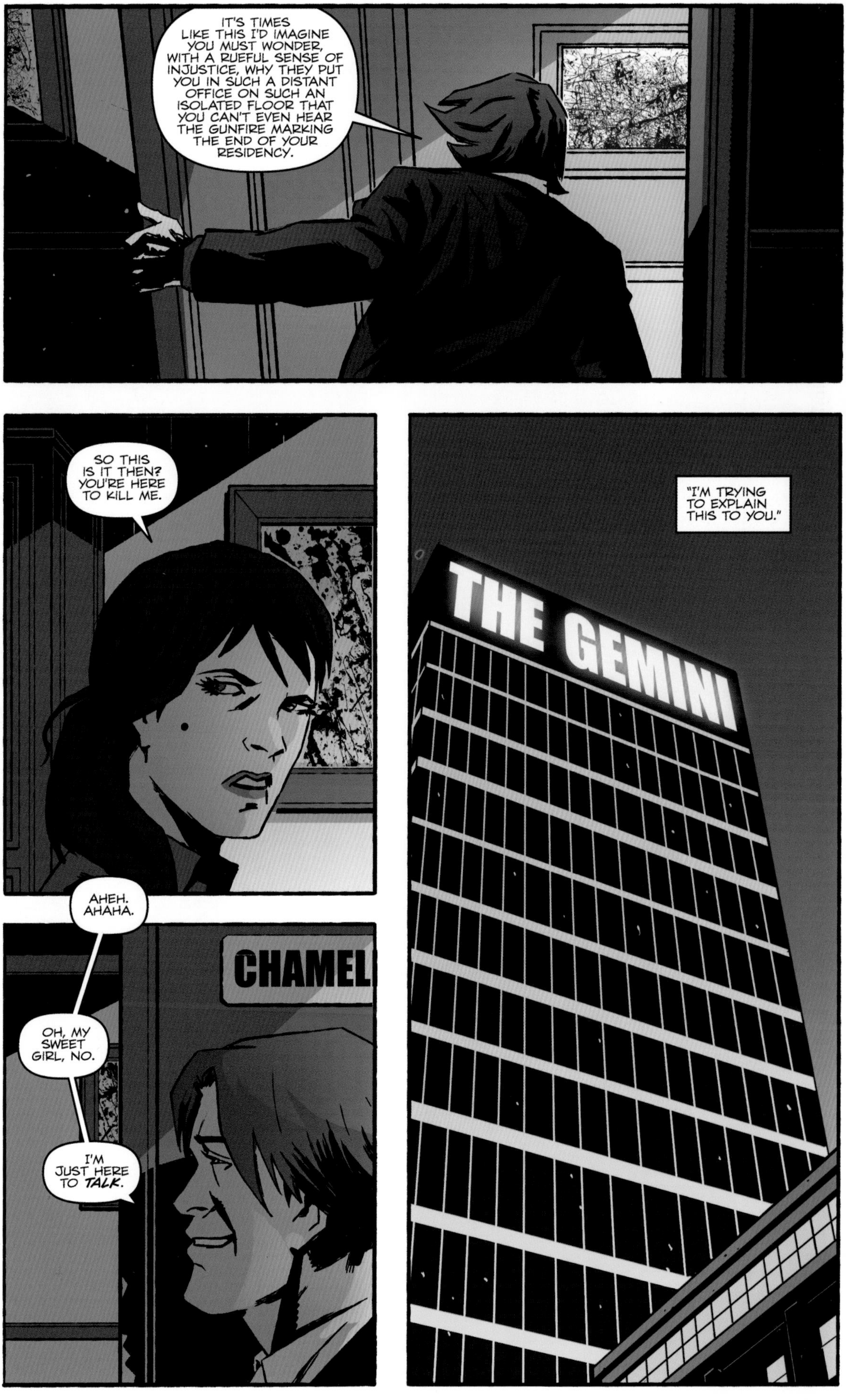
IT'S TIMES LIKE THIS I'D IMAGINE YOU MUST WONDER, WITH A RUEFUL SENSE OF INJUSTICE, WHY THEY PUT YOU IN SUCH A DISTANT OFFICE ON SUCH AN ISOLATED FLOOR THAT YOU CAN'T EVEN HEAR THE GUNFIRE MARKING THE END OF YOUR RESIDENCY.
SO THIS IS IT THEN? YOU'RE HERE TO KILL ME.
AHEH. AHAHA.
CHAMEL
OH, MY SWEET GIRL, NO.
I'M JUST HERE TO *TALK*.
"I'M TRYING TO EXPLAIN THIS TO YOU."
THE GEMINI

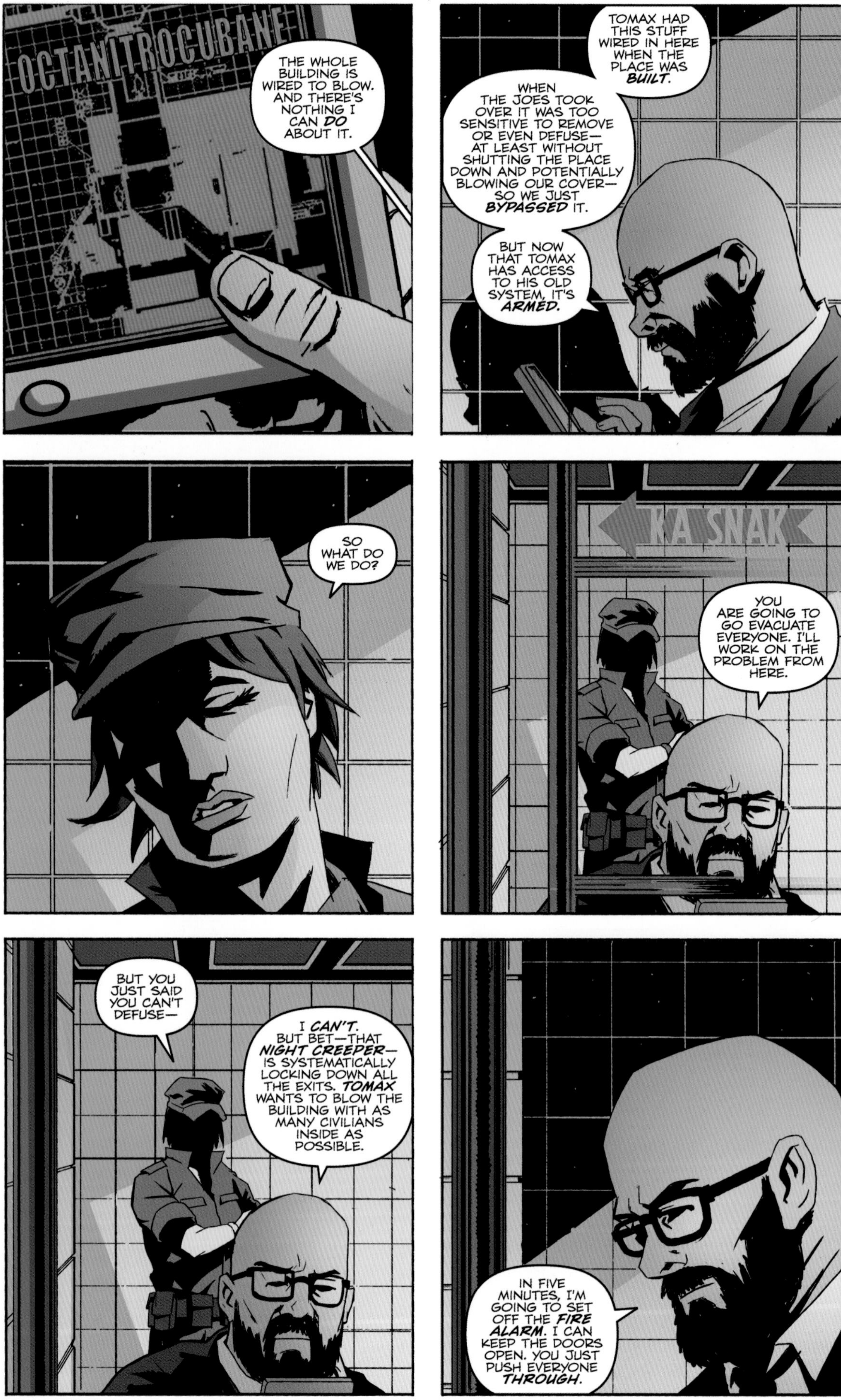
OCTANITROCUBANE
THE WHOLE BUILDING IS WIRED TO BLOW. AND THERE'S NOTHING I CAN *DO* ABOUT IT.
TOMAX HAD THIS STUFF WIRED IN HERE WHEN THE PLACE WAS *BUILT*.
WHEN THE JOES TOOK OVER IT WAS TOO SENSITIVE TO REMOVE OR EVEN DEFUSE—AT LEAST WITHOUT SHUTTING THE PLACE DOWN AND POTENTIALLY BLOWING OUR COVER—SO WE JUST *BYPASSED* IT.
BUT NOW THAT TOMAX HAS ACCESS TO HIS OLD SYSTEM, IT'S *ARMED.*
SO WHAT DO WE DO?
KA SNAK
YOU ARE GOING TO GO EVACUATE EVERYONE. I'LL WORK ON THE PROBLEM FROM HERE.
BUT YOU JUST SAID YOU CAN'T DEFUSE—
I *CAN'T*. BUT BET—THAT *NIGHT CREEPER*—IS SYSTEMATICALLY LOCKING DOWN ALL THE EXITS. *TOMAX* WANTS TO BLOW THE BUILDING WITH AS MANY CIVILIANS INSIDE AS POSSIBLE.
IN FIVE MINUTES, I'M GOING TO SET OFF THE *FIRE ALARM*. I CAN KEEP THE DOORS OPEN. YOU JUST PUSH EVERYONE *THROUGH*.

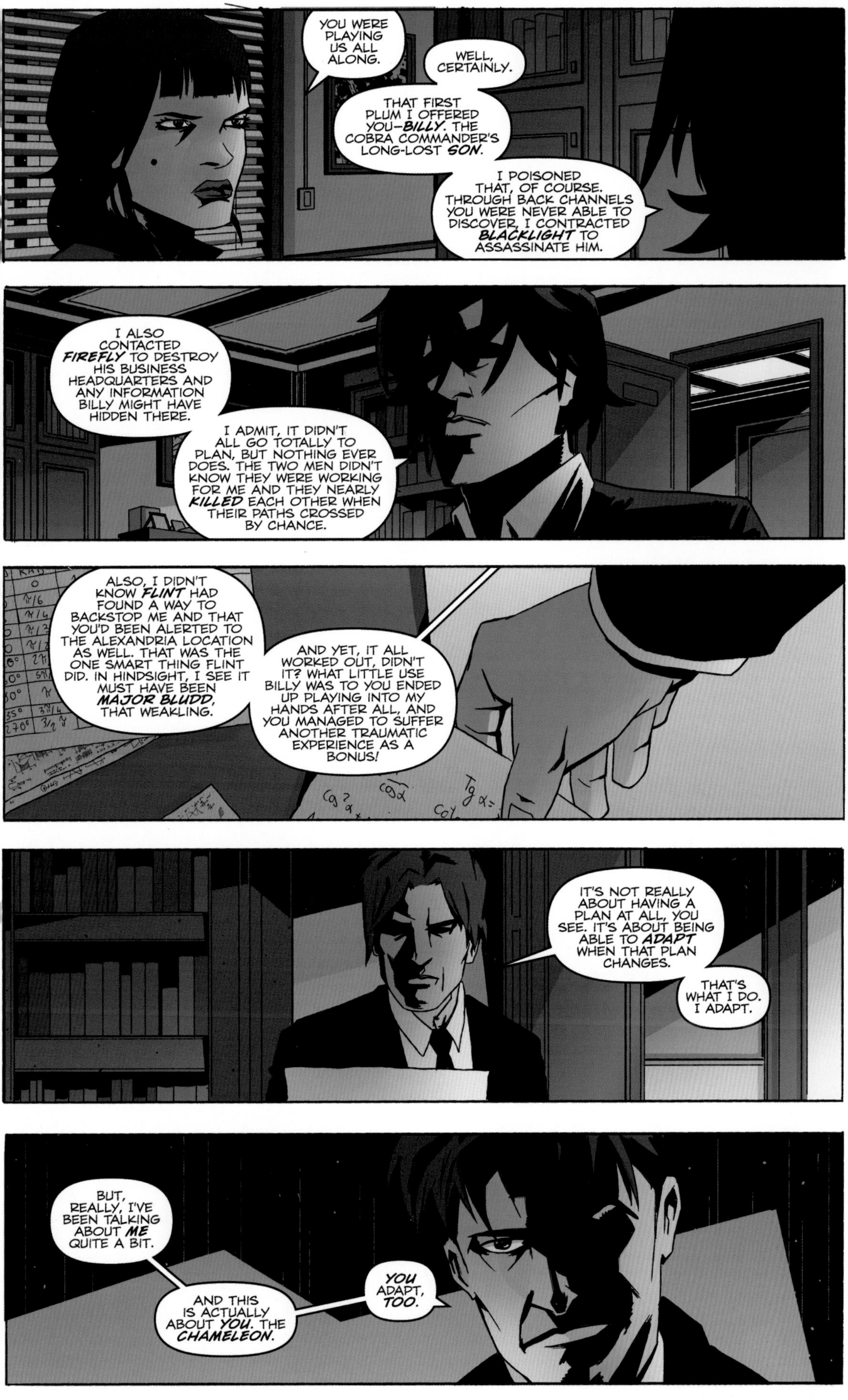
YOU WERE PLAYING US ALL ALONG.
WELL, CERTAINLY.
THAT FIRST PLUM I OFFERED YOU—BILLY. THE COBRA COMMANDER'S LONG-LOST SON.
I POISONED THAT, OF COURSE. THROUGH BACK CHANNELS YOU WERE NEVER ABLE TO DISCOVER, I CONTRACTED BLACKLIGHT TO ASSASSINATE HIM.
I ALSO CONTACTED FIREFLY TO DESTROY HIS BUSINESS HEADQUARTERS AND ANY INFORMATION BILLY MIGHT HAVE HIDDEN THERE.
I ADMIT, IT DIDN'T ALL GO TOTALLY TO PLAN, BUT NOTHING EVER DOES. THE TWO MEN DIDN'T KNOW THEY WERE WORKING FOR ME AND THEY NEARLY KILLED EACH OTHER WHEN THEIR PATHS CROSSED BY CHANCE.
ALSO, I DIDN'T KNOW FLINT HAD FOUND A WAY TO BACKSTOP ME AND THAT YOU'D BEEN ALERTED TO THE ALEXANDRIA LOCATION AS WELL. THAT WAS THE ONE SMART THING FLINT DID. IN HINDSIGHT, I SEE IT MUST HAVE BEEN MAJOR BLUDD, THAT WEAKLING.
AND YET, IT ALL WORKED OUT, DIDN'T IT? WHAT LITTLE USE BILLY WAS TO YOU ENDED UP PLAYING INTO MY HANDS AFTER ALL, AND YOU MANAGED TO SUFFER ANOTHER TRAUMATIC EXPERIENCE AS A BONUS!
IT'S NOT REALLY ABOUT HAVING A PLAN AT ALL, YOU SEE. IT'S ABOUT BEING ABLE TO ADAPT WHEN THAT PLAN CHANGES.
THAT'S WHAT I DO. I ADAPT.
BUT, REALLY, I'VE BEEN TALKING ABOUT ME QUITE A BIT.
AND THIS IS ACTUALLY ABOUT YOU. THE CHAMELEON.
YOU ADAPT, TOO.

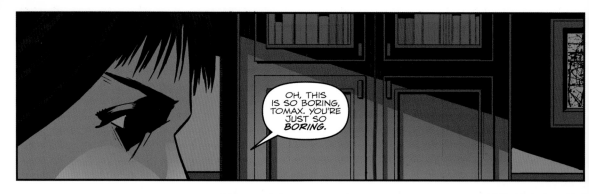

OH, THIS IS SO BORING, TOMAX. YOU'RE JUST SO *BORING*.

YOU COME IN HERE TO GLOAT TO ME ABOUT WHAT AN EVIL GENIUS YOU ARE. HOW WE'RE ALL YOUR PUPPETS. THEN JUST AS YOU THINK MY RIGHTEOUS INDIGNATION IS CRESTING, YOU PLAY THE HOARY "YOU AND ME ARE JUST THE SAME" CARD.

I DON'T *LISTEN* TO WHAT YOU *SAY*, TOMAX. AND I DON'T *BELIEVE* YOU. YOU'RE *SCUM*. THAT'S ALL.

MY MOTHER ABANDONED ME TOO, YOU KNOW.

MYSELF AND MY BROTHER.

ARE YOU KIDDING ME WITH THIS?

OUR FATHER DIED WHEN WE WERE TODDLERS AND SHE SOLD US TO THE *UNIONE CORSE*. SHE'D TAKEN UP WITH ANOTHER MAN AND HE DIDN'T WANT TO RAISE SOMEONE ELSE'S CHILDREN.

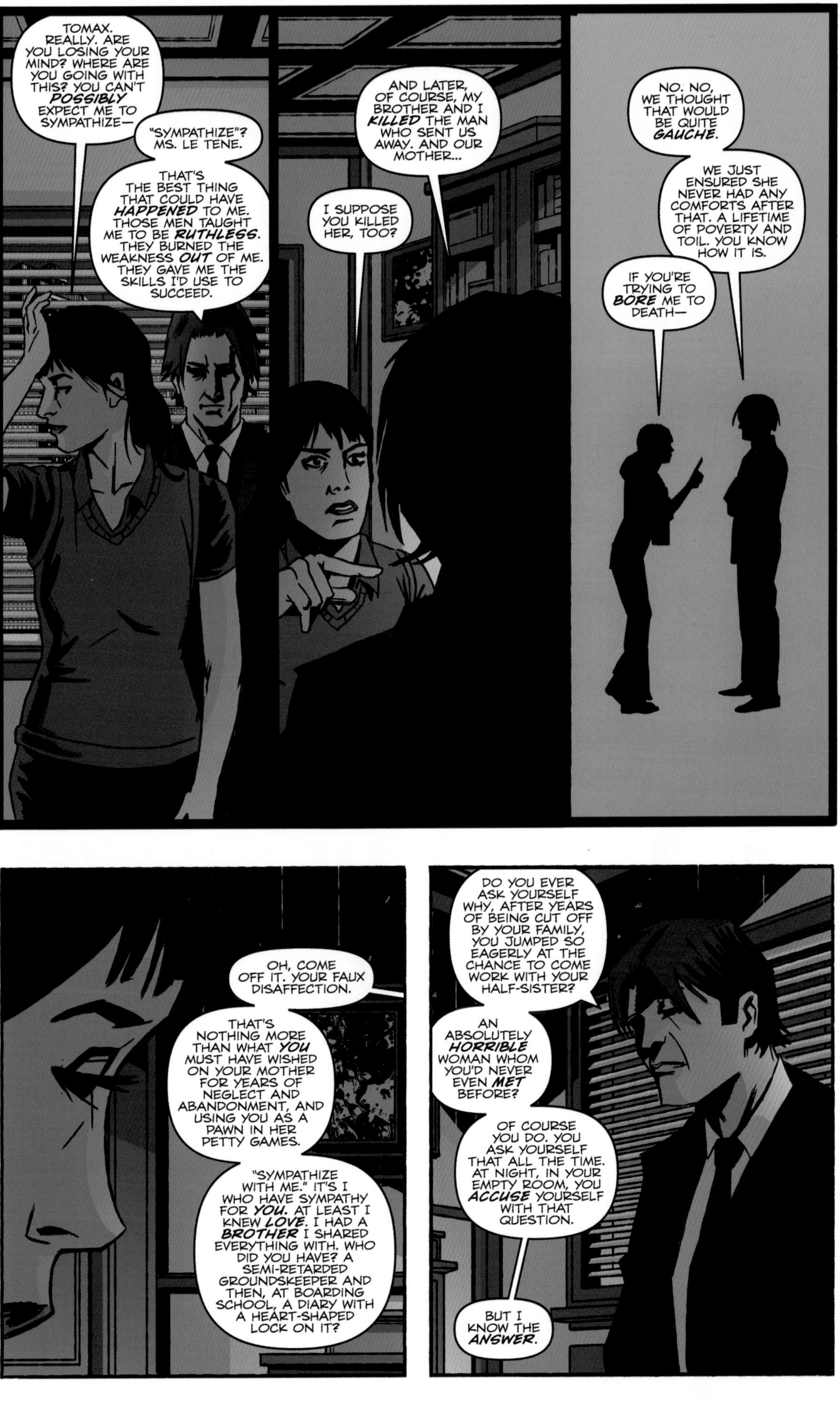
TOMAX. REALLY. ARE YOU LOSING YOUR MIND? WHERE ARE YOU GOING WITH THIS? YOU CAN'T POSSIBLY EXPECT ME TO SYMPATHIZE—
"SYMPATHIZE"? MS. LE TENE.
THAT'S THE BEST THING THAT COULD HAVE HAPPENED TO ME. THOSE MEN TAUGHT ME TO BE RUTHLESS. THEY BURNED THE WEAKNESS OUT OF ME. THEY GAVE ME THE SKILLS I'D USE TO SUCCEED.
AND LATER, OF COURSE, MY BROTHER AND I KILLED THE MAN WHO SENT US AWAY. AND OUR MOTHER...
I SUPPOSE YOU KILLED HER, TOO?
NO. NO, WE THOUGHT THAT WOULD BE QUITE GAUCHE.
WE JUST ENSURED SHE NEVER HAD ANY COMFORTS AFTER THAT. A LIFETIME OF POVERTY AND TOIL. YOU KNOW HOW IT IS.
IF YOU'RE TRYING TO BORE ME TO DEATH—
OH, COME OFF IT. YOUR FAUX DISAFFECTION.
THAT'S NOTHING MORE THAN WHAT YOU MUST HAVE WISHED ON YOUR MOTHER FOR YEARS OF NEGLECT AND ABANDONMENT, AND USING YOU AS A PAWN IN HER PETTY GAMES.
"SYMPATHIZE WITH ME." IT'S I WHO HAVE SYMPATHY FOR YOU. AT LEAST I KNEW LOVE. I HAD A BROTHER I SHARED EVERYTHING WITH. WHO DID YOU HAVE? A SEMI-RETARDED GROUNDSKEEPER AND THEN, AT BOARDING SCHOOL, A DIARY WITH A HEART-SHAPED LOCK ON IT?
DO YOU EVER ASK YOURSELF WHY, AFTER YEARS OF BEING CUT OFF BY YOUR FAMILY, YOU JUMPED SO EAGERLY AT THE CHANCE TO COME WORK WITH YOUR HALF-SISTER?
AN ABSOLUTELY HORRIBLE WOMAN WHOM YOU'D NEVER EVEN MET BEFORE?
OF COURSE YOU DO. YOU ASK YOURSELF THAT ALL THE TIME. AT NIGHT, IN YOUR EMPTY ROOM, YOU ACCUSE YOURSELF WITH THAT QUESTION.
BUT I KNOW THE ANSWER.

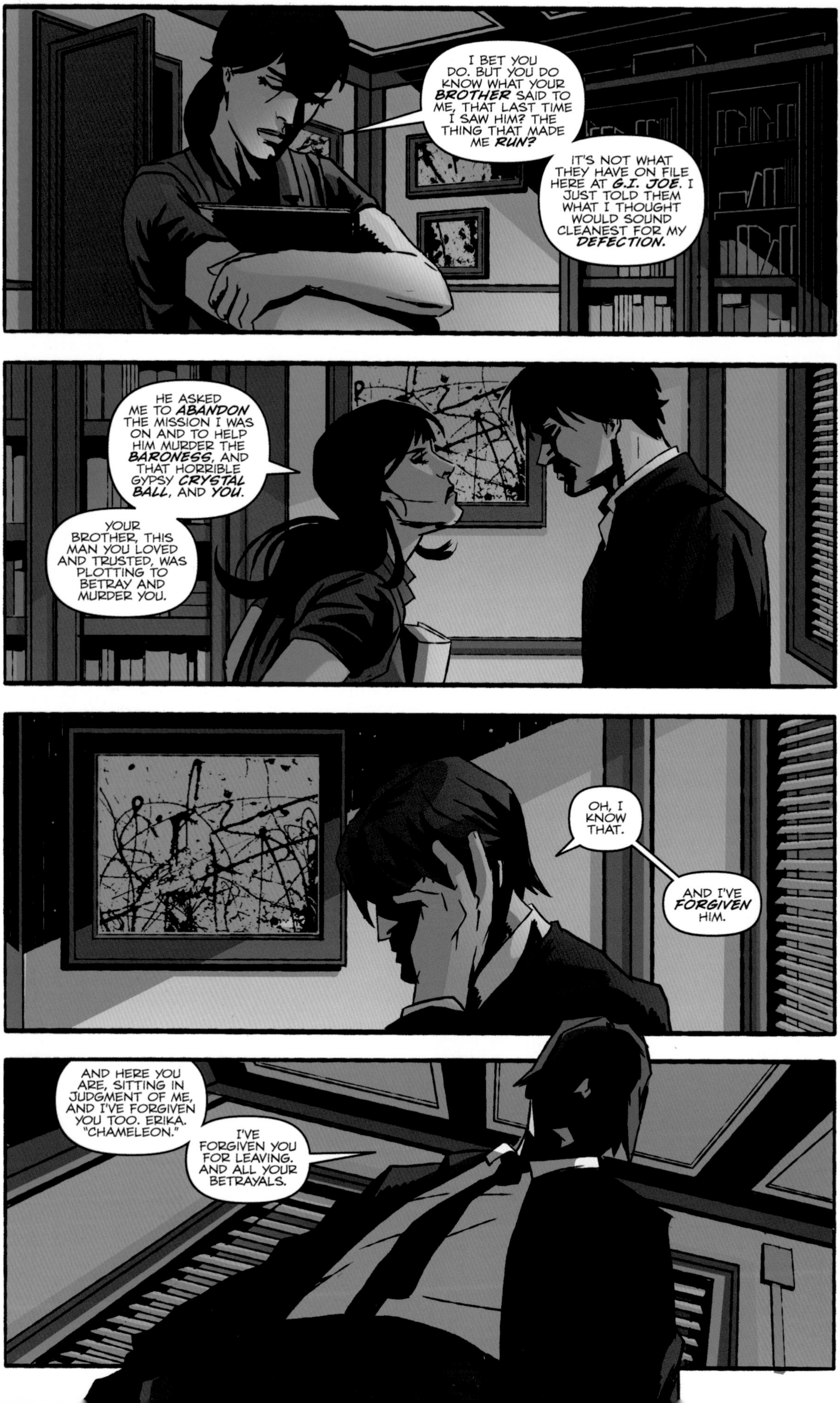
I BET YOU DO. BUT YOU DO KNOW WHAT YOUR BROTHER SAID TO ME, THAT LAST TIME I SAW HIM? THE THING THAT MADE ME RUN?
IT'S NOT WHAT THEY HAVE ON FILE HERE AT G.I. JOE. I JUST TOLD THEM WHAT I THOUGHT WOULD SOUND CLEANEST FOR MY DEFECTION.
HE ASKED ME TO ABANDON THE MISSION I WAS ON AND TO HELP HIM MURDER THE BARONESS, AND THAT HORRIBLE GYPSY CRYSTAL BALL, AND YOU.
YOUR BROTHER, THIS MAN YOU LOVED AND TRUSTED, WAS PLOTTING TO BETRAY AND MURDER YOU.
OH, I KNOW THAT.
AND I'VE FORGIVEN HIM.
AND HERE YOU ARE, SITTING IN JUDGMENT OF ME, AND I'VE FORGIVEN YOU TOO. ERIKA. "CHAMELEON."
I'VE FORGIVEN YOU FOR LEAVING. AND ALL YOUR BETRAYALS.

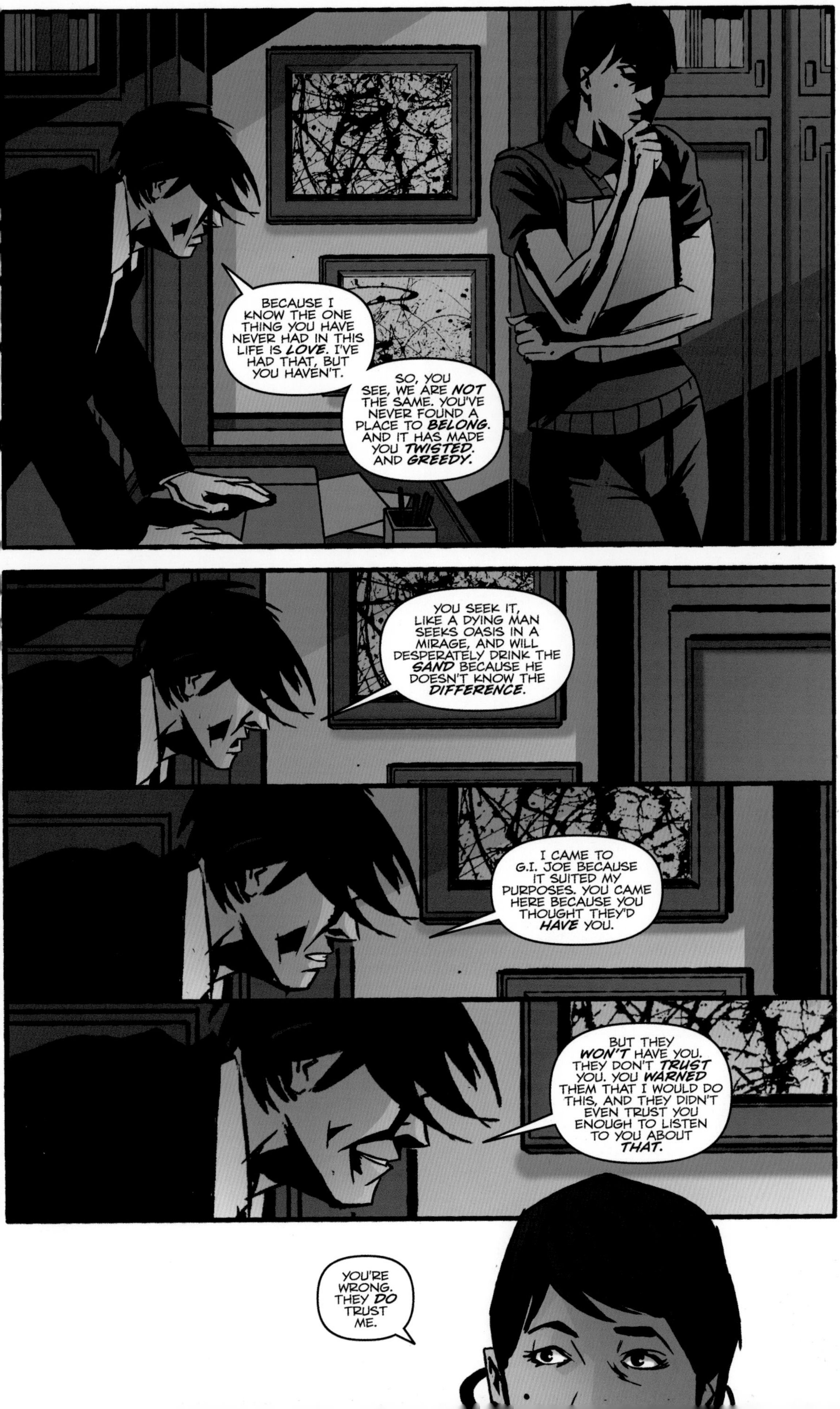
BECAUSE I KNOW THE ONE THING YOU HAVE NEVER HAD IN THIS LIFE IS LOVE. I'VE HAD THAT, BUT YOU HAVEN'T.
SO, YOU SEE, WE ARE NOT THE SAME. YOU'VE NEVER FOUND A PLACE TO BELONG. AND IT HAS MADE YOU TWISTED. AND GREEDY.
YOU SEEK IT, LIKE A DYING MAN SEEKS OASIS IN A MIRAGE, AND WILL DESPERATELY DRINK THE SAND BECAUSE HE DOESN'T KNOW THE DIFFERENCE.
I CAME TO G.I. JOE BECAUSE IT SUITED MY PURPOSES. YOU CAME HERE BECAUSE YOU THOUGHT THEY'D HAVE YOU.
BUT THEY WON'T HAVE YOU. THEY DON'T TRUST YOU. YOU WARNED THEM THAT I WOULD DO THIS, AND THEY DIDN'T EVEN TRUST YOU ENOUGH TO LISTEN TO YOU ABOUT THAT.
YOU'RE WRONG. THEY DO TRUST ME.

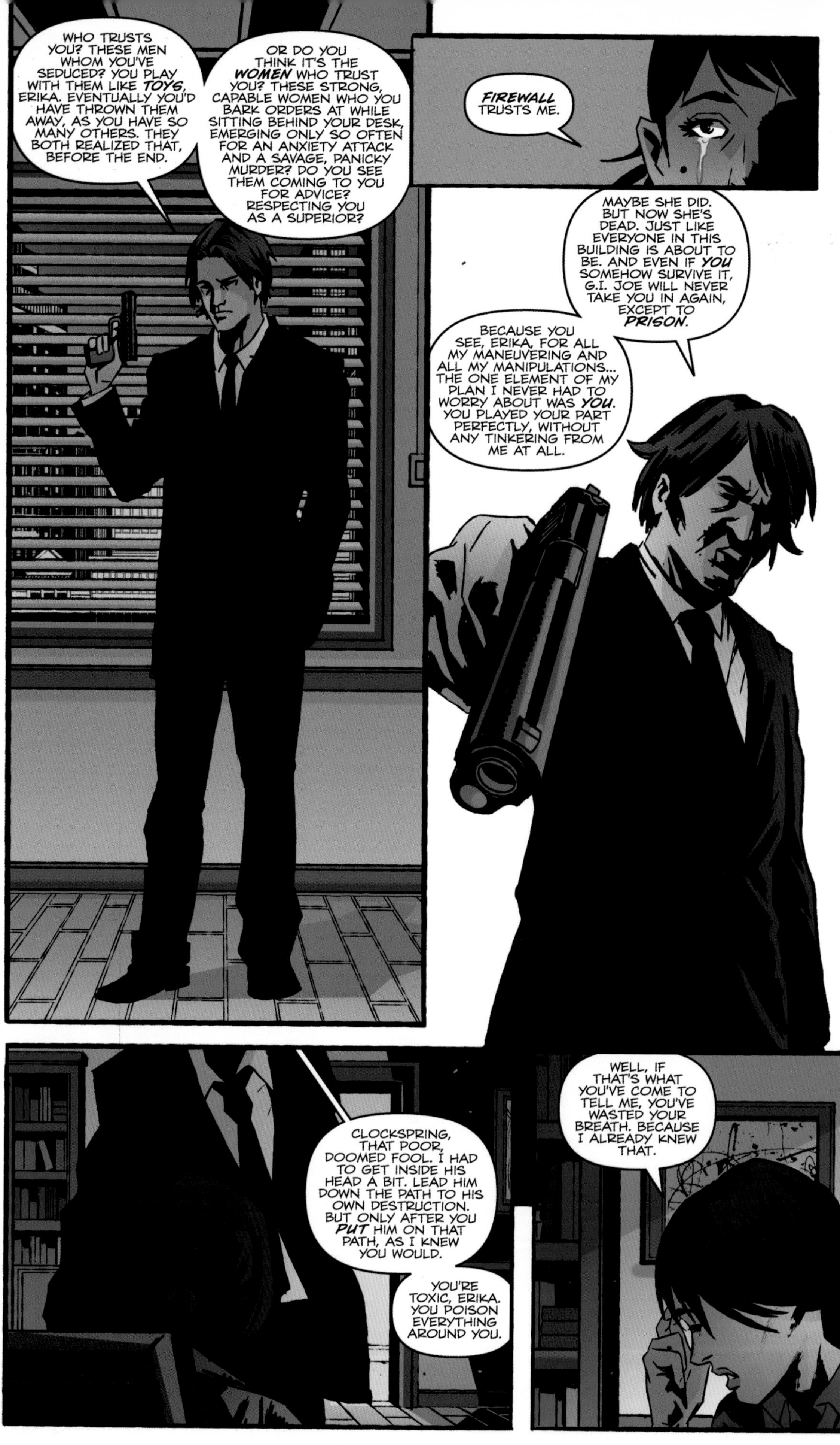
WHO TRUSTS YOU? THESE MEN WHOM YOU'VE SEDUCED? YOU PLAY WITH THEM LIKE TOYS, ERIKA. EVENTUALLY YOU'D HAVE THROWN THEM AWAY, AS YOU HAVE SO MANY OTHERS. THEY BOTH REALIZED THAT, BEFORE THE END.
OR DO YOU THINK IT'S THE WOMEN WHO TRUST YOU? THESE STRONG, CAPABLE WOMEN WHO YOU BARK ORDERS AT WHILE SITTING BEHIND YOUR DESK, EMERGING ONLY SO OFTEN FOR AN ANXIETY ATTACK AND A SAVAGE, PANICKY MURDER? DO YOU SEE THEM COMING TO YOU FOR ADVICE? RESPECTING YOU AS A SUPERIOR?
FIREWALL TRUSTS ME.
MAYBE SHE DID. BUT NOW SHE'S DEAD. JUST LIKE EVERYONE IN THIS BUILDING IS ABOUT TO BE. AND EVEN IF YOU SOMEHOW SURVIVE IT, G.I. JOE WILL NEVER TAKE YOU IN AGAIN, EXCEPT TO PRISON.
BECAUSE YOU SEE, ERIKA, FOR ALL MY MANEUVERING AND ALL MY MANIPULATIONS... THE ONE ELEMENT OF MY PLAN I NEVER HAD TO WORRY ABOUT WAS YOU. YOU PLAYED YOUR PART PERFECTLY, WITHOUT ANY TINKERING FROM ME AT ALL.
CLOCKSPRING, THAT POOR, DOOMED FOOL. I HAD TO GET INSIDE HIS HEAD A BIT. LEAD HIM DOWN THE PATH TO HIS OWN DESTRUCTION. BUT ONLY AFTER YOU PUT HIM ON THAT PATH, AS I KNEW YOU WOULD.
YOU'RE TOXIC, ERIKA. YOU POISON EVERYTHING AROUND YOU.
WELL, IF THAT'S WHAT YOU'VE COME TO TELL ME, YOU'VE WASTED YOUR BREATH. BECAUSE I ALREADY KNEW THAT.

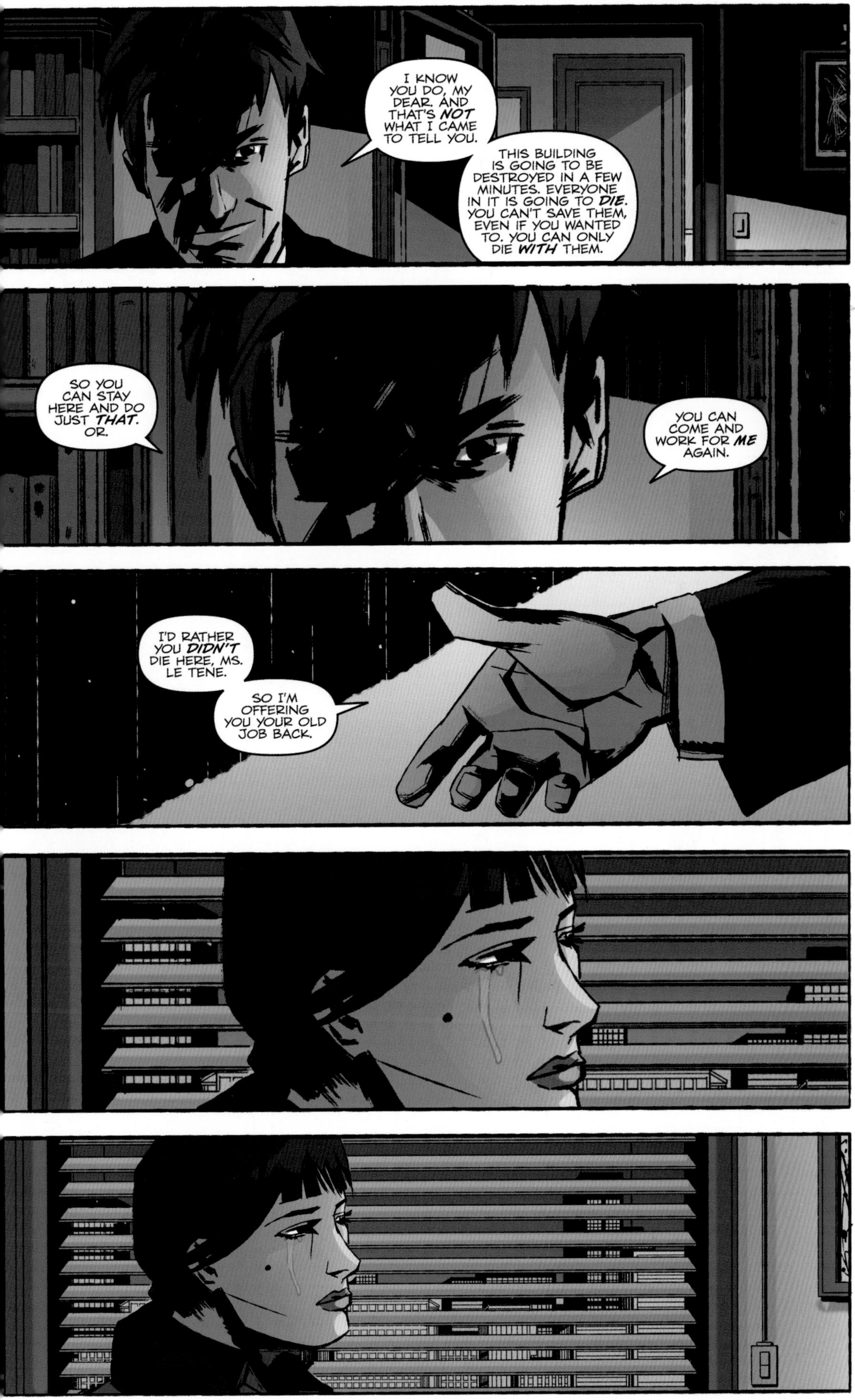
I KNOW YOU DO, MY DEAR. AND THAT'S NOT WHAT I CAME TO TELL YOU.
THIS BUILDING IS GOING TO BE DESTROYED IN A FEW MINUTES. EVERYONE IN IT IS GOING TO DIE. YOU CAN'T SAVE THEM, EVEN IF YOU WANTED TO. YOU CAN ONLY DIE WITH THEM.
SO YOU CAN STAY HERE AND DO JUST THAT. OR.
YOU CAN COME AND WORK FOR ME AGAIN.
I'D RATHER YOU DIDN'T DIE HERE, MS. LE TENE.
SO I'M OFFERING YOU YOUR OLD JOB BACK.

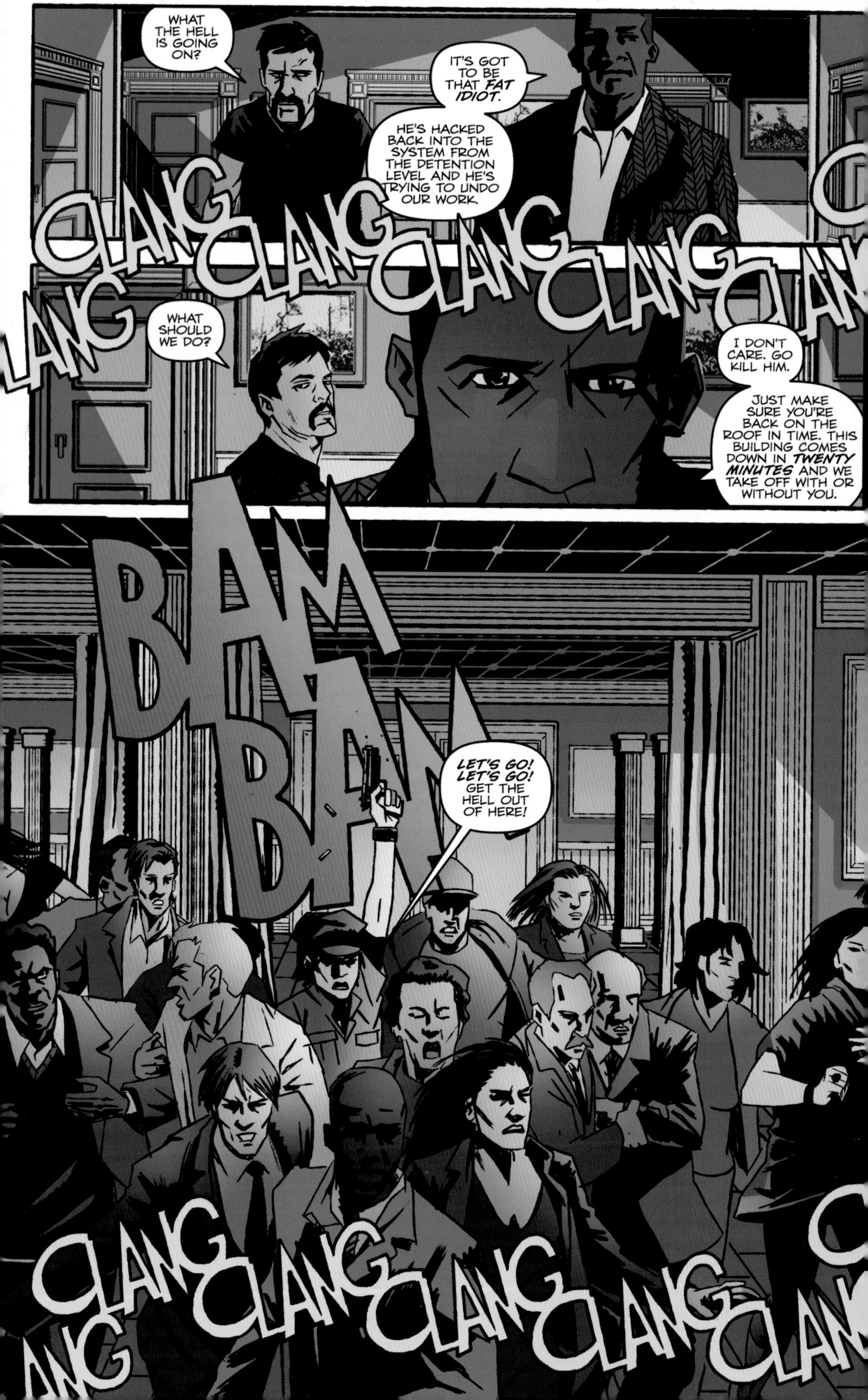
WHAT THE HELL IS GOING ON?
IT'S GOT TO BE THAT *FAT IDIOT*.
HE'S HACKED BACK INTO THE SYSTEM FROM THE DETENTION LEVEL AND HE'S TRYING TO UNDO OUR WORK.
CLANG CLANG CLANG CLANG CLANG CLANG CLANG CLANG CLANG CLANG CLANG
WHAT SHOULD WE DO?
I DON'T CARE. GO KILL HIM.
JUST MAKE SURE YOU'RE BACK ON THE ROOF IN TIME. THIS BUILDING COMES DOWN IN *TWENTY MINUTES* AND WE TAKE OFF WITH OR WITHOUT YOU.
BAM BAM
LET'S GO! LET'S GO! GET THE HELL OUT OF HERE!
CLANG CLANG CLANG CLANG CLANG CLANG CLANG CLANG CLANG CLANG

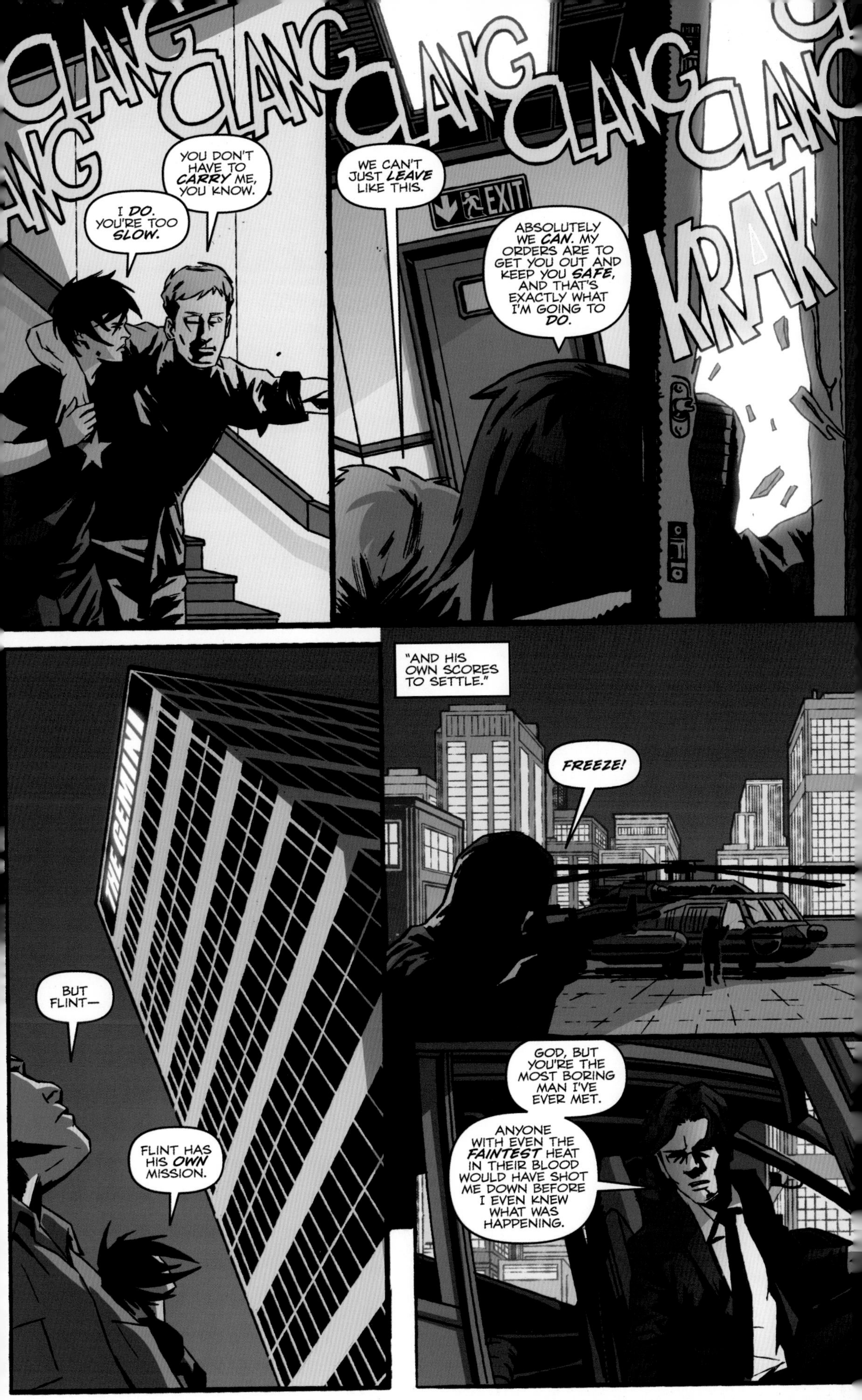
CLANG CLANG CLANG CLANG CLANG
YOU DON'T HAVE TO CARRY ME, YOU KNOW.
I DO. YOU'RE TOO SLOW.
WE CAN'T JUST LEAVE LIKE THIS.
EXIT
ABSOLUTELY WE CAN. MY ORDERS ARE TO GET YOU OUT AND KEEP YOU SAFE, AND THAT'S EXACTLY WHAT I'M GOING TO DO.
KRAK
THE GEMINI
BUT FLINT—
FLINT HAS HIS OWN MISSION.
"AND HIS OWN SCORES TO SETTLE."
FREEZE!
GOD, BUT YOU'RE THE MOST BORING MAN I'VE EVER MET.
ANYONE WITH EVEN THE FAINTEST HEAT IN THEIR BLOOD WOULD HAVE SHOT ME DOWN BEFORE I EVEN KNEW WHAT WAS HAPPENING.

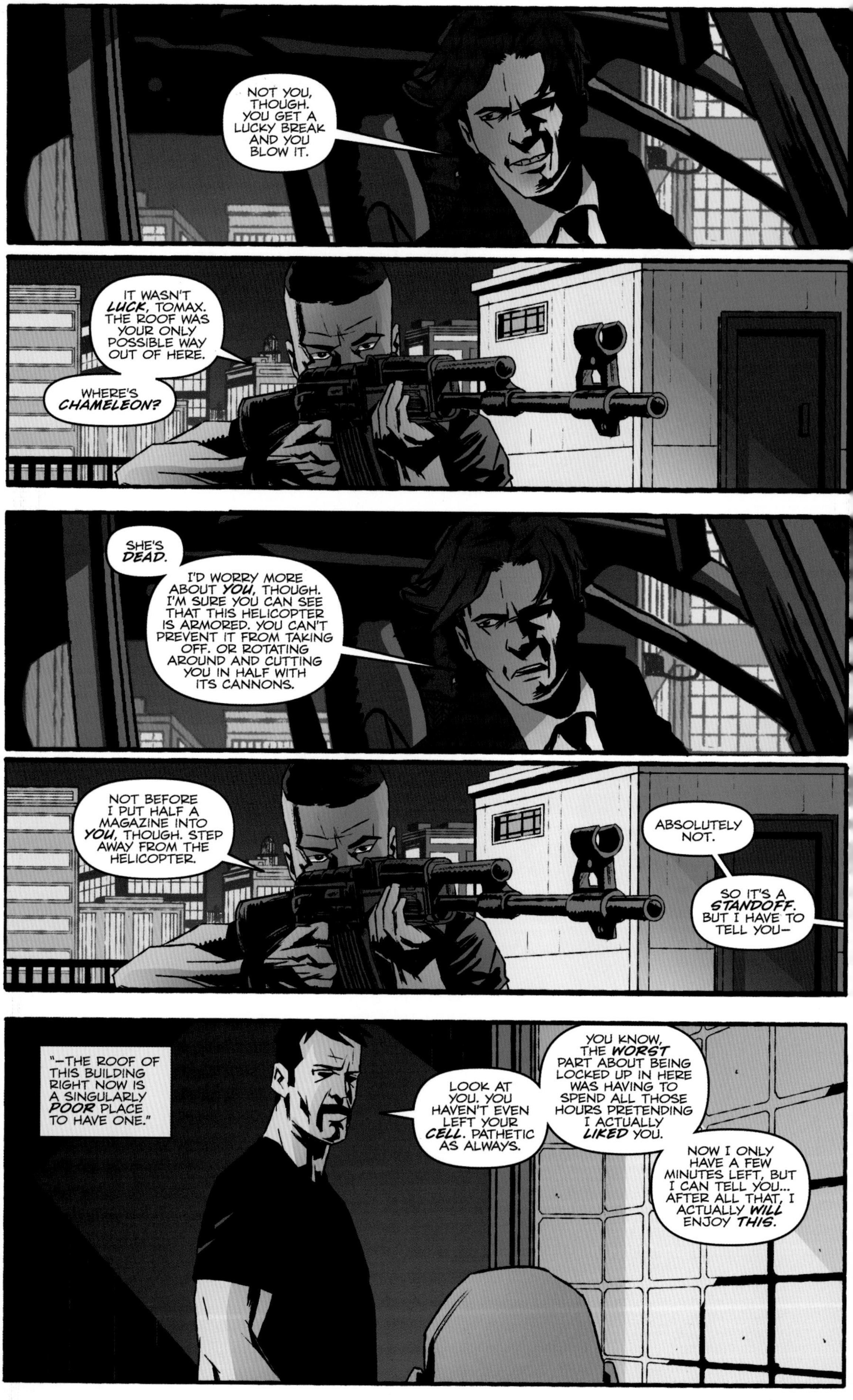

NOT YOU, THOUGH. YOU GET A LUCKY BREAK AND YOU BLOW IT.
IT WASN'T LUCK, TOMAX. THE ROOF WAS YOUR ONLY POSSIBLE WAY OUT OF HERE.
WHERE'S CHAMELEON?
SHE'S DEAD.
I'D WORRY MORE ABOUT YOU, THOUGH. I'M SURE YOU CAN SEE THAT THIS HELICOPTER IS ARMORED. YOU CAN'T PREVENT IT FROM TAKING OFF. OR ROTATING AROUND AND CUTTING YOU IN HALF WITH ITS CANNONS.
NOT BEFORE I PUT HALF A MAGAZINE INTO YOU, THOUGH. STEP AWAY FROM THE HELICOPTER.
ABSOLUTELY NOT.
SO IT'S A STANDOFF. BUT I HAVE TO TELL YOU—
"—THE ROOF OF THIS BUILDING RIGHT NOW IS A SINGULARLY POOR PLACE TO HAVE ONE."
LOOK AT YOU. YOU HAVEN'T EVEN LEFT YOUR CELL. PATHETIC AS ALWAYS.
YOU KNOW, THE WORST PART ABOUT BEING LOCKED UP IN HERE WAS HAVING TO SPEND ALL THOSE HOURS PRETENDING I ACTUALLY LIKED YOU.
NOW I ONLY HAVE A FEW MINUTES LEFT, BUT I CAN TELL YOU... AFTER ALL THAT, I ACTUALLY WILL ENJOY THIS.

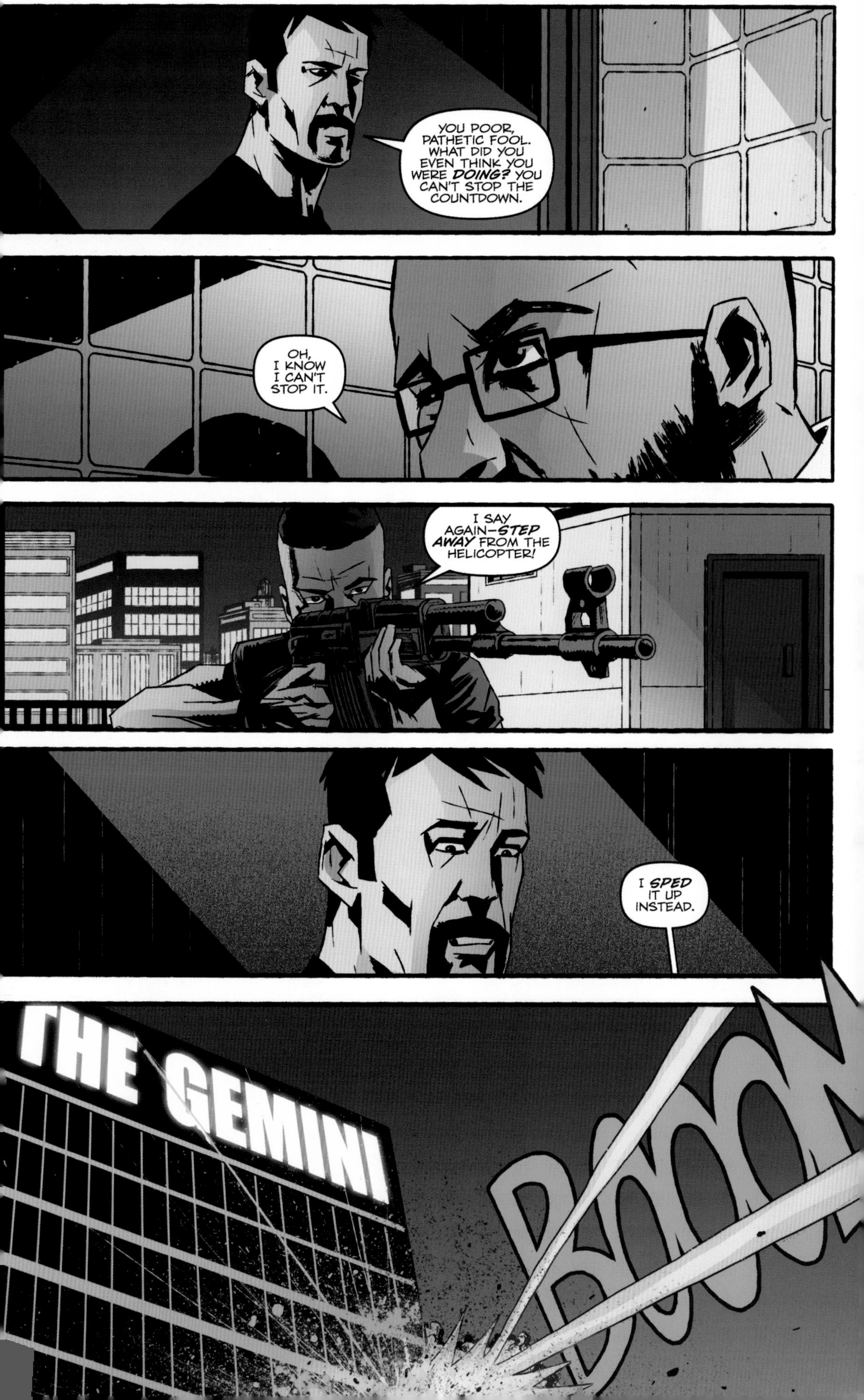
YOU POOR, PATHETIC FOOL. WHAT DID YOU EVEN THINK YOU WERE ***DOING?*** YOU CAN'T STOP THE COUNTDOWN.
OH, I KNOW I CAN'T STOP IT.
I SAY AGAIN—***STEP AWAY*** FROM THE HELICOPTER!
I ***SPED*** IT UP INSTEAD.
THE GEMINI
BOOOO

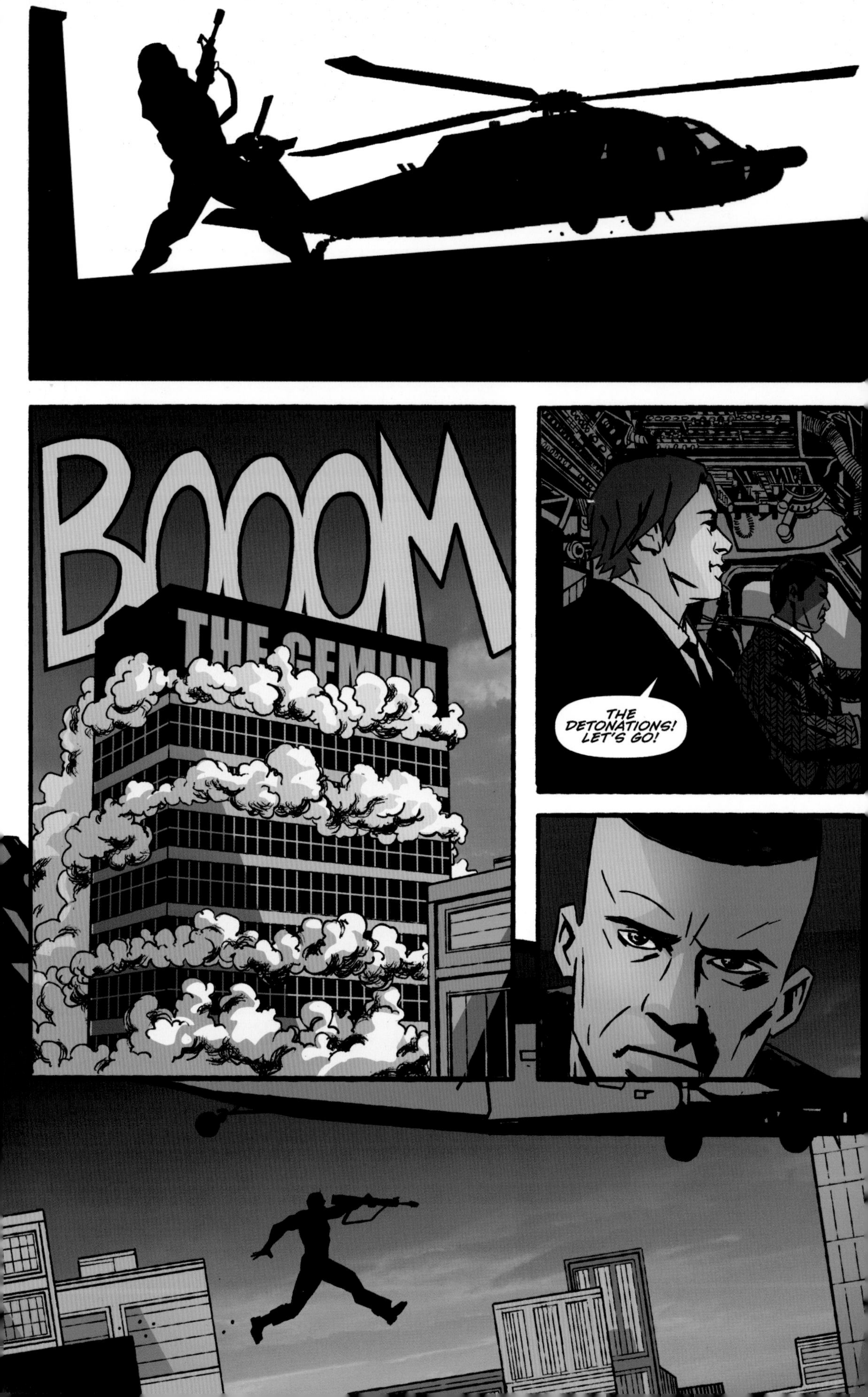
BOOOM
THE GEMINI
THE DETONATIONS! LET'S GO!

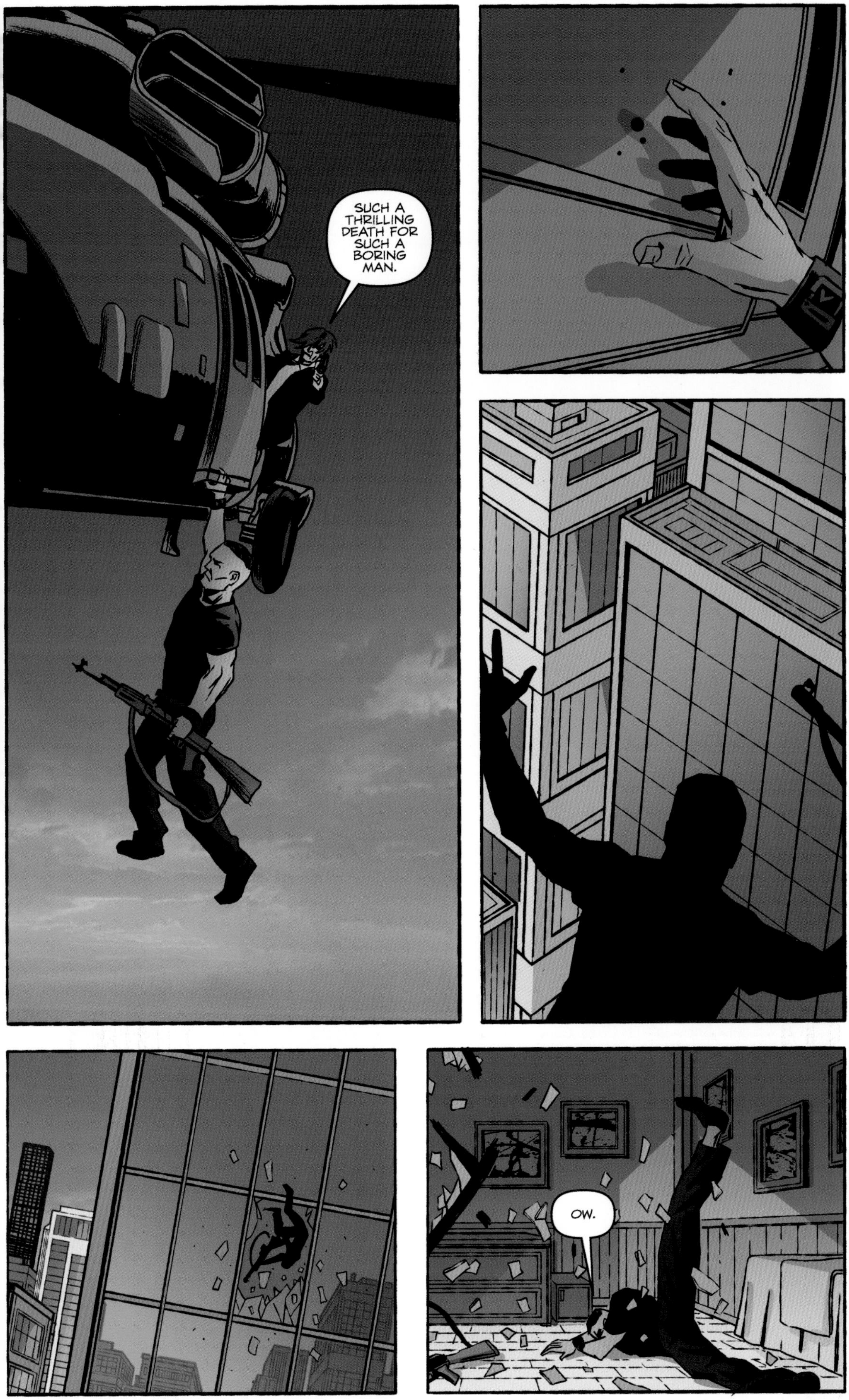
SUCH A THRILLING DEATH FOR SUCH A BORING MAN.
OW.

HM. I CAN'T DENY THAT WAS IMPRESSIVE.

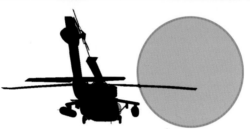

GOD.

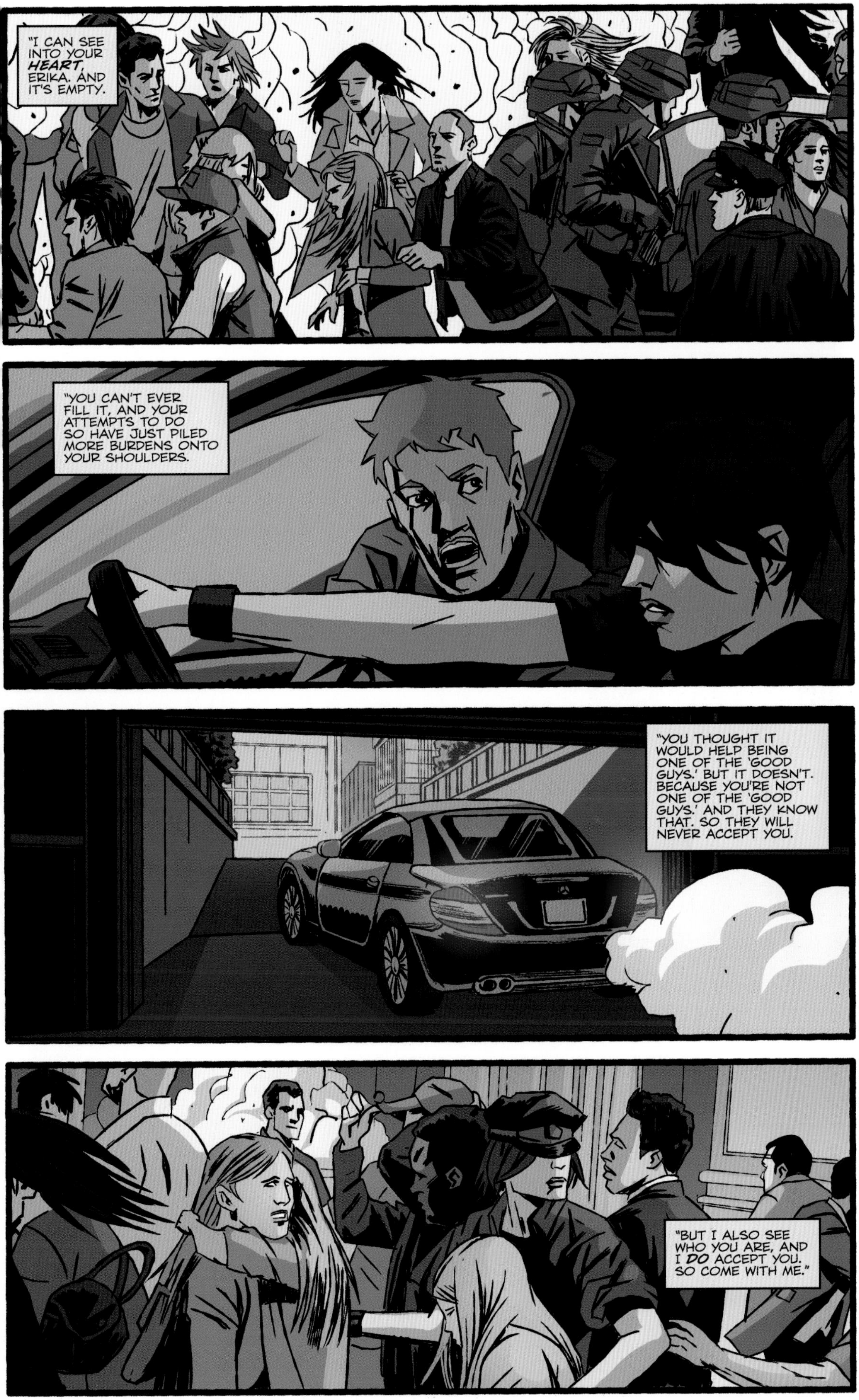
"I CAN SEE INTO YOUR *HEART*, ERIKA. AND IT'S EMPTY.
"YOU CAN'T EVER FILL IT, AND YOUR ATTEMPTS TO DO SO HAVE JUST PILED MORE BURDENS ONTO YOUR SHOULDERS.
"YOU THOUGHT IT WOULD HELP BEING ONE OF THE 'GOOD GUYS.' BUT IT DOESN'T. BECAUSE YOU'RE NOT ONE OF THE 'GOOD GUYS.' AND THEY KNOW THAT. SO THEY WILL NEVER ACCEPT YOU.
"BUT I ALSO SEE WHO YOU ARE, AND I *DO* ACCEPT YOU. SO COME WITH ME."

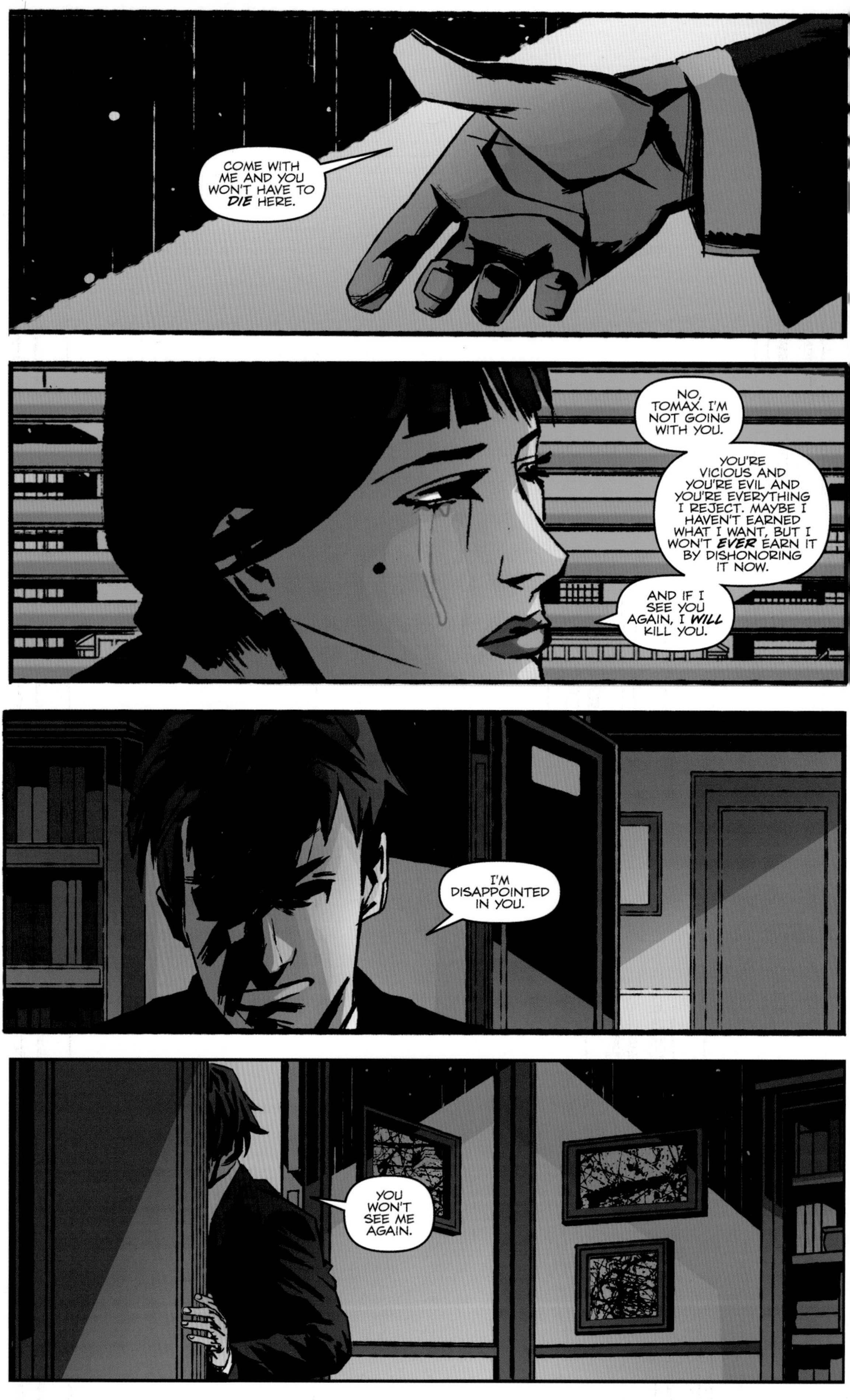
COME WITH ME AND YOU WON'T HAVE TO **DIE** HERE.
NO, TOMAX. I'M NOT GOING WITH YOU.
YOU'RE VICIOUS AND YOU'RE EVIL AND YOU'RE EVERYTHING I REJECT. MAYBE I HAVEN'T EARNED WHAT I WANT, BUT I WON'T **EVER** EARN IT BY DISHONORING IT NOW.
AND IF I SEE YOU AGAIN, I **WILL** KILL YOU.
I'M DISAPPOINTED IN YOU.
YOU WON'T SEE ME AGAIN.

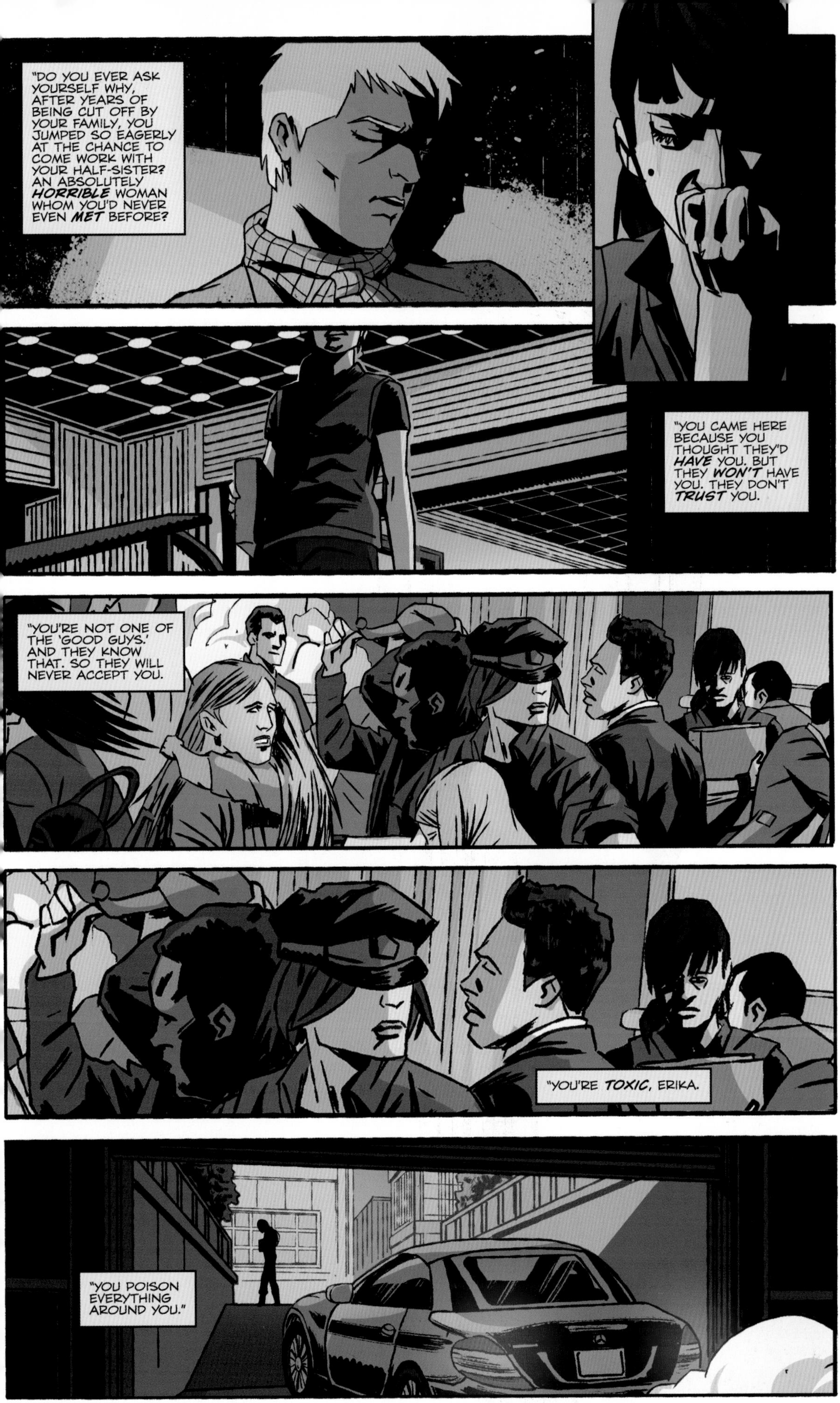
"DO YOU EVER ASK YOURSELF WHY, AFTER YEARS OF BEING CUT OFF BY YOUR FAMILY, YOU JUMPED SO EAGERLY AT THE CHANCE TO COME WORK WITH YOUR HALF-SISTER? AN ABSOLUTELY HORRIBLE WOMAN WHOM YOU'D NEVER EVEN MET BEFORE?
"YOU CAME HERE BECAUSE YOU THOUGHT THEY'D HAVE YOU. BUT THEY WON'T HAVE YOU. THEY DON'T TRUST YOU.
"YOU'RE NOT ONE OF THE 'GOOD GUYS.' AND THEY KNOW THAT. SO THEY WILL NEVER ACCEPT YOU.
"YOU'RE TOXIC, ERIKA.
"YOU POISON EVERYTHING AROUND YOU."

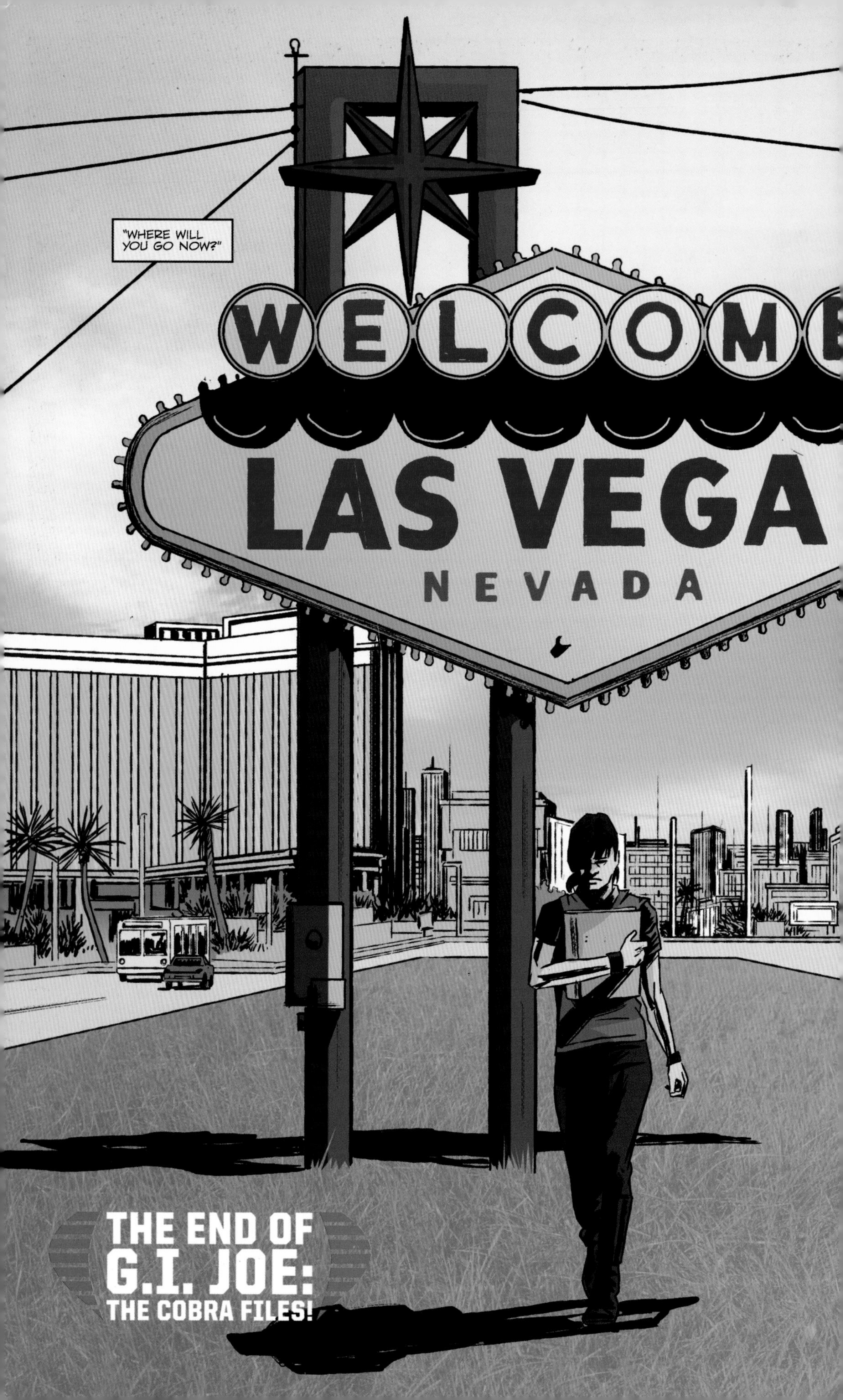
"WHERE WILL YOU GO NOW?"
WELCOME
LAS VEGA
NEVADA
THE END OF G.I. JOE: THE COBRA FILES!

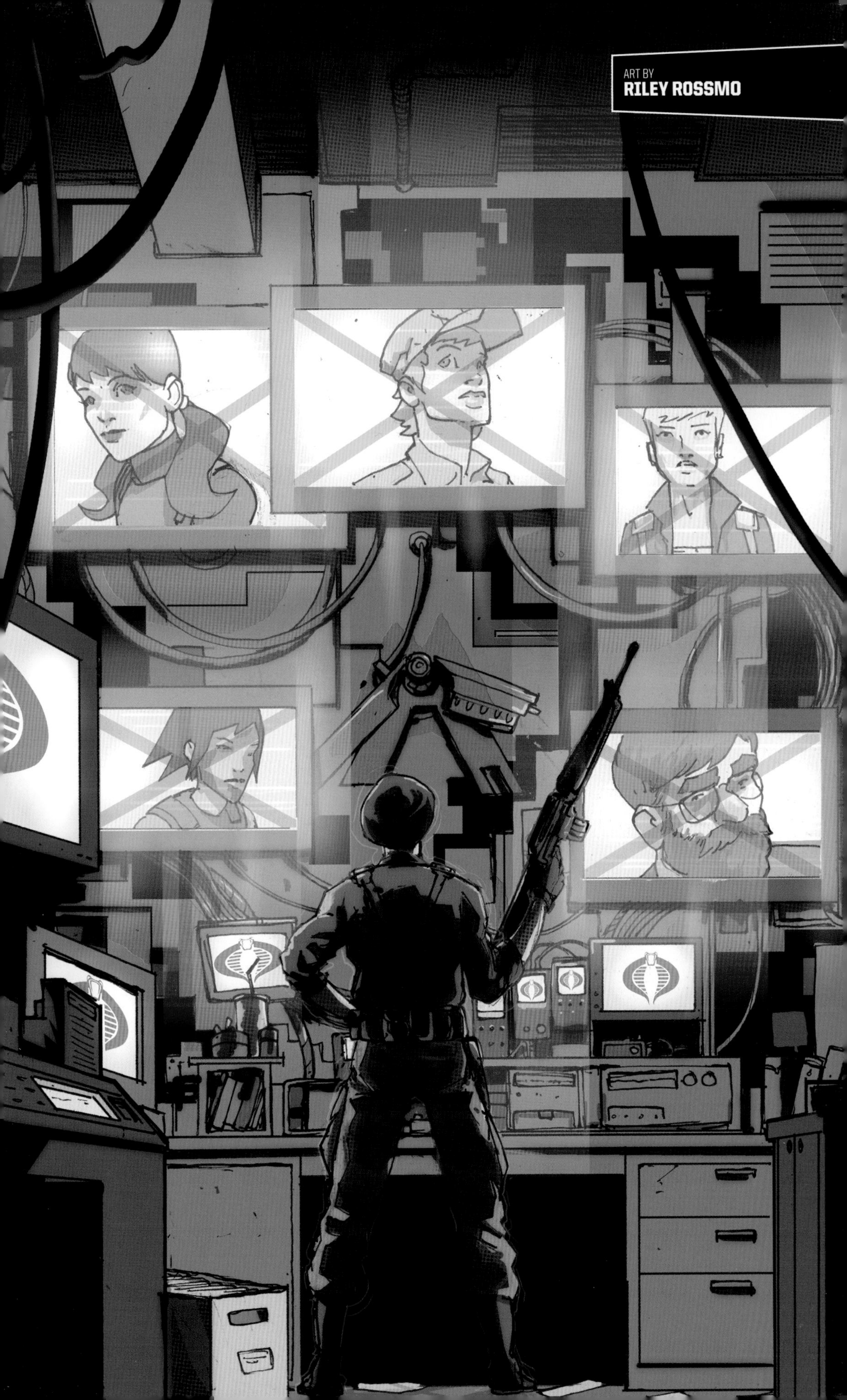

ART BY
RILEY ROSSMO

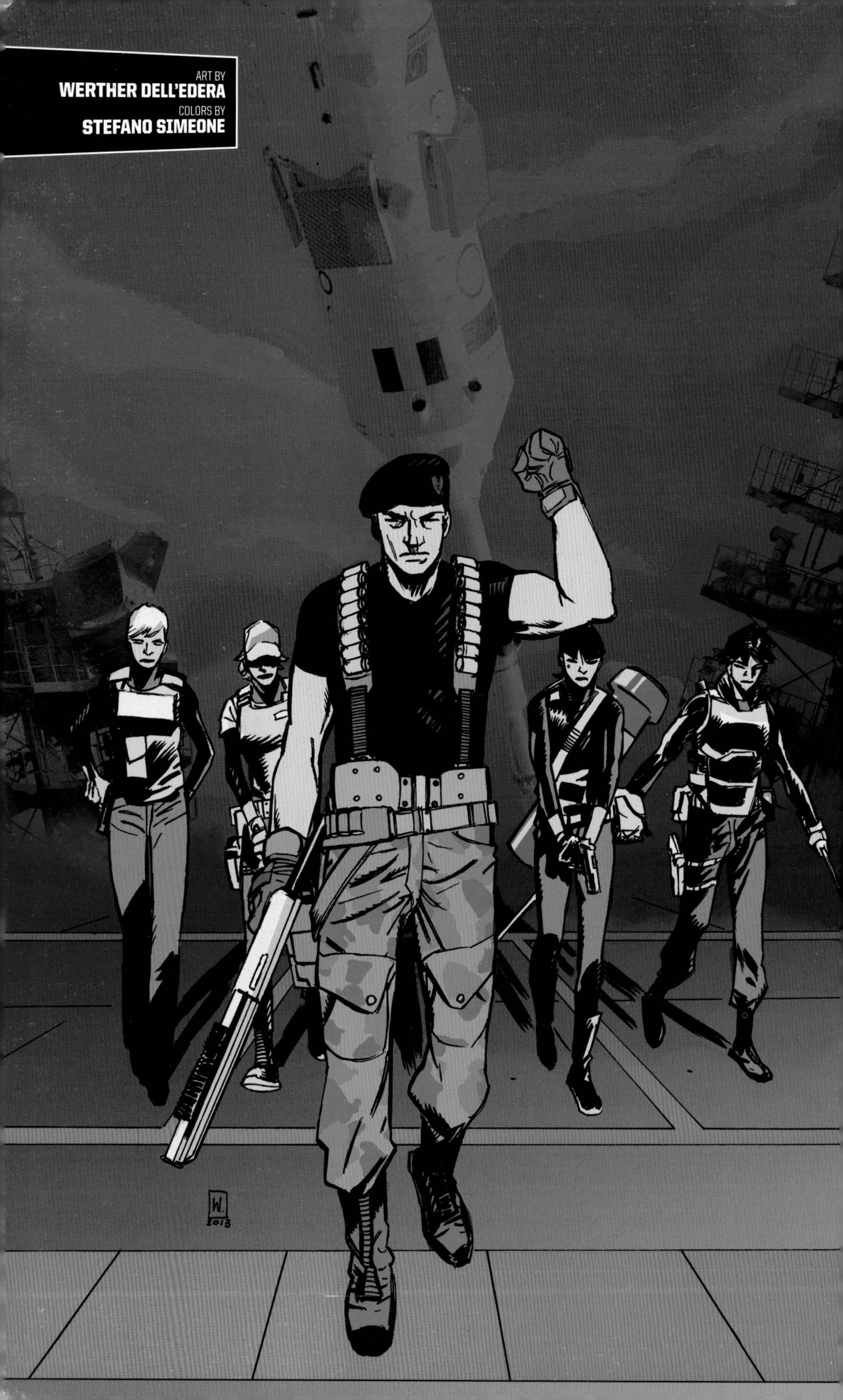
ART BY
WERTHER DELL'EDERA
COLORS BY
STEFANO SIMEONE